Anonymous

**Abridgement of the Minutes of the Evidence**

Anonymous

**Abridgement of the Minutes of the Evidence**

ISBN/EAN: 9783744760584

Printed in Europe, USA, Canada, Australia, Japan

Cover: Foto ©ninafisch / pixelio.de

More available books at **www.hansebooks.com**

# Number III.

# ABRIDGMENT

OF THE

MINUTES OF THE EVIDENCE,

TAKEN BEFORE A

COMMITTEE OF THE WHOLE HOUSE,

TO WHOM IT WAS REFERRED TO CONSIDER OF THE

SLAVE-TRADE,

1790.

OF THE

# MINUTES OF THE EVIDENCE,

TAKEN BEFORE A

SELECT COMMITTEE OF THE WHOLE HOUSE,

TO WHOM IT WAS REFERRED TO CONSIDER OF THE

# SLAVE-TRADE, 1790.

NUMBER III.

Witneſs examined—Captain WILSON.

Was between five and ſix months in Africa, between Cape Blanco and the River Gambia, in 1783 and 1784, as commander of the ſhip Racehorſe, and reſided chiefly at Goree, where he learnt how ſlaves were generally procured for the trade, as matter of publick notoriety, from frequent converſations with many reſpectable inhabitants, themſelves traders in ſlaves, (p. 13.) who ſpoke the French, Engliſh, and negro languages; and who were frequently at his table.

1790. Part II. P. 3. P. 4.

Slaves are principally procured for the ſlave-trade by inteſtine wars; kings breaking up villages; crimes, or imputed crimes; and kidnapping.

Villages are broken up by the king's troops ſurrounding them in the night, and ſeizing ſuch of the inhabitants

1790.　inhabitants as fuit their purpofe. This practice moft
Part II. common when there is no war with another ftate.

P. 5.　It is univerfally acknowledged, and he firmly believes, that free perfons are fold for real or imputed crimes, for the benefit of their judges.

Soon after his arrival at Goree, the king of Damel fent a free man to him for fale, and was to have the price himfelf. A king's guard being afked whether the man was guilty of the crime imputed to him, anfwered, that was of no confequence, or ever inquired into. Captain W. returned the man.

P. 6.　Kidnapping was acknowledged by all he converfed with to be generally prevalent. It is the firft principle of the natives, the principle of felf-prefervation, (p. 17.) who never go unarmed while a flave-veffel is on the coaft; and on being afked the reafon, alledge their fears. A courier of Captain Lacy, his predeceffor, though a Moor, a Muffulman, a free man, a native of Senegal, fpoke the French language fluently, and had difpatches in his pocket on his Britannick Majefty's fervice, (for particulars fee the

P. 7.　Minutes) was kidnapped, fold to a French veffel, and his releafe with difficulty obtained by the witnefs. The French captain endangered the man's life by his inhumanity.

P. 8.　Never heard of flaves being bred for fale.

Never heard of the practice of eating human flefh in Africa, and is morally certain that it did not exift on the part of the coaft where he was.

Was informed, that the governments near Goree were abfolute, but more or lefs fo according to the ftrength of the princes. King's dues feem to be

P. 9.　very regularly collected in every village: they were always paid by the fhip commanded by witnefs, and he doubts not are required from others. Has heard that when payment has been refufed, boats and men have been feized, (p. 17.)

Fully believes Africans to be equal to Europeans in capacity. They have various manufactures, chiefly for home confumption. They make cotton

cloths

cloths beautifully fine, under every want of machi- | 1790.
nery; alfo very curious ornaments of gold, and | Part II.
weapons, and tools of iron, which their experience
makes them prefer to thofe fent from hence, which | P. 141.
are made for them. On this account, unmanufac-
tured iron is preferred by them in their barter with
us. They have feveral manufactures in cane and | P. 10.
leather. They fupplied the fhips and Goree with
every thing they could raife, produce, or with fafety
catch, and entirely found them with provifions.
Perceived no indifpofition to labour or commerce in
the Africans.

According to his experience, the Africans are
grateful and affectionate. They treated him moft
kindly when many miles up their country, and unprotected, and numbers fhed tears on his departure.

The natives dare not explore Africa during the
continuance of the flave-trade, which fubjects them to
the rifk of being kidnapped.

Has boarded flave-fhips when a midfhipman—the | P. 11.
ftench intolerable—fuch a ftench proceeded from two
(he believes French) which anchored to windward of
his fhip, that he ordered them to leeward for fear of
infection, and alfo ordered that no part of their
crews fhould be fuffered to board her.

Believes the flave-fhips are not a fource of fupply | P. 12.
to the Royal navy. He never would recruit his fhip
from them, even when fhort of his compliment, to
which he attributes not having loft a man while on
the coaft, out of a crew of about 100. The Guinea
failors, who offered themfelves to him, befides their
cadaverous looks, were the moft filthy vagabonds he
ever faw. Rather than take into his fhip feven men
who were wrecked in a Guinea-man, he fed them on
fhore, and fent them home in fome tranfports.

When he prefided in a court at Goree, a Maraboo | P. 13.
fwore, with an energy which evinced the truth of his
evidence, that his brother, another Maraboo, had
been kidnapped in the act of drinking, facred by
their religion, at the inftigation of a former governor,

1790.  nor, who had taken a diflike to him: and two or
Part II. more flaves being offered for his releafe, declared
that he would not liberate him for any confideration.
This was a matter notorious at Goree.

  The natives would enter a king's fhip on her arrival off any part of the coaft, and traverfe her with as much eafe and confidence as if they had been on fhore, but he never faw a canoe board a flave-fhip, and concludes this arofe from the reafonable fears of the Africans.

P. 14. The flaves employed by the Africans live with their mafters, and are fo treated as fcarcely to be diftinguifhable from them.

  Guinea failors frequently applied to be taken by witnefs, and do not feem attached to their fhips as in other trades.

  Has been in moft of the Weft India iflands, in 1762, 1781, and 1782. The new-imported flaves appeared dejected, and very different from thofe in Africa. The country flaves appeared more dejected, and bore ftronger marks of flavery than the town
P. 15. flaves, many of whom (the domeftic ones) were fat and faucy. A great proportion of the flaves were indelibly marked with the lafh. Has feen runaways working in clogs and pothooks. Has relieved negroes placed by the road-fide, in the moft abject ftate, and from inquiries on the fpot, fully believes, that, being unfit for labour, they are turned off by their mafters to fubfift on charity. It was generally underftood, that where planters refided, the flaves were better treated than when under overfeers. Heard from refpectable merchants at Kingfton, that importing flaves was preferable to breeding them, but does not know the general opinion of the refident planters. So far from the flaves appearing as happy as
P. 16. the lower orders in Britain, &c. he never faw any figns of happinefs among the imported flaves, except at their funerals, when they fhew extravagant joy from a perfuafion that the deceafed is efcaped from flavery

to

to his native country. In Africa their funerals are attended with the moſt mournful cries.

Has been great part of his life in America, and always thought the ſlaves better treated and clothed, more domeſtic and happy, marriages among them more frequent, and fewer imported in proportion than in the Weſt India iſlands.

Has ſeen ſome branded with letters, which he thought were not made in Africa, but theſe were not common.

Has long entertained a moſt decided opinion againſt the juſtice and humanity of the ſlave-trade.

In 1762 he was a midſhipman, in 1781, 1782, a firſt lieutenant in the navy. Never reſided on ſhore or lodged on a ſugar-plantation, but made his obſervations wherever he occaſionally viſited. Was frequently on ſhore at ſeveral plantations in 1781, 1782, where he was a few days at Antigua, and five or ſix months at Jamaica.

1790.
Part II.

P. 17.

P. 18.

---

### Witneſs examined——Wadstrom.

Mr. Wadſtrom is a native of Sweden, and the Chief Director of the Aſſay Office there. Was in Africa near 3 months, in 1787, 1788, (p. 37) with Dr. Spaarman, engaged by the King of Sweden to make diſcoveries. The department allotted to witneſs was mineralogy, antiquities, and what regards the ſtate of man. They had the protection of the Senegal Company, obtained through the French miniſter, at the requeſt of the Swediſh Ambaſſador, as appears from letters produced.

Witneſs viſited the coaſt from Senegal almoſt to Gambia, thoſe parts being then in the hands of the French. Was on ſhore at different times ſeveral days, and once or twice ſeven or eight days, and was up the river Joal. He made it his buſineſs to obtain information, and could always converſe with the natives

P. 18.
P. 19.
P. 20.
P. 21.

1790.    natives by means of the English, French, and Dutch
Part II. languages, which are generally spoken by the chief
negroes.    He offered to produce a journal kept at
P. 22.   the time, in which the facts he should deliver in
evidence were noted down.

He thinks he knows perfectly how slaves are obtained, between Senegal and Gambia, viz. by the general pillage, robbery by individuals, stratagem, or deceit.

The general pillage is executed by the king's troops, armed and on horseback, who seize the unwary. Parties were sent out for this purpose by king Barbessin almost every day during the week. He was at Joal, accompanying one of those embassies, which the French Governor used to send every year, with presents to the black kings, to keep up the
P. 23.  commerce. It is customary for the king to make a return for these presents, by a gift of slaves; and though unwilling to pillage, he was excited to it by means of a constant intoxication, kept up by the French and Mulattoes of the embassy, who generally agreed every morning on taking this method to effect their purpose. When sober, he always expressed a reluctance to harrass his people; thought it hard that he should be obliged continually to do so; complained that the inhabitants of Goree, continually coming under pretence of trade, took occasion to make him insignificant presents, which he neither liked nor wished for: that they then came upon him with long accounts, debts said to be due, and pretensions without end: that the Governor of Goree
P. 24.  living among them listened too readily to their tales and complaints, and thought little of the sufferings of the negroes; and that he must have been imposed upon to suffer his name to be used on such occasions. This speech was interpreted on the spot, and put in a journal by witness, who also heard the king hold the same language on different days, and yet he afterwards ordered the pillage to be executed. Witness has no doubt but that he also pillages in other parts

of

of his dominions, since it is the custom of the Mu- 1790.
latto merchants (as both they and the French officers Part II.
declare) when they want slaves, to go to the kings,
and excite them to pillages, which are usually practised in all that part of the coast.

King of Sallum practises the pillage. Witness
saw 27 slaves from Sallum, 23 of whom were women and children, thus taken. Was told by captains P. 25.
and merchants that this was the usual practice.

Was told by merchants at Goree, that the king of
Damel practises the pillage.

Robbery, in which individuals seize on each other, P. 25.
was a general way of taking single slaves. Mentions P. 26.
a woman whom he saw in the Captiveries, and a
boy, who belonged to a French officer. The latter
was taken in the interior part above Cape Rouge by
stealth from his parents, and declared that such rob-
beries are very frequent in his country. The former
was taken at Rufisque, from her husband and children. The children are themselves articles of merchandize, if not so far from the shore as to be incapable of walking to it. Could state several instances
of this robbery: very often saw negroes thus taken
brought to Goree. Ganna of Dacard was a noted
man-stealer, and employed as such by the slave
merchants at Goree. Witness was very near being
in danger of being taken by this man to the king of
Damel, then at war with the French, who would
have demanded a high ransom for his release; he
having agreed to travel to Senegal with Ganna, but
the great Maraboo of the village cautioned him to
beware, and on his return to Goree, he was congra-
tulated on his escape by several of the inhabitants.

As instances of stratagem being a way of obtaining slaves, witness mentions a negro whom he saw
brought from Dacard, where he was on a visit. A
French merchant taking a fancy to him, persuaded
the village to seize him. He was taken from his P. 27.
wife, who wished to accompany him, but the merchant had not merchandize enough to buy both.
                                                    The

1790.
Part II.

P. 28.

P. 29.

The village agreed with the merchant about his price. Witnefs faw him at Goree on the day of his arrival, chained, and lying on the ground, exceedingly diftreffed. The king of Sallum prevailed on a woman to come into his kingdom, and fell him fome millet. On her arrival, he feized and fold her to a French officer, with whom witnefs faw this woman every day during his ftay at Goree.

Was on the ifland of St. Louis in the Senegal, and on the Continent near the river.

All the flaves fold at Senegal are brought down the river, except thofe taken by the robbery of the Moors in the neighbourhood, which is fometimes conducted by large parties in what are called petty wars. Thefe wars are promoted by prefents given to the Moorifh kings regularly every year by the Senegal Company, to engage them to procure as many negroes as poffible, and to prevent gum-arabic from being carried to the Englifh at Portandick. Witnefs heard this from the inhabitants and French officers at Senegal, and from the Moors, even in the prefence of the Director of the Company.

King Dalmanny having been brought up as a Grand Maraboo, prohibited ftrong liquors, and alfo the flave-trade, fo as not even to fuffer the paffage of flaves through his dominions; nor would he receive fome valuable prefents fent by the Company, to induce him to alter his refolution. Witnefs was fhewn the prefents by the Director, on their return. The king's dominions, including both fides of the Senegal, his prohibition ftopped the whole trade with Galam, and prevented the Company from receiving 800 flaves, which they had purchafed there. In order to obtain their compliment of flaves they had recourfe to their ufual method on fimilar occafions, bribing the Moors, and fupplying them with arms and ammunition, to feize king Dalmanny's fubjects. By January 12th, 1788, when witnefs arrived at Senegal, 50 were taken, whom the king defired to ranfom, but they were already fent to Cayenne.

Cayenne. Some were brought in every day afterwards, and put in the Company's slave-hole, in a miserable state, the greater part being very much wounded by sabres and balls. The Director conducted the witness thither, with Dr. Spaarman, whom he consulted as a medical man in their behalf. Witness particularly remembers one, lying in his blood, which flowed from a wound made by a ball in his shoulder. *[1790. Part II. P. 30.]*

Mentions an instance of a slave-taker being himself taken.

Though the Company, for many reasons, seldom purchased Moors, being now pressed for slaves, to fulfill their agreement, according to their charter with Government, they took all of whatever quality. This witness heard from the Director, and immediately noted it down in his journal.

Was told by the French officers, that European ships, particularly Dutch and English, frequently carry off natives, by treachery, from the coast. *[P. 31.]*

Was informed at Goree, by Captain Wignie, from Rochelle, who was just arrived from the Gambia, that a little before his departure from that river, three English vessels were cut off by the natives, owing to the captain of one of them, who had his cargo, being tempted by a fair wind to sail away with several of the free negroes, then drinking with the crew. Soon afterwards the wind changed, and he was driven back, seized, and killed, with all his crew, and two other vessels. Witness has by accident met with the insurer of two of these vessels, in London, who confirmed the above facts.

Witness has very often seen the merchants defraud the negroes in their dealings with them. There are many methods of deceiving the negroes in almost every article.

Thinks the negroes understandings capable of equal improvement with whites. *[P. 32.]*

Thinks the Africans very honest and hospitable; often passed days and nights alone with them, with-

1792.
Part II.

out the least fear, and was treated with all civility and kindness; he never was deceived by them.

Is clearly convinced, that the negroes surpass such Europeans as he has known, in affection, and are capable of being soon brought into the state of society enjoyed by Europeans.

Has been surprised at their industry in manufacturing cotton, indigo, iron, soap, wood, pottery, leather, and other articles. They work gold so well, that witness never saw better wrought trinkets and ornaments in Europe. They manufacture cloth and leather with uncommon neatness. The latter they tan and work into saddles, sandals, and a variety of useful and ornamental articles. The former they dye blue, yellow, brown and orange. The blue is produced from indigo. The indigo grows abundantly all over the country, so as to spoil their ground for millet and rice plantations; and equal, in the opinion of merchants, &c. who have been in America, to the best in Carolina. The yellow and brown dyes are produced from vegetable productions noticed by Dr. Spaarman. Witness has in his collection, a kind of bean used in dying, and carried in quantities on camels to Morocco. The whole army of the king of Damel, is clothed in cloth dyed orange, and brown. They forge iron very dexterously, on anvils of a remarkably hard and heavy wood, when they cannot get stone for the purpose.

P. 32.
P. 33.

Witness offered to shew specimens of the productions of Africa, raw and manufactured, which he had brought with him.

P. 34.

The canoes are generally made by negroes near the shore; but wood of a sufficiently close texture being seldom found there; this is brought without being hollowed, from the interior parts, being drawn by a great number of negroes (for weeks together) each village generally undertaking to drag it to the next, and receiving in return, partly European merchandise, and partly fish and salt. Salt is prepared from sea-water by the negroes. The ropes are made

of

of a kind of aloe, and when well made, are exceedingly strong, this aloe grows abundantly on the coast.

1790.
Part II.

The Africans have an extraordinary genius for commerce and industry, fully equal to the supply of their wants. They would extend their cultivation and manufactures, if in some degree civilized (which it would be easy to effect, were not the slave trade the only means of commerce; and it would be greatly promoted by European settlers not going thither as at present, with the sole view of making a fortune shortly, and then returning home) and if the slave trade did not occupy the minds of the natives, who are continually incited, and the merchants to engage in it, and have no encouragement to cultivate their country.

P. 35.

Slaves are kept by the natives at Goree and Senegal, but scarcely any on the continent. They are very well treated, and never sold, left there should be an insurrection among their fellow slaves. Even the French officers at Goree and Senegal, generally observe the rule of not selling them, very strictly.

The island of Goree is supplied by free negroes with provisions, from the continent.

Rice of an excellent quality, with a brownish husk, but very white kernel, is cultivated in great quantities, south of Sallum, as far as Gambia, and especially at the River Caramansa; but there is but little north of Sallum. Witness has seen many small vessels and boats, loaded with it, for the supply not only of Goree and Senegal, but of the shipping there; has samples of it.

P. 35.
P. 36.

Doctor Spaarman declared, he found a great part, if not the whole, of the materia medica in Africa, and drugs for various manufacturing uses.

The slave trade makes it dangerous for the negroes to pass from one part of their country to another, and is the chief hindrance to the improvement of their cultivation, since they never venture into the fields, unless very well armed.

B 2                                                 The

1790. The negroes print their cotton cloths with wood-
Part II. en ſtamps; has patterns of cloths ſo printed.

He reſided in all about three weeks on the continent. At Joal he was his greateſt diſtance from the ſhore, about ſix miles. When there, he went to ſeveral villages, Dacard, Bain, &c. When on ſhore, he viſited the interior, as far as he could in one or two days (as his time permitted) and at Dacard and Bain he was quite alone for ſeveral days, and went with the negroes five or ſix miles up the country. He was about a week at Senegal, and went ſometimes to the continent.

P. 38. His evidence is the reſult of obſervation and information on the ſpot, except as to the names of the veſſels and their captains, which were cut off in the Gambia; particulars which he learnt in England.

Kidnapping is not allowed by the laws in Africa, but it can ſcarcely be diſcovered by the kings, and he never heard of an inſtance of its being puniſhed; if diſcovered it would be puniſhed, he believes, and particularly if ſome European trader were preſent at the trial. He was preſent at a trial for ſome offence at Joal, when the king was incited to condemn by the Mulattoes of Goree, who wiſhed to purchaſe the man when convicted; but the king acquitted him.

There are ſome ſlaves by birth on the coaſt, particularly at Sallum, but few higher up the coaſt; and on the continent oppoſite Goree, very few. The wealth of great men is not eſtimated from the number of ſlaves they poſſeſs, but at Sallum from the ſilver and European merchandize; and higher up the coaſt, from the quantity of millet, and of their
P. 39. cattle, camels and horſes. The king of Sallum generally takes ſilver for his ſlaves, and generally kidnaps his neighbours; but higher up the coaſt, the kings kidnap their own ſubjects.

Was informed by the mulattoes at Goree, that 1200 ſlaves were procured at Joal, but he believes the real number is not ſo great. He was informed that more than 1000 ſlaves were procured at Senegal.
The

The manufactures specified are carried on from 1790. Senegal down to Goree. The negroes are particu- Part II. larly skilful in manufacturing iron and gold. They probably derived their art, with regard to the latter, P. 39. from the Moors, but now are themselves the artists; P. 40. witness seeing but one Moor work in that branch. They are equal to any European goldsmith in fillagree, and even other articles, as buckles, except the chafes, tongues, and anchors. The best manufacture of cotton cloths is at Sallum, which is probably chiefly owing to the goodness of the cotton, this becoming better and better lower down the coast. Witness has samples manufactured from the principal parts of the coast where he was.

The Maraboos in some parts deal in slaves, but generally not. They support themselves in the same way as other negroes.

The French excite not only petty wars, but man- P. 43. stealing, in order to obtain slaves. Witness has heard that the English and Dutch frequently do so. The English possessed the coast he visited, previously to P. 44. its belonging to the French. He never heard that the practices he has mentioned in his evidence, were newly introduced.

As far as he knows, all the sabres on the coast are P. 43. from Europe.

Except working in gold, the Moors are known for no industry, except seizing on negroes, and collecting gum arabic.

At Joal the king has a certain interest in the trade, but no particular taxes; king Damel has some taxes, but no regular system of taxation: what they receive is in cattle and millet, which they sell in great quantities at Goree.

Never heard of any instance of the king's sending out parties to enforce the payment of taxes in arrear.

At Sallum the trade in slaves is almost entirely in the hands of the king. At Sin the king has the
principal

1790.
Part II.
P. 44.

principal share, but suffers his subjects to trade also. King Damel has no prerogative in this trade.

Was told by two French captains, and French merchant, that the French Guinea ships are provided with poison, with which they may destroy their negroes, if subjected to a calm, short provisions, or contagious sickness; and captain Le Loup instanced a vessel from Brest, the commander of which was obliged to poison his slaves, in a passage of two or three months; but 20 reaching the Cape out of a cargo of 500.

### Witness Examined—GEORGE ROOKE.

P. 45.   Was at Goree from May 6th to August 16th, 1779.

Never saw the pillage executed by the king of Damel on his villages, or wounded people brought from thence; he always understood that when he wanted slaves for sale, he made war to procure them, and does not know whether this war was of the nature of a marauding expedition or not.

P. 46.

He knew that kidnapping took place in the neighbourhood of Goree. It was spoken of as a common practice. It was reckoned disgraceful there, but cannot speak as to the opinion on the continent. As instances of kidnapping, he remembers two or three negroes being brought to Goree, but he could not discover by whom. At their request he immediately sent them back.

P. 46, 47, 48.

It was proposed to him by three captains of English slave ships lying under the fort of Goree to kidnap 100 or 150 men, women, and children, the king of Damel's subjects, (some of whom were Maraboos) who came to Goree in consequence of the friendly intercourse between him and Damel. He refused, and was much shocked by the proposition. They

said

said such things had been done by a former governor, 1790. but the chief Maraboo at Rufisque did not recollect any such event. Part II.

As to the natives being fraudulently taken off, recollects being informed by a Maraboo, that four or five of the king of Damel's subjects were on board a merchant ship. He had them brought on shore, and sent to the king. The captain said in excuse, that they came on board drunk, and that he meant to send them ashore. P. 46.

---

Witness examined—ROBERT NORRIS, Esq.

Says, that the evidence delivered by him before the Privy Council (in their Report to the House of Commons) is, he thinks, to the best of his recollection, a correct account of the information he then gave: cannot speak with precision, but supposes that the printed account of the evidence delivered by him at the bar of the House of Commons, on the Bill for regulating the transportation of Slaves, is a correct statement of the information he then gave. P. 50.

Had several interviews with the Rev. Mr. Clarkson at Liverpool, latter part of 1787, who expressing a wish to have the slave trade abolished, told him of some part of his plan; which was, to encourage by bounties a trade with Africa for its natural produce; and to subject vessels in the slave-trade to a licence tax, from which to defray the said bounty: also spoke of making a settlement on the coast, and thinks that he (Mr. Norris) proposed Caramansa river, as a proper place: that slave ships should be restricted from bringing home West India produce was also a part of Mr. Clarkson's plan; of which he has now given the substance. Believes he said in reply, that confining slave-ships entirely to the slave-trade, would give greater latitude to ships trading in African produce. Thinks he could not suppose the plan proposed P. 51.

P. 52.

1790. proposed, could abolish the slave-trade, but encou-
Part II. rage a trade in the productions of the country. Mr.
Clarkson appeared to have two objects, viz. to confirm his good opinion of the trade for the natural products of Africa, and to discover the abuses in the slave-trade. He discovered an anxious solicitude to effect the abolition of the slave-trade, but Mr. N. could not conceive that he could accomplish it, and it was not an immediate but a gradual abolition which he understood him as aiming at; for he recollects, that he (Mr. C.) wished him to get a particular friend (Mr. Falconbridge) recommended to the command of a slave ship.

Understood abolition of the slave-trade to be the avowed object of Mr. C. but by a gradual operation. Really does not recollect what he then thought the propositions from that gentleman would effect; presumes he thought they tended to a gradual abolition.

P. 53. He gave his opinion of them at the time to Mr. C. who is, he dares say, more able than himself, at this distance of time, to recollect what he stated his impressions to be ; but as well as he recollects, it was, that they tended to a gradual abolition ; and he gave him every information that he possessed frankly on this subject, Mr. C. will, he dares say, do him the justice to say, he heard him with temper ; and though he could not think an immediate abolition practicable or politick, yet he withheld no advice on the subject from him.

He did express his concurrence with Mr. C. in his object as stated of gradual abolition, and still entertains the same opinion, that the slave-trade will gradually come to the abolition he wished for.

As to the propositions above alluded to, believes he suggested one of them himself, and the others he thought conducive to the end proposed.

He could approve of no abolition of the slave-trade that was not compatible with the situation of the West India islands ; and when the necessities of planters there no longer required the aid of labourers
from

from Africa, he has always reckoned that the trade will ceafe of itfelf. 1790. Part II.

Is not cafuift enough to decide on the merits or demerits of the flave trade on any other ground, than that of political and commercial neceffity.

Previous to the period referred to, he had formed his own private opinion; which was, that the fubjects of that trade are in general more happily fituated in the colonies, than at home; and when conducted with propriety, thinks it confiftent with his notions of humanity: conceived the neceffities of the Weft India iflands ought to prefcribe the continuance of the flave-trade; for, he confidered flavery as a condition of mankind in every age, and in every country; and whilft the neceffities of the Weft India iflands require a fupply of African flaves (convinced that their ftate there, is in general as happy as it was at home) and whilft thofe neceffities exift, he does not difcover that the caufe of humanity is violated by continuing that trade. P. 54.

Did not think the neceffities of the Weft Indies fhould prefcribe the extent to which the flave trade fhould be carried on, as well as the continuance of it; for, whilft the colonies of other ftates require a fimilar fupply (which they would endeavour to get for themfelves) as a commercial man he confiders we fhould relinquifh an important fhare of our commerce, were we to regulate it by the neceffities of the Britifh colonies alone. Declares, he does not recollect whether any thing paffed in his intercourfe with Mr. C. at Liverpool, about preventing our fhips from fupplying fettlements of foreign powers with flaves; but if there did, is perfuaded that Mr. C. can inform the Committee, but fo far as his memory ferves, believes they had no converfation on that point.

Really does not recollect, whether Mr. C. made at the time, any minutes of what paffed in the converfation.

1790.
Part II.
P. 55.

As to the neceffities of the colonies for flaves, prefumes his opinion then was the fame as now; that the iflands want a fupply of 10 or 12,000 annually, and as to the time fuch fupply may be wanted, it was then as impoffible for him to define it as now. As to the flave trade being carried on for the purpofe only of keeping up the flaves then in the iflands, he cannot recollect his opinion, in a converfation that he has almoft entirely forgotten; but it is his opinion, that along with what is wanted to keep up the ftock, an additional ftrength of labourers is requifite to extend the cultivation of the iflands.

Was informed by Mr. C. that he had been at Briftol, to collect what he could, relative to the abufes faid to have been committed in the flave-trade, with a view of bringing thofe officers and mafters to juftice who had treated their feamen harfhly.

Underftood the object of his journey was, to redrefs the injuries faid to be fuftained by individuals, and gave him credit for the attempt; but does not recollect his mentioning any other object of his inquiry there than to difcover what violences had been committed by the officers againft the feamen.

Underftood he had the fame object in view at Liverpool, together with his plan for an eftablifhment in Africa, and gradual abolition of the flavetrade.

P. 56.

Conceived the redrefs of the injuries fuffered by feamen, to be his immediate object, the other parts of his plan he conceived to be a more diftant confideration, as they could not be effected immediately.

Is not competent to anfwer what was his main object.

The converfation before alluded to with Mr. C. was at Liverpool in 1787, probably at his own houfe. Was not before acquainted with Mr. C. had feen his book on the Commerce of the Human Species. Mr. C. was introduced to him by a Mr. Rathbone, a merchant, as defirous of fome information refpecting the African flave-trade, in which he (Mr. N.) had
been

been long engaged: he replied that he would give 1790.
him what information he knew, and shew him a ma- Part II.
nuscript respecting Africa.

Does not recollect if it was then mentioned that P. 57.
Mr. C. was pursuing the object of an abolition of the
trade. Believes there was then no mention made of
the Society instituted in London for that purpose, either by Mr. Rathbone or any other of the party.
Does not recollect, whether the interview, in which
the propositions for the gradual abolition of the
slave-trade were discussed, was by appointment or
not.

As to being supposed, from what he said before,
to concur with Mr. C. in his design and wish for the
abolition of the slave-trade, or only to declare his
opinion that the propositions if adopted would tend
to that effect. Says, that Mr. C. being introduced
to him by a friend whom he respected, he wished to
treat him with courtesy. He found him strongly
impressed with the accomplishing of a particular
object. Courtesy to a stranger induced him to acquiesce in, rather than discuss the merits of the question, and it was his opinion that the propositions if
adopted, would tend to that effect. At that time he
had no idea of ever seeing Mr. C. again, nor could he
interest himself either in the abolition of the slave-
trade, or the emancipation of the negroes in the
West Indies, which was also one of his propositions;
but the redress of abuses of seamen was an object that
he desired as earnestly as Mr. C.

He acquiesced as well from complaisance to a P. 58.
stranger, as from a conviction which he still entertains, that a day will come when the slave-trade will
cease. Could not but approve of Mr. C's. philan-
thropy, though he doubts of the policy of reducing
his principles to practice; if he was to point at any
thing reprehensible in Mr. C's. conduct, it is the
abusing a private conversation, in the manner he
suspects he has done, by making him stand here to
sustain an examination upon it nearly three years

after

1791. after it passed; he little expected ever to have heard
Part II. any future mention of it.

Could not but condemn the measure if carried on with precipitation, as ruinous to the commerce of this country, and to the cultivation of the islands; but at same time courtesy to a stranger, whom he never expected to see again, prevented him from debating the merits or demerits of the measure.

As to whether he understood Mr. C's. object to be precipitate and immediate, or gradual abolition, does not recollect the whole of his object; their conversations on the subject were much too short for a full explanation of so important a measure; but believes a gradual abolition, to be precipitated by his plan, was one object of his inquiries at Liverpool: he gave Mr. C's. heart full credit for the philanthropic measure which he pursued, without weighing (in his opinion) the political and commercial inconveniencies annexed to it; and civility to a stranger induced him to acquiesce in the measure, rather than condemn it. Does not recollect that he used any arguments with Mr. C. to dissuade him from pursuing his object of gradual abolition, for he found him to cherish it so warmly, that any attempt would have been fruitless.

P. 59.

Cannot recollect when Mr. C. left Liverpool, nor after what interval he was appointed delegate, which was in his absence, and without his knowledge.— From his first seeing Mr. C. to his appearing before the Privy Council, might perhaps be six months.

Does not recollect the particular abuses in the conduct of the slave trade, the correction of which Mr. C had in view, except as before intimated, too much severity said to be practised by the officers, and also the regulation of the price of slops, and the custom of paying half the wages in the currency of the West Indies He gave him all the information on that head that he possessed. Differed from him in

P. 60.

in opinion as to the frequency of ill treatment. Mr. C. quoted more inftances than had ever come within his knowledge. Never heard of many inftances in 15 years experience. Some he has known.

Thinks one fingle inftance would juftify Mr C's. endeavours: conceives wanton feverity always merits punifhment; the inftances he has heard of not occurring under his own eye, he cannot judge of the provocation that might occafion them; but if they were, as reprefented, he fhould heartily embrace Mr C's. fentiments refpecting them.

Does not recollect that he gave any opinion to Mr. C. as to the general practice of kidnapping in Africa by natives, though he might have mentioned it: for, a few months after, he ftated, in his evidence before the Privy Council, that he fufpected it was practifed in fome inftances between the unconnected tribes of the Windward Coaft.

Does not recollect ftating his opinion to Mr. C. upon the utility of the flave-trade confidered as the fource of fupply to the marine of Great Britain; but if he did, he probably coincided on that as on other points to the opinions which that gentleman entertained, rather than harrafs his feelings, by difputing opinions which he cherifhed.

The inhabitants of the vicinity of Cape Appolonia, are fubject to nearly a fimilarly oppreffive tyranny with the ftate of Dahomy. Thefe are the only two arbitrary governments which he has vifited; the other diftricts of the Gold Coaft have a milder government.

Whether from the condition of the inhabitants of Dahomy or Appolonia, any fair conclufions can be drawn as to the people of Negroland in general, obferves, that in drawing fair conclufions, they fhould be taken from the particular countries, and not by general comparifon. Thefe two countries are not a ftandard by which to judge of the adjoining nations on the fea coaft, and he knows but little of the interior country.

As

1790.
Part II.

As to the weight of a bafket or crue of rice on the Windward Coaft,—a bafket is an indefinite weight; when brought aboard in bafkets, it is meafured in a crue, which is about 20 lb.

Has read the entries from Capt. Frafer's journal, mentioned in the examination of Mr. Falconbridge, before the former Select Committee on the Slave Trade.—The date of the firft entry is 19th Sept. of the laft 10th of November. The amount of the total rice mentioned in thefe two entries, is not quite $12\frac{1}{2}$ tons, not quite 6 tons of which appears to have been gotten at Junk. The daily confumption of the fhip's company, and of the few negroes on board, during the period mentioned, was, he believes, not included in the quantity ftated in Captain Frafer's journal.

P. 62.

Whether the abolition, for which Mr. Clarkfon wifhed, was an abolition to be accelerated by means to be ufed for that purpofe, and not merely a difcontinuance of the trade, from the circumftance of the Weft India iflands ceafing to want any further fupply, he cannot at this diftance of time take upon him to fay; nor does he recollect more of it, (Mr. C's. plan) than a gradual abolition of the flave-trade, and the emancipation of the negroes now in the iflands.

Might be led, from the perufal of Mr. C's. Effay on the Slavery and Commerce of the Human Species, and from his converfation, that he had in view the accelerating of the abolition; but, with refpect to the concurrence which he has ftated to have expreffed, with Mr. C. in his object, he calls his conduct in all his communications with that gentleman, rather an acquiefcence from deference to a ftranger of his character and functions, than a concurrence with his meafures.

Even had he difapproved of that object, which he fuppofed Mr. C. to be in purfuit of at the time, he would have fuggefted means which, in his own opinion,

opinion, conduced to the attainment of it; becaufe Mr. C. could not reafonably fuppofe him totally ignorant of the trade which he was inveftigating, and if he had withheld every hint or communication, he would have been charged with not treating a ftranger, (introduced to him by a friend he refpected) with that civility and hofpitality which he wifhed to do, during his vifit to Liverpool. Befides, one part of Mr. C.'s plan met his moft fincere concurrence, that of redreffing the abufes faid to be practifed towards feamen, and he found it impoffible to converfe with him on the one fubject without being infenfibly led to the other.

He found Mr. C. fo zealous on the fubject, that his acquaintance with him would not juftify his prefuming to reafon with him againft a fyftem ruinous to the commerce of this country, and which he thought at the time he could not poffibly effect. He conceived it to be a fine fpun theory of humanity, and could not bring himfelf to think, that men and meafures were fo powerfully combined, as he has fince found them, to promote his (Mr. C's.) views.

Cannot fay now, that he was of opinion that any of thofe propofitions in which he concurred, and which he apprehended to tend to accelerate the abolition of the trade, would tend alfo to accelerate that period at which the Weft India Iflands would ceafe to require any further fupply of flaves. Does not recollect that at that time any fuch confideration occurred.

As to the period, he may be fuppofed to have fixed in his mind for the abolition, when he ftated that fuch an event would gradually take place, it would have been prefumption in him to have fixed any; for in all his converfations with Mr. C. on a fubject, which he deemed equally imprudent and impolitic, he had fcarcely one ferious confideration, beyond being commonly civil to him.

The grounds upon which he entertained the opinion, that the African flave-trade will gradually come
to

1791. Part II.
P. 64.

to be abolished, are, the restrictions already laid upon the trade, and the measures so ably and unremittingly pursued in this country to effect it.

Whether, as a commercial man, he thinks it would be for the interest of this country to furnish the colonies of other powers with slaves, after our own have ceased to need further supply, this being matter of opinion, should he live to see the day when the British islands have ceased to require any further supply, he will be more competent to form a judgment on the question than at present.

But he fancies there is not a politician or merchant in this country but will admit that such a commerce would be to the advantage of this country; for it would be securing to the merchant that profit which would otherwise center with other merchants and manufacturers that continued it.

Whether " The African slave-trade is carried on " as much to the ease and comfort of those that are " the subjects of it, and also of those that conduct it, " as it is possible for human ingenuity to devise:" begs leave to object to the question, because it is a quotation from a pamphlet, which he does not think it incumbent on him to support before the committee.

P. 65.

Has no reason to doubt, that all the ships in that account from Liverpool, which he delivered to the committee, stated to have been laid up in consequence of the act, commonly called the Slave-carrying Act, were actually driven out of the trade by the operation of that law.

Has recently received an account of a late rapid increase in the French trade to and from the Coast of Africa, which states, that there had sailed, or were fitting out, between 1st June, 1789, and 18th January, 1790, for the African trade, from Nantes 42 vessels; Rochelle 12; Bourdeaux 32; St. Maloes 4; Harfleur 8; Marseilles 4; and from Havre 28; in all 130 vessels, in seven months and an half, or thereabouts. His information does not specify whether any of these vessels are employed in trade for the

the productions of the country, in contradiction to the slave-trade; which induces him to believe that the slave-trade only is meant.

1790. Part II.

---

Witness examined,—Rev. THOMAS CLARKSON.

Went, in company with Mr. Rathbone, of Liverpool, to Mr. Norris's house, but not finding him, was introduced to him upon change, as the author of an Essay on "the Slavery and Commerce of the Human Species;" and as coming to Liverpool for information on the slave trade. Mr. Norris said, he had read his book with much satisfaction, adding, as near as he can recollect, that it contained the truth. He promised him also every information as to the object of his journey, and appointed Sunday following, for a meeting at his own house.

P. 66.

Was afterwards at his house 6 times; and was waited upon also by Mr. Norris, 3 or 4. Each time they had long conversations on the slave trade. On the first of these (Sunday) witness read a manuscript, intitled, " An account of the wars and customs of the " Dahomans," which Mr. Norris lent him. Afterwards, on same day, in speaking of productions of Africa, Mr. Norris stated them such, as they were afterwards set down, in consequence of his evidence in the Privy Council report. He affirmed also, the almost universal way in which such became slaves, as he had transported from the coast, was this, That they were kidnapped (by the natives, p. 68) either as they were travelling on the roads, or fishing in the creeks, or cultivating their little spots, which history he had learnt from themselves. In future conversations also, as to this being an universal mode, his reply was, " Undoubtedly, no person can deny " it."

P. 67.

At a future time, Mr. Norris gave him some black pepper, brought with him from Whydah, as one argument

1790.
Part. II

P. 68.

argument of the impolicy of the flave trade. Being shewn alfo copies of fome mufter-rolls of Briftol Guineamen, which witnefs had collected, he faid, he would find nearly the fame lofs of feamen in thofe of Liverpool, as in thofe then fhewn him.

At another time, when informed by witnefs, that he was on point of difcovering a murder by captain Brown, on Peter Green, a feaman; he allowed great cruelties practifed on feamen in flave trade. Called afterwards on witnefs with a journal of a voyage in that trade, to convince him he had not been deceived in information collected on that point; and to confirm witnefs more, of his being of the fame mind with himfelf, invited him to his houfe, to communicate on claufes for a bill, that would bring about abolition of flave trade. Witnefs went, and after fome converfation, Mr. N. dictated, and witnefs wrote. He wrote the claufes with Mr. N's own pen and ink, and in his own room.

Witnefs had fuch confidence in Mr. N. as a man of veracity, and a zealous friend to the abolition of flave trade, that on making a fecond edition of his work, " On the Slavery and Commerce of the Hu-" man Species," he inferted the circumftance of kidnapping, as well as that of the king of Dahomy breaking up a village when he wanted flaves, as before communicated to him by Mr. Norris. As a farther proof, when he waited upon Mr. Pitt, to exprefs his hopes, that the committe of the Privy Council (then about to examine into the flave trade) would examine witneffes on both fides of the queftion. He mentioned Mr. Norris having material information on that fide of the queftion, which related to the abolition; repeating the fubftance of his different converfations with him on the produce of Africa; the new trade that could be eftablifhed there; the lofs of feamen, and cruelties exercifed on them in the flave trade; mentioning, at the fame time, the claufes which Mr. N. had given him for a bill for its abolition. Was afraid, however, that

Mr.

Mr. N. on being written to only by an individual like himself, would not come to London, connected as he was at Liverpool; though he knew his heart to be engaged on that side; wished therefore an order to be sent him by the committee, which would take off the risk of disobliging connections there. On being told by Mr. Pitt, that attendance to such order could not be enforced, witness wrote himself to Mr. N. at Liverpool, but was answered by Mr. Rathbone, that he Mr. N. was then in London.

On this information, witness wished much to find him out, to intreat him to persevere in the same line of conduct, as manifested to him at Liverpool. Found his address, but before he could see him, was told by the bishop of London, very greatly to his surprise, that Mr. Norris " had come up as a Liverpool delegate, in support of the slave trade." Witness upon this, tells his lordship, and afterwards states in writing, how Mr. Norris had behaved, as above stated. Distressed at the time, and balancing between the thought of violating the rights of hospitality, by exposing Mr. Norris, and the duty due to the cause he had undertaken, he asked his lordship how to act; who advising him to call personally on Mr. N. to explain the reasons of his conduct, he went, but not finding him at home, left his card. Soon after Mr. N. waited upon witness, who was out, and left the following letter, which the committee desired to be produced, and taken down.

" My dear Sir,
" The letter, which you did me the honour to
" address to me at Liverpool, missed me there, and
" reached me here only a few days ago; being
" brought to me by a gentleman from thence, who
" was so obliging as to charge himself with the care
" of it. It gave me the sincerest pleasure to receive
" this testimony of the regard of a gentleman, whom
" I shall ever respect and esteem, and whose phi-
" lanthropy claims the admiration of every person
" whose

1790.
Part. II.

P. 71.

"whose bosom contains a spark of humanity. Upon
"my return to my lodgings last night, I was ho-
"noured with your card, announcing your address,
"and resolved to wait upon you this morning; but
"the arrival of a packet from the West Indies,
"which called on its way at Charleston, has brought
"me letters from my connections there, which
"oblige me to relinquish my intention, from avo-
"cations which require my immediate attention
"elsewhere; and as I am under an engagement to
"visit a friend in the country to-morrow, and shall
"not return till Monday, I find I shall not be able
"to enjoy the pleasure of waiting on you until some
"day early in the ensuing week.

"Since we parted last, the subject of our con-
"versation has frequently employed my thoughts;
"and the force of your arguments, and the justice
"and humanity of your sentiments, have impressed
"on my mind a due deference for your opinions;
"but we differ in some points: from commercial
"and political considerations, I am induced to
"think, that the benevolence of your plan cannot be
"acceded to in toto. If you will be pleased to turn
"to my favourite author, the Abbé Raynal, vol. 1.
"p. 9, you will see a strong argument against one
"part of it; and other objections occur to myself;
"but I assure you, that whatever my own private
"opinions may be, I should gladly have declined
"any publick interference in this business, could I
"have refused it with propriety. The present in-
"vestigation will, I hope, tend to correct whatever
"abuses exist in the African trade, as well as to im-
"prove the condition and situation of that unhappy
"part of our fellow-creatures, whose unfortunate
"lot it is, perhaps, for some wise, though inscruta-
"ble purpose of our Creator, to toil for their breth-
"ren; and every idea, tending to so desirable a pur-
"pose is, I trust, as dear to me as it can be to any
"person whatever.

"Your

" Your kind remembrance of Mrs. Norris, claims 1790.
" my warmeſt thanks, and I am, with every ſenti- Part II.
" ment of reſpect and friendſhip,

" Dear Sir,

" Your obliged and moſt obedient ſervant,

Salopian, 29th Feb. 1788.   " ROBERT NORRIS."

P. S.  " I am ſo preſſed for time, that I muſt beg
" you will excuſe this very incorrect letter, which I
" aſſure you I have not leiſure to copy."

The Rev. Thomas Clarkſon, No. 10, Gerrard-Street,
Soho.

Witneſs ſays, that he ſtated this conduct of Mr. N. to Sir William Dolben, ſo early as the time of his regulating bill: as alſo 2 or 3 times to Mr. Cruden, to ſee if Mr. Cruden, who was preſent at the firſt converſation at Mr. Norris's houſe, and knew Mr. Norris's great pains to give him intelligence, perfectly recollected it, and if ſuch conduct did not appear equally ſtriking to him as to witneſs. Mr. Cruden's reply to witneſs, in the preſence of another perſon or perſons, was, " My opinion of Mr. Norris, whom I P. 72.
" have known for years, is of the higheſt kind, but I
" confeſs his conduct to you at Liverpool, and ſince
" as a Liverpool delegate, embarraſſes me much."

Says, Mr. Norris could not but have known his object at Liverpool to be abolition of ſlave trade, even had he not heard it from himſelf. It was notorious that witneſs went there with that view, he dining daily in publick, and merchants pointing at him as he paſſed the change, as a perſon of that deſcription.

Is ſure the information he is now giving, is preciſely what he received from Mr. Norris; for as to the two facts relative  " to kidnapping, and the king
" of

1790.
Part II.

"of Dahomy," before related, he put them down in a book, soon after the conversation, he kept for that purpose; and as to the clauses given him by Mr. N. for a bill for abolition, he put them down also, with this difference, that he put down the latter with Mr. Norris's own pen and ink, and own room; has that book to produce, if necessary.

The committee requesting the book to be produced, the following clauses were taken from it.

P. 73.
1. "Make every slave vessel take out a licence, "and let the sum paid for such licence, be at least £50.

2. "Let no slave vessel, under severe penalties, "be suffered to take a tooth, a puncheon of palm "oil, or any of its productions, from the coast.

3. "Let no slave vessel be permitted to bring a "bale of cotton, a hogshead of sugar, or even a pas- "senger, from the West Indies.

4. "£1000 fine for a vessel that supplies the "Spaniards and French.

5. "Let every vessel that goes to Africa for the "natural productions of the country, receive a "bounty. £500 for bounty would be adequate to "the wages of seamen, their provisions, and the "stores of a vessel of 200 tons, for 8 months; £300 "to be paid at outset, £200 at her return.

6. "The Bananas to be head quarters and first "settlement; they belonged to one Cleland, a mu- "latto; perhaps his family, who remain, would "sell it.

7. "That the De Loss Islands be the second "from Sierra Leone to Cape Mount. To wind- "ward of Sierra Leone there is a tract, where the "blacks are descendants of the Portuguese; these "people are industrious at present, more civilized "than the natives, good boatmen, craftsmen, &c. "They are free, and not dependant on the Portu- "guese; a sort of mulattoes, and would easily be "brought over.

8. "The

8. " The River Caramanca, on the Windward, 1790.
" or Gold Coaft, runs parallel to the fea, and would Part II.
" be a moft eligible fituation, both in point of de-
" fence and productions.

9. " Thefe regulations will deftroy the flave P. 74.
" trade in a few years."

Says, the claufe relative to a licence for flave fhips, came from Mr. N. that relative to a bounty, from himfelf; though Mr. N. calculated the fums annexed to it; that relative to hindering flave fhips from taking off the produce of Africa, came from himfelf alfo; but that for hindering them from taking Weft India produce, &c. from Mr. N. As to that relative to the trade carried on for the French and Spaniards, cannot fay who propofed it; but Mr. N. mentioned the fine of £1000, faying, this branch of it ought immediately to be abolifhed, as fupplying foreigners at the expence of the Englifh marine. The fettlements alfo were mentioned by Mr. N. in the order in which they ftand, though witnefs cannot fay pofitively whether propofed as neceffary by Mr. N. or himfelf. Mr. N. however, gave his fanction to the whole, for witnefs put down no claufe not approved of by Mr. N. after converfation on the propriety of it.

Recollects Mr. Norris ftated the flave-trade to be a lofing trade, in prefence of Meffrs. Cruden and Copeland, the latter of whom had been a flavemerchant.

Was introduced to Mr. N. he fuppofes, in the P. 75. beginning of Septemb. left him the end of October, and in the February following was told that Mr. N. had come up as a Liverpool Delegate.

Never afked Mr. N. to procure a flave-fhip for Mr. Falconbridge. Should have thought he would have fuffered in Mr. N's. opinion from fuch a propofal. Befides, Mr. F. had previoufly declared to witnefs at Briftol, before a gentleman, that he had left the trade from principle. Adds that the object of Mr. Falconbridge's journey to Liverpool, was to
aid

1790.
Part II.

aid him in procuring facts for abolition of the slave trade: nor did he make such a proposal to any other person. Thinks it not improbable he might have told Mr. N. that as the slave-trade could not immediately be abolished, it was a pity that humane men should not be selected to command slave-ships in the interim, but does not even recollect this.

P. 76.
Says there were very few meetings of himself and Mr. N. at which Mr. F. was present. Does not recollect being at the Exchange with Mr. F. and Mr. N. or of seeing Mr. F. at the Exchange at any distance, when with Mr. N. though this might have happened. Was about six weeks at Liverpool.

P. 77.
Thinks, in his calls on Mr. N. found him at home five or six times; dined with him twice; saw him in a morning, when he shewed him copies of the Bristol muster-rolls; received from him another morning, at his house, the pepper from Whydah: saw him also when he went to tell him of the probability of proving the murder of Green, by Capt. Brown: a sixth time was, when he received from him the clauses.

Was of opinion, that Mr. N. did not consider the abolition as an extraordinary plan, but as one which ought to be executed. His whole conduct to him, (Mr. C.) at Liverpool, made him believe so.

Recollects Mr. N. shewed him some papers, and gave him one, viz. " An Invoice for a Cargo to " Whydah;" but none about the loss of seamen. Must, however, do Mr. N. the justice to say, he has heard him state the loss of seamen in his own ship to be little or nothing This, however, he did not state, to shew Mr. C. had been deceived, but that there were ships that went to the coast without any material loss; and Mr. C. considered it as a proof of Mr. N's. own humanity.

Understood kidnapping, from Mr. N. to be the general practice, as far as he, Mr. N. could judge from his own experience, except only Dahomy, for that king was said by him not to kidnap, but to

seize

seize on a village, when in want of slaves. Mr N. never discriminated between kidnapping by hostile nations or by individuals. His words were, (which witness will never forget) " that on inquiry into the history of those whom he had taken from Africa in his own vessels, their almost universal answer was, that they were kidnapped either as they were travelling, or fishing, or cultivating their little spots." On returning from Mr. Norris's he put down these words in his journal, produced yesterday. Says it is impossible for him ever to have misunderstood Mr. N. on this particular; was never clearer of any thing in his life. Says also, that though he inserted the circumstance into the second edition of his " Essay on the Slavery and Commerce of the Human Species," he did not insert it as the basis upon which he built the assertion there, that kidnapping was a general practice, but only to corroborate other circumstances mentioned in the former edition of that book.

Does not recollect that Mr. N. alluded to any particular period, when he stated the slave-trade to be a losing one.

Never heard Mr. N. express any approbation or disapprobation of his, (witness's) measures to redress abuses of Guinea seamen. Knows only Mr. N. concurred with him, that such enormities were practised, and the seamen were worse used in that than any other trade, which Mr. N. not only expressed at his own house, but when he lent him the journal before described, (p. 67.)

As to any plan said to have been communicated by him to Mr. N. for freeing of the negroes, says he was never so absurd as to think of such a plan. His sole object at Liverpool was to collect facts for the abolition of the slave-trade. This distinction between abolition and emancipation he set out with as a first principle, and has preserved till now.

As to the supposition that Mr. N. could not be serious in condemning a trade he had long pursued, witness believes he sincerely meant the abolition of

1790. the trade in many branches, as neither juftifiable on
Part II. the principles of humanity nor policy; and witnefs's
conduct, as explained yefterday, proves he thought
fo; for he not only mentioned him to Mr. Pitt, as he
then ftated, as a proper evidence for abolition, but
even wrote him to come to London in that capacity.

On being afked the character of Mr. Rathbone,
witnefs replied, that he was recommended to him as
to a very worthy man, and found him fo; and being
afked again, if civility to a ftranger, recommended
by Mr. Rathbone, might not prevent Mr. N. from
controverting opinions, which he, witnefs, warmly
efpoufed, replied, in his opinion, civility to a ftranger,
ought not to prevent any man from telling the truth;
neither does he believe it did him, becaufe Mr. R.
repeatedly told witnefs Mr. N. condemned the trade.

---

Witnefs examined—Dr. THOMAS TROTTER,

A Surgeon in the Royal Navy.

P. 80.  Was a voyage in the African flave-trade, from
Liverpool, in 1783, furgeon of the Brookes, Clement
Noble, mafter. Ten months on the coaft, from the
time they reached Cape Palmas, till the cargo was
P. 81. completed at Anamaboe. Made many inquiries into
the mode of procuring flaves, of flaves themfelves,
of traders, and particularly of Accra, a trader at
Cape la How, who was a moft intelligent man, of
uncommon modefty and gentlenefs, and well known
as a man of great integrity. The information received was, that the natives were fometimes flaves
from crimes, but the greater part of flaves were what
they called prifoners of war. Of their whole cargo
recollects only three criminals, one fold for adultery,
and one for witchcraft, whofe whole family fhared
his fate. One of the firft faid he had been decoyed
by a woman, who told her hufband, and he was
fentenced

sentenced to pay a slave; but being poor, was sold himself. Such stratagems are frequent: the fourth mate of the Brookes was so decoyed, and obliged to pay a slave, under threat of stopping trade.

1790. Part II.

Of the family sold for witchcraft, consisting, he thinks, of the man, his mother, wife, and two daughters; the women shewed the deepest affliction, the man a sullen melancholy: said, that having quarrelled with the Cabbosheer of Salt-pan, he, in revenge, had accused him of witchcraft: he refused food: early next morning it was found he had attempted to cut his throat; the wound was sewed up, but the following night he had not only torn out the sutures, but had made a similar attempt on the other side: from the ragged edges of the wound, and the blood upon his finger ends it appeared to have been done with his nails, for though strict search was made through all the rooms, no instrument was found. He declared he never would go with white men, uttered incoherent sentences, and looked wishfully at the skies. His hands were secured, but persisting to refuse all sustenance, he died of hunger in eight or ten days.

P. 82.

Has often asked Accra, what he meant by prisoners of war. Found they were such as had been carried off by a set of marauders, who ravage the country for that purpose. The bush-men making war to make trade, (meaning it seemed to make slaves) was a common way of speaking among the traders. The practice was also confirmed by the slaves who shewed by gestures how the robbers had come upon them; and in the Brookes, during the passage, some of the boy (slaves) played a game, which they called slave-taking, or bush-fighting; shewing the different manœuvres thereof in leaping, sallying, and retreating. Inquiries of this nature put to the women, were answered only by violent bursts of sorrow. Upon asking Accra, what they made of their slaves when the English and French

P. 83.

1790. were at war, he simply answered, " Suppose ship no
Part II. " come, massa, no take slave."

Had many boys and girls on board, who had no relations in the ship; many of them told him they had been kidnapped in the neighbourhood of Anamaboe, particularly a girl of about 8 years, who said she had been carried off from her mother, by the man who sold her to the ship.

Once saw fat Sam, their gold taker, send his canoe to take 3 fishermen, employed in the offing, which were immediately brought on board, and put in irons, and about a week after, he was paid for them. Remembers another man taken in the same way from on board a canoe along side. Fat Sam very frequently sent slaves on board in the night, which, from their own information, he found, were every one of them taken in the neighbourhood of Anamaboe: he remarked, that slaves sent off in the night, were not paid for till they had been some time on board, lest, he thinks, they should be claimed; for some were really restored; one in particular, a boy, was carried on shore by some near relations; which boy told him, he had lived in the neighbourhood of Anamaboe, and was kidnapped (p. 90.)

As to kidnapping by Europeans, has only heard of it; but the master of the Brookes, urged his gold-takers daily, to get him slaves by any means.

P. 84. Slaves in the passage are so crowded below, that it is impossible to walk through them, without treading on them; those who are out of irons, are locked spoonways (in the technical phrase) to one another; it is the first mate's duty to see them stowed in this way every morning; those who do not get quickly into their places, are compelled by the cat. In this situation, when the ship had much motion, they were often miserably bruised. In the passage, when the scuttles must be shut, the gratings are not sufficient for airing the rooms; he never himself could breathe freely, unless immediately under the hatchway. Never saw ventilators used in these ships; a wind-

sail

sail was often tried on the coast, but he remembers none used in the passage. Has seen the slaves drawing their breath with all those laborious and anxious efforts for life, which is observed in expiring animals, subjected by experiment to foul air, or in the exhausted receiver of an air pump; has also seen them, when the tarpawlings have inadvertently been thrown over the gratings, attempting to heave them up, crying out, " Kickeraboo, kickeraboo," i. e. " We " are dying;" on removing the tarpawlings and gratings, they would fly to the hatchway with all the signs of terror, and dread of suffocation; many whom he has seen in a dying state, have recovered, by being brought thither, or on the deck; others were irrecoverably lost, by suffocation, having had no previous signs of indisposition.

Slaves, on being brought on board, shew signs of extreme distress and despair, from a feeling of their situation, and regret at being torn from friends and connections; many retain those impressions for a long time; in proof of which, the slaves being often heard in the night, making an howling melancholy noise, expressive of extreme anguish; he repeatedly ordered the woman, who had been his interpreter, to inquire the cause; she discovered it to be owing to their having dreamed they were in their own country, and finding themselves when awake, in the hold of a slave ship. This exquisite sensibility was particularly observable among the women, many of whom, on such occasions, he found in hysteric fits.

They sailed after dark in the night, when the slaves were secured below, to prevent their shewing signs of discontent at leaving the coast; he thinks this the reason, because every ship that left the road while the Brooks was there, left it in the night; has heard the custom is general.

Thinks they bought upwards of 600 slaves, and lost about 70 in the voyage.

As to insurrections among the slaves; a number of the strongest men in their ship had one night
sawed

1790. sawed off their irons with an old knife, notched for
Part II. the purpose, furnished by a woman from the cabin;
but were detected by the information of another
slave.

 A man jumped overboard at Anamaboe, and was
drowned; another, in the Middle Passage, who was
taken up; a woman was, for some time, chained to
the mainmast, after being taken up; being let loose,
made a second attempt; was taken up and died
under the floggings given her in consequence.

 Believes the practice of dancing them is general
in the trade; in the Brookes it was not used till
exercise became absolutely necessary for their health;
those in irons were ordered to stand up, and make
what motions they could, leaving a passage for such
as were out of irons, to dance round the deck. Such
as did not relish the exercise of dancing, were compelled to it by the cat; but many still refused,
though urged in this way to a severe degree.

P. 87.  Besides the instance already given, of a slave starving himself to death—remembers another. A woman was repeatedly flogged, and victuals forced into
her mouth; no means however could make her
swallow, and she lived the 4 last days in a state of
torpid insensibility.

 The cargo was disposed of in Jamaica, p. 94, by
what is called the scramble. The buyers stand
ready, when the signal is given for opening the sale,
to rush all at once upon the slaves, and affix their
tallies to those they wish to have; this unexpected
manœuvre, had an astonishing effect; the slaves were
heard crying out for their friends, in language expressive of the deepest affliction. Some husbands and
wives were parted, and many other relations.

 The seamen lay, in the Middle Passage, under the
booms, according to custom, and, when the weather
was bad, were certainly exposed very much.

 During the Middle Passage, some of the seamen
were most cruelly flogged by the master, so much so,
that on one occasion he saw from the quarter deck,
               some

some of the sailors coming aft from the forecastle, to rescue a man, upon which the master let him go, and never afterwards punished any of them in that manner. Same master was carrying, in a former voyage, 12 paroquets to the West Indies; they died, and suspecting a sailor of having killed them, ordered the man to be lashed to one of the topmasts for 12 days, in which time he had no other food but one of those birds, and a pint of water a day; though wonderful, the man survived this. He was a native of Philadelphia, and was discharged in the West Indies. Has heard the master who perpetrated this wanton barbarity, relate it in a publick company, with triumph.

From what he has seen, he should suppose the minds of Africans very capable of cultivation; some part of his evidence shews them susceptible of all the social virtues; has seen no bad habits, but among those engaged in trade with white men; of those, Accra an exception.

Food of the slaves on the passage was, rice, horsebeans, and unclean corn, with usual condiments of palm-oil, salt and pepper: the beans from England, the rice was got to windward, and the Indian corn at Anamaboe: they had abundance of cheese: a quantity of the Indian corn was sold in the West Indies. At Anamaboe it was in such plenty, that many canoes of it were sent away after their corn room was full. The rice was a very wholesome food; had a red husk, but white within.

Does not remember the surf was too high, during the whole time they were on the coast, for canoes to come off (nearly 10 months) except two or three days.

The 3 fishermen, before-mentioned to have been seized, said they were free men. Another case is mentioned of a man taken out of a canoe along-side: both done with so much indifference, that he thinks the practice was frequent, of seizing and selling free men.

As

1790.
Part II.

P. 90.

P. 91.

P. 92.

P. 93.

P. 96.

P. 98.

As to the 3 fishermen complaining of the illegality of their capture; all communication is prevented between the slaves on board and the traders; and canoe-men who come to sell slaves; hence it could not be supposed that any of their connections were informed of their situation. Traders are not allowed to go forward after the barricado, and they cannot, from its height, look over it; nor are they permitted to look over the ship's side.

As to the case of the child reclaimed, before-mentioned, it is probable that the trader who sold him, perhaps not being the kidnapper, had informed the boy's relations.

The man who attempted to cut his own throat, had all the appearance of a sullen melancholy, but was by no means insane; believes a degree of delirium might come on before death; but when he came on board, believes him to have been in his perfect senses.

Cannot be positive as to the particular amount of the mortality on board the Brookes.

Engaged to go as surgeon in the Brookes, in the spring of 1783, at the close of the war.

Is at present surgeon to the Edgar M. W. Had his medical education at the University of Edinburgh, and also his doctor's degree.

Many slaves died of the scurvy; thinks only a very quiet passage saved half the cargo; for between 2 and 300 were tainted with this disease on their arrival at Antigua. Does not think their food was such as would have produced this disease, independent of other causes, viz. their peculiar confinement; the contaminated atmosphere of the ship, with all those depressing passions, inseparable from the state of a human being, torn from all that is to be valued in life.

Was often thwarted (by the master) in his prescriptions for the sick, who in violent bursts of anger, swore they fell victims to his medicines: his (the master's) contradictions, were particularly observable

servable when the scurvy broke out; he treated with contempt the proposal of carrying out a great quantity of fresh fruits; of which not a 20th part of what was necessary, was in the ship at leaving the coast; the event justified the proposal, for when a liberal supply of fruits was had at Antigua, the recovery of slaves was rapid beyond example.

Among the slaves, were many related in different degrees; remembers two or three husbands and wives; one of these had a child, which he often carried from the mother to the father, who always received it with much affection: it died on the passage.

Any intercourse between husbands and wives on board, is carried on by the boys which run about, and are allowed occasionally to go aft: other relations, of the same sex, commonly wished to mess together, and their affection to each other was certainly very conspicuous, particularly when diseased; in some instances their feelings were such, as would bear a comparison with those of any civilized people.

Boys and girls, under the age of puberty, generally kept separate; boys with the men, girls with the women.

First heard the master relate the story of his punishing the Philadelphia seaman (by having him tied to the topmast, and fed on a paroquet a day, as already mentioned) on a Saturday night, when he had company, in the Road of Anamaboe; does not recollect who were present; the fact itself, as related, struck him so forcibly, that he thought of nothing else at the time; he was so shocked, that he immediately left the cabin, and told the story to one of the mates; shall never forget the impression it left upon his mind at the time, and he has since mentioned it among his friends, as a piece of unparalleled cruelty (p. 98.)

1790.
Part II.

Witness examined—WILLIAM DOVE.

P. 100. Mr. William Dove, of Plymouth, was 1769 on the coast of Africa, from Sierra Leone down to Piccipini Sisters on board the Lily, Captain Saltcraig, from Liverpool.

P. 101. Respecting the mode of getting slaves, he observed an instance of a girl that was kidnapped being brought on board by one Ben Johnson, a black trader, who had scarcely left the ship in his canoe with the price of her, when another canoe with two black men came in a hurry to the ship, and inquired concerning the girl. Having been allowed to see her, they hurried down to their canoe and hastily paddled off. Overtaking Ben Johnson, they brought him back to the ship, got him on the quarter deck, and calling him " teeffee" (which implies thief), to the captain, offered him to sale. Ben Johnson remonstrated, asking the captain, if he would buy him grand trading man; to which the captain answered, if they would sell him he would buy him, be he what he would, which he accordingly did, and put him into irons immediately with another man. Was led to think from that instance, that slaves were kidnapped, and as well as from having seen children brought separately on board, and men and women without fresh wounds, or marks of old ones on them.

P. 102. They had on board between 30 and 40 children, boys and girls, some on their mothers breasts; four or five were born during the passage.

The slaves in his ship were in general very well treated, as well as any ship on the coast, two or three instances of great cruelty excepted.

Captain Saltcraig coming on board one evening somewhat intoxicated, scolded the officers for not manning the sides to receive him, then with a rope's end beat many white people on deck; he then stretched a rope across, and ordering a negro, a stout fellow, out of irons, made him stand on one side

side of the rope, while he stood on the other, and setting his foot to the black man's, squared as if to box him, saying, that he would learn him how to fight, and signified to the black fellow to make a blow at him again, which, though at first he knew not how to do, at last he did, and gave the captain a terrible blow; the captain turned about, went to the cabin, brought up a horse-whip, and beat him most unmercifully, first with the lash, then with a full sweep with the but end, till the black man evacuated both by urine and excrement, insomuch that the ship's company thought he could not survive it.

The other instance; the black men between decks had drawn the staple of the fore lazaretto where the horse-beans were kept, and taken as witness supposes through hunger, two or three gallons; at night they were overheard eating them; five were severely whipped by the captain's order, two of the ringleaders thumbscrewed; a punishment so severe, that while under it, the sweat ran down their faces, and they trembled as under a violent ague fit.

The men slaves were fettered all the Middle Passage till in sight of Desida, a West India island, except a few sick slaves who were let to walk the deck, and taking great care to recover them. This confinement may be necessary from their great superiority of numbers. Has known men fettered together quarrel in the night; but this was put to rights by the second mate or boatswain's going down.

As to capacity among the negroes, he observed some that seemed apt at taking any thing. Two boys from a little oakum given to them, would very dexterously work a curious fishing-line, twisting it only on their knees; it was used often to catch cat fish; there were others not so apt. In the West Indies he has seen them at different handicrafts, make as good workmen as white people.

Was not on shore in Africa to observe their disposition either to agriculture or trade, but in the West Indies he has seen some diligent and attentive to the duties

1790.
Part II.

duties required of them; others there are of a lazy cast, just as our common people at home. He has no doubt but that a trade might be cultivated with them in Africa. Sierra Leone afforded rice to the ship; they took about two tons. Pine apples, plantanes, bananas, and yams, were brought to them in abundance; some honey also, and a few bottles of the juice of the sugar-cane. Both natives and the ship's boats brought them off, but chiefly the natives.

The African rice is in quality equal to the Carolina; is thought to go farther; it has a redness in it, which, when the husk is taken off, does not penetrate the grain, but lies as a little dust upon its surface.

The tarpaulins are only put on in case of rain; when taken off there is a steam comes up between the gratings, by which means the air is communicated to them below, and has relieved them when they have been panting for breath.

P. 105. Treatment of sailors on board with him was in general oppressive, particularly in one or two instances; the chief mate finding a leak in a barrel of tar, told the captain, who called the boatswain to account for it; the boatswain saying it was not his fault, for that tar would run in that warm climate; the captain told him he would make him prevent it, and then took an end of a rope, and beat him in so unmerciful a manner, that he did not recover for some weeks.

Another instance; John Coffee, assistant surgeon was taken ill of a disorder prevalent among the whites, which first seizes them with a sleepy heaviness and disinclination to move. A swelling of the legs soon takes place, which makes it painful even to stand or walk; this the captain said was idleness, and that if they would exert themselves, they would soon get well, and to make them do so, repeatedly beat them with a rope's end. In this manner he treated Coffee, and when at last he could not stand, insisting on it that he would make him, he ordered one of the

hands

hands to seize him up to the shrouds, where, after a few minutes in that position, Coffee begged him for God's sake to shoot him and put him out of pain; to which, in a most brutish manner the captain answered, "No, no, do you think I'll be hanged for you?" Coffee repeatedly begged him either to let him down or shoot him, yet still he kept him there for near three hours. When loosed he lay down on his bed upon the deck, and in about two hours he expired.

In the outward bound passage they were tolerably well off in point of provisions: they had 4 lb. of bread a week, 1 lb. of salt beef a day, with a proportion of potatoes, which being out when they arrived on the coast, they felt it a little sharp, but caught cat-fish to supply their place; this however the captain forbid, and refused also to add half a pound of bread to the week's allowance. Once a week they had stock-fish, with only a little vinegar, chiefly on the Middle Passage. On the most part of the outward bound passage they had a breakfast also of oatmeal boiled thick, called Burgou, which was very comfortable.

From the year 1774 to 1783, he resided at Boston and New-York. There are there many negro slaves and free blacks; half the inhabitants may be black. In general the slaves were treated very well there, as are servants here. There was not a single importation of slaves while he resided in either of those places. Thinks the numbers did not decrease, and from the great multitude of black children running about the streets, he infers that population was kept up. He never saw nor heard of a driver in America. Negroes are not punished ordinarily there with whipping; beating was never found to answer the purpose; they are transferred to other masters, such as they like themselves, for they have liberty to choose.

He was paid two months advance-money on the ship's sailing from Liverpool, which was accounted for in West India currency, on his arrival in West Indies.

Having

1790.
Part II.

Having soon left Liverpool, he does not know whether captain Saltcraig was discharged for his drunkenness and misconduct. He was repeatedly requested by Mr. Rice, one of the owners, to remain in the service and promised promotion in it, but he objected because of the ill treatment of the ship's company, and not only so, but because he did not like the traffick. He had an assurance afterwards, from Mr. Rice, that Saltcraig should be prevented in future from using the ship's company as before. Mr. Dove had made a point of stating it to the owners himself.

He does not know whether Piccinini, Sisters, and Wappoa, are distinct states, nor while there, did he hear of any hostility between them.

He never heard of families sold on account of witchcraft, nor heard of such a thing as witchcraft while on the coast.

Upwards of half the ship's crew were landmen.

He has often eaten horse-beans, and thought them an excellent mess.

He went to Boston as cooper of His Majesty's ship Preston, under Admiral Graves; at New-York he was cooper to the same ship under Com. Hotham.

At Boston white people cultivate the land as well as negroes; and they indiscriminately work together. Both at Boston and New-York he was appointed to offices on shore, where he accordingly resided during the whole war, till 1783, and that has afforded him an opportunity of being so particular in his observations.

He thinks an English constitution equal to field-labour at Boston. He has not a doubt, that were there a sufficient number of white people there, the country could be cultivated without any negroes at all.

1790.
Part II.

Witnefs examined—CLEMENT NOBLE.

Has been nine voyages to Africa, two as a mate, and feven as a mafter. P. 108.

Recollects the voyage when Mr. Thomas Trotter was furgeon, they failed 3d June, 1783, and arrived at Liverpool in Auguft 1784. Had no previous knowledge of Doctor Trotter; who was recommended by one of his friends, to one of the owners of the fhip. Thought him often very remifs in his duty, and fpent a great deal too much time in drefs, which he often reproved him for. P. 109.

Veffel about 300 tons; bought 638 flaves; loft 19 on the coaft, 33 on the paffage, and 6 in Kingfton harbour, in all 58. In preceding voyage, bought 666, buried 26 in whole.

In the voyage with Mr. Trotter, had 49 feamen, one died in the fmall-pox ten days from Liverpool, another fell overboard from a boat and was drowned, another a natural death; total lofs three, which he thinks might be the average of all his voyages. P. 110.

Does not remember a dead man and a living ever being found chained together, nor flaves fuffocated from the tarpaulins laid over the gratings through inattention, which it is impoffible can happen, for flaves are always ready enough to call to the people on deck to put the tarpaulin either up or down as they feel heat or cold. Rain is kept out of the rooms by a tarpaulin or awning fpread 10 or 12 feet above the deck from maft to maft, like the roof of a houfe.

Has been often at Cape la Hou; trade is there chiefly carried on by the Dutch; Englifh or French fhips ftop a day or two only, perhaps fometimes a week. Believes flaves cannot be taken off the coaft, that have not been fold under the laws of the country. Never knew an inftance.

Really

1790.  Really does not believe slaves could be kidnapped
Part II. with impunity on the Gold coast.

Remembers a man slave on board his ship attempting to destroy himself, and believes the man was perfectly mad, is sure of it. Did not appear so at first, or he should not have bought him; it appeared some few days after; he stormed and made a great noise, worked with his hands, &c. and shewed every sign of being mad. Believes he generally refused sustenance. Had no conversation with him, except at times when he seemed to be rather better than at others. He gave no reason at all for his violent conduct; could seldom get him to speak (p. 113.)

Has known many slaves fall overboard by accident, but generally picked up. Remembers one
P. 111. only in the voyage Dr. Trotter was with the ship, who was subject to fits, and fell out of the fore chains in a fit and was drowned; also a woman who was insane and very troublesome, believes she did jump overboard once or oftener. Ordered her to be confined to prevent her from doing it again, but punished her no other way. Does not recollect whether she died or not.

Never had any slaves die on board in consequence of correction.

His officers and seamen were in general desirous to sail again with him.

Remembers, in the voyage Mr. Trotter was with him, flogging a sailor for abusing the slaves, and being insolent to himself. Believes it was the only time a seaman was flogged in the voyage; same man came home from Jamaica with the ship, and behaved well, and offered to go again with Mr. N. in preference to any other ship (p. 112 and 120.)

Does not know Mr. Trotter ever expressed himself dissatisfied with any occurrence on the voyage, and has no reason to think he would not have gone with him, but the ship was laid up (p. 116.)
P. 112.  Does remember a voyage, when he had a number of paroquets on board, it was in 1774, they were all killed

killed in one night, by a black man of the ship (not a slave) who told some of the people he would do as much for him (Mr. N.) the next night; when asked if he said so, he said, yes, with all the insolence in the world; he was ordered to be confined, and by advice of the officers of the ship, who judged it unsafe to keep him below, he was sent to the mast head; at two days end he sent to say he was sorry for what he had done, and hoped to be let come down; he was immediately ordered to be brought down and let out of irons; but for the remaining part of the voyage he (Mr. N.) took care to have the cabin door made fast in the night: the man was very turbulent, and at Kingston was caged almost every night till he went off the island: when so confined he sent every morning to Mr. N. for money to relieve him: he never blamed Mr. N. for sending him to the mast head, but told many of the sailors it was very fortunate he was so confined, otherwise he was sure he would have murdered Mr. N. for his resolution was fixed.

Does not recollect he had ever any trouble with his sailors, employing attornies, or any thing of that sort.

Did not often receive slaves in the night; but every now and then; that the other captains should not see them come on board, he judged was the cause, for the traders wished to keep on good terms with all the captains.

He was nine months and eight days on the coast.

Does not remember receiving three men that were fishing in the offing, but has frequently seen them taken out of canoes and sold: they were slaves to be sure. The greater part of those that paddle the canoes, and go afishing, are slaves.

Believes persons in the condition of slaves on the coast, may be sold to the ships, without being convicted of any crime: always understood they had a right by the laws of the country to do what they pleased with their own property. Never made any inquiry whether the slaves brought for sale, were the property

1790. property of the sellers; they being usually brokers
Part II. only; never enquired how these brokers came by
them, thinks there is no occasion; always supposed,
and did not doubt, but they had a right to sell them.

Instances of slaves falling overboard in Guinea
ships are not very frequent; it happens every now
and then.

Is not at present engaged in the African trade;
quitted the sea above four years since.

P. 116. Some of the slaves appear dejected when brought
on board, but in general soon mend of that, and are
in very good spirits while on board.

Now and then met with sulky ones that would not
eat without force, then endeavoured to persuade them,
and if that would not do, to force them to it.

Has been often below when the slaves were all in
their rooms: they had room enough to lie down,
and were as comfortable as could be expected on
board a ship: could walk among them without treading upon them, it is done every night by the officers
P. 117. after they go to rest: all the ships he has had, had
platforms. It was much hotter below at some times,
than at others; that depends chiefly on the weather:
when calm it is sure to be very warm. Never found
any bad effects from the air: the air cannot surely be
so good as upon deck: it is rather foul and offen-
sive, but more so in calm weather than at other times.

Refers in what he has said of the state of the ship
between decks, &c. to the voyage that Dr. Trotter
was with him.

Cannot say with certainty how many slaves were
in the mens room in this voyage: from the number
on board thinks there must have been something
short of 300; cannot say the exact proportion of
males in the cargo, but should suppose about two-
thirds males, and one-third females.

Cannot recollect number of boys; in general they
reckon in their accounts, without distinguishing;
they had many of both boys and girls.

Does

Does not remember the length of the mens room, the breadth about 26 feet: there were in the breadth 4 rows of slaves on the deck, and one on each platform: stowed on their backs or sides as they chose to lie: chief mate and boatswain generally stow them in the mens room: never measured, nor calculated what room they had; they had always plenty of room to lie down in, and had they had 3 times as much they would all lie close jammed together; they do so before the room is half full: the space in the middle between the two rows of slaves varies according to the lengths of the slaves; in some places perhaps a foot, in some more, in some less: sometimes when the weather is cool they will lie as near the side as they can, and when it is warm crowd more under the gratings. Cannot recollect how they were distributed as to numbers; are divided so as not to throng one room more than another: they were he believes distributed as the cargo usually is on board of Guinea ships, where he understood it the rule to distribute them equally fore and aft: there were men stowed in the boys room adjoining to the mens; which is generally the case (p. 120.)

1790.
Part II.
P. 118.

The slaves were sold in the West Indies after this manner: the men are on the main, and the women all on the quarter deck; the buyers come in at the gangway between, where they remain till the sale is opened, when they rush in fore and aft, and suit themselves as they can, clapping their tallies on whoever they mean to take.

Believes this is the common way of selling a cargo of slaves by scramble in Jamaica; in other islands it differs.

P. 119.

Remembers the slaves being in great distress, and making grievous outcries on the sale by scramble in this particular voyage; the cause of it is, because they are parting; it is a general cry and a noise throughout the whole ship; but more particularly so with some that think they are going to be parted from their husbands, wives, mothers, children, &c.

1792. but the purchasers are always very particular in
Part II. making exchanges, so that husbands, wives, mothers,
and children, and even acquaintances, shall go together. Never knew it otherwise.

The men slaves take exercise during the passage;
a drum is beat, and they jump or dance to it, as
well as their situation will admit; the stout men are
all in irons, and a right leg and a left, and their
hands the same: a chain fastens the greatest part of
them to the deck, a few days before leaving the
coast, and a few days after; then those chains are
taken away, and many of the slaves let out of irons;
they are always very ready and very fond of dancing,
except a few sulky ones; but in general there are
very few of them. As to the means used to compel
them to dance when sulky, the master or people that
are among them endeavour to persuade them, and if
they will not, they let them do as they please.

P. 120. He was supplied with rice or corn by the natives
while on the coast.

---

### Witness examined—ISAAC PARKER.

P. 122. Isaac Parker, Ship-keeper of the Melampus Frigate,
sailed in 1764 from Liverpool to the River Gambia,
in the Black Joke, Captain Pollard, who treated the
slaves well, but who dying off St. Jago, was succeeded by Capt. Marshall, who did not behave so
well to them, but pinched them in provisions and
water, while there was plenty in the ship. One exception to Captain Pollard's good treatment was, a
child of nine months old which refused to eat, for
which the captain took it up in his hand, and flogged
it with a cat, saying at the same time, " Damn you,
I'll make you eat, or I'll kill you."

The same child having swelled feet, the captain
ordered them to be put into water, though the ship's
cook told him it was too hot. This brought off the
skin

skin and nails. He then ordered sweet oil and cloths, which Isaac Parker himself applied to the feet; and as the child at mess time again refused to eat, the captain again took it up and flogged it, and tied a log of mango-wood 18 or 20 inches long, and of 12 or 13 lb. weight round its neck as a punishment. He repeated the flogging for four days together at mess time; the last time after flogging he let it drop out of his hand, with the same expressions as before, and accordingly in about three quarters of an hour, the child died. He then called its mother to heave it overboard, and beat her for refusing. He, however, forced her to take it up, and go to the ship's side, where holding her head on one side to avoid the sight, she dropped her child overboard, after which she cried for many hours.

The crew consisted of 13 of whom only 5 survived.

In 1765, he sailed again from Liverpool, in the Latham, captain Colly, to Old Calabar, and there, for want of provisions, left the ship, which, though bound for the West Indies, lay windbound then upon the bar. He went with the surgeon to buy slaves, with the goods that were left, to Newtown, where Dick Ebro, a king's son, who knew of the ill treatment given the crew by captain Colly, concealed him for three days in a room till the ship was gone. He then came out, and employed himself in fishing, cleaning their arms, &c. and remained there for five months.

When there, Dick Ebro' asking him to go to war with him, he complied, and accordingly having fitted out and armed the canoes, they went up the river, lying under the bushes in the day when they came near a village; and at night flying up to the village, and taking hold of every one they could see. These they handcuffed, brought down to the canoes, and so proceeded up the river, till they got to the amount of 45, with whom they returned to Newtown, where sending to the captains of the shipping, they divided them among the ships. About a fortnight

|        |                                                                                                                                                                                                                                                                                                                                   |
| ------ | ----------------------------------------------------------------------------------------------------------------------------------------------------------------------------------------------------------------------------------------------------------------------------------------------------------------------------------- |
| 1790.  | night after they went again, and were out eight or nine days, plundering other villages higher up the |
| P. 125.| river. They seized on much the same number as before, brought them to Newtown, gave the same notice, and disposed of them as before among the |
| P. 133.| ships. They took man, woman, and child as they could catch them in the houses, and except sucking children, who went with their mothers, there was no care taken to prevent the separation of the children from the parents when sold. When sold to the English merchants, they lamented, and cried that they were taken away by force. |
| P. 135.| Dick Ebro' was certainly not at war with the people up the river, nor had they made any attack upon him. Slaves were very slack in the back country, at that time, and were wanted when he went on these |
| P. 135.| expeditions. He took no goods with him in the canoes. He was not at war with any body, nor did J. P. hear that there had been any war before his coming there. The old town and new town of Calabar were at peace with one another. |
| P. 133.| Dick Ebro' had many slaves of his own, whom he employed in cutting wood and fishing, &c. but he treated them always very well. |
| P. 132.| The Guinea captains fixing on a certain price, agreed to lie under a £50 bond, if any one of them should give more for slaves than another; in conse- |
| P. 133.| quence of which, the natives did not readily bring slaves on board, to sell at those prices; upon which the captains used to row guard at night, to take the canoes as they passed the ship, and so stopping the slaves from getting to their towns prevent the traders from getting them. These they took on board the different ships, and kept them till the traders agreed to slave at the old price. |
| P. 133.| He has known presents made by the captains to |
| P. 135.| the black traders to induce them to bring slaves. Captain Colly in particular gave them some pieces of cannon, which he himself saw landed. |
| P. 134.| Captain Colly did not behave so well to the ship's crew |

crew after his arrival on the coaſt as during the voyage. He kept them on ſhort proviſions, giving them only fiſh for four months, with nothing but palm oil to it, and ſometimes not that. He gave alſo 4 lb. of bread by the week. The quantity of fiſh, when boiled, was not ſufficient for a meal, and the reſt of the day they were forced to go without victuals. When up in the country, he took a yam from off the coppers, for which the captain charged him a ſhilling againſt his wages.

He has been more than once in the Weſt Indies; and in Jamaica, Barbadoes, Antigua, and the Grenadas, has ſeen ſeamen ſick, with ſwelled feet, and begging for want of food and employment; and theſe informed him that the ſhips they came from were Guineamen.

He did not know, when he went out with captain Pollard, that any part of his wages was to be paid in Weſt India currency, and accordingly objected to receiving it in that manner when there; declaring to capt. Marſhall, that " he would not go home with the ſhip if he did not give full pay;" upon which the captain threw him and ſome others of the crew into priſon, where they lay two or three days, and then agreed to go with him, on the captain's paying their gaol fees. The governor, though applied to, gave the ſailors no redreſs.

Since his return to England, in 1766, he has been ſome time in the coaſting trade, and ſome time in his Majeſty's ſervice, and in 1768, entered the Endeavour bark, in which he went round the world with captain Cook, as boatſwain's mate. He ſerved after in the Monarch, captain Joſhua Rowley, and is now by appointment of the maſter-attendant of Plymouth dock, ſhip-keeper of the Melampus.

The ſlaves on board ſhips very often refuſe to eat; they take ſick, and will not eat: blows make them only more ſulky, and in general they ſeem very melancholy and dejected.

1790. Part II.

P. 134.

P. 135.
P. 136.

P. 131.

P. 136.
P. 137.

Witneſs

Witness examined—Rev. JOHN NEWTON,
Rector of St. Mary, Woolnoth.

1790.
Part II.
P. 137.

Made five voyages to Africa, the last in 1754, as master of a slave-ship. Lived ashore about a year and a half, chiefly at the island of Plantanes, at the mouth of the river Sherbro.

The Purrow, the legislative and executive power there. A sort of free-masonry, to which the obedience paid may be a mixture of superstitious charms, and submission to government.

P. 138. Always judged, that, with equal advantages, the natives capacities would be equal to ours. Has known many of real and decided capacity. The Sherbro people are in a degree civilized, often friendly, and may be trusted where not previously deceived by Europeans. Has lived in safety among them, when the only white man there. The best people he met with were on the R. Gaboon and at C. Lopas. These had then the least intercourse with Europe. Believes they had then no slave-

P. 139. trade, and has heard them speak against it. They traded in ivory and wax. One great man said, " If I was to be angry and sell my boy, how should I get my boy back when my anger was gone?"

Has known ships and boats cut off, but never at Gaboon or C. Lopas. Sometimes at Sherbro, usually in retaliation.

Natives, having few wants, make fewer exertions; but he does not think them naturally indolent.

P. 140. Many of them hired to work in our boats and ships. On the Windward Coast, they cultivate the land, not only to supply themselves, but the ships with rice.

Polygamy being practised, the affections may possibly not be so strong as in other countries; but he never heard of a mother selling her children.

They are generally worse in their conduct in pro- 1790.
portion to their acquaintance with us. Part II.
Believes the African trade very fatal to seamen,
from exposure to weather, intemperance, and ill
treatment. Thinks in a trade in African produce
they would not necessarily be exposed to weather so
much, and that the slave-trade is a great cause of
their hard treatment. The real or supposed necessity
of treating the negroes rigorously, gradually be-
numbs the heart, and renders most of those engaged
in it too indifferent to their fellow creature's sufferings. He has seen them when sick, beaten for lazi-
ness till they have died under the blows. P. 141.
Once when on shore, the traders suddenly put him
into his long-boat, telling him that a ship just
passed, had carried off two people. Had it been
known in the town, he would have been detained.
Has known many other such instances; but after 36
years cannot specify them. It was a general opinion,
founded on repeated and indisputable facts, that depredations of this sort were frequently committed by
the Europeans. (p. 147.)
Knows little of punishments, except the selling
offenders for slaves. Believes many were sold for
slaves, whose punishment otherwise would have been
trifling.
Many considered frauds as a necessary branch of P. 142.
the slave-trade. Has known them put false heads
into powder-casks, cut off two or three yards from
the middle of a piece of cloth, greatly adulterate
the brandy, and sometimes steal back articles delivered.
The men slaves always fettered. He never put
them out of irons, till they saw the land in the W.
Indies. Thinks the ship would not otherwise have
been safe. Two or three plots, in his ship, were
timely discovered. He was mate of a ship where
one white man and three or four negroes were killed,
in an insurrection.
The slaves had more room in his ship, because

Numb. 3. H

1790.
Part II.

never compleated his purchase; but their situation in a full ship is uncomfortable indeed, being kept constantly in irons, crowded in their lodging, and often, in bad weather, almost destitute of air to breathe; besides what they suffer from the ships motion, in their irons, and the difficulty in the night of getting to their tubs, which are sometimes overset.

P. 143. In plots or insurrections, they suffer most generally severe floggings, to which the masters of some ships he has been on board of, added thumb-screws. A captain told him repeatedly, that he had put negroes to death, after an insurrection, by different cruel tortures. In many ships the sufferings of the women were aggravated by the brutality of the crews. He knew many women in Sherbro, whom he thought modest, but knows not how to compare their modesty with that of women in other countries.

The slaves are fettered in pairs, not chained. He has often, in the morning, seen one of the pair dead.

He has known pawns taken off the coast by European traders. Individual Europeans were thought well of by the natives, but they had no good opinion of them upon the whole, and sometimes when charged with a fraud or crime, would say, " What, do you think I am a white man?"

Small slaves, from 8 to 16 years of age, used to constitute about 1-4th of the cargo.

P. 144. He was at three slave sales in the West Indies, and at one in South Carolina. Relations were separated as sheep and lambs are separated by the butcher.

His concern in the slave-trade was not profitable to his employers. There were more losing than gainful voyages. The trade was generally considered as a sort of lottery.

He made three voyages as commander of a slave-ship. He first went on board a slave-ship as a fore-mast-man at Madeira, in 1745, having been discharged from a man of war; but was made steward for about six months. He was left by her when the ship

ship sailed with a person who was part owner, on 1790. the coast, where he lived perhaps 18 months, as a servant to white traders. He left the coast in the end of 1747, as passenger in a ship which called at Gaboon, and arrived in England 1748. He counts all that time his first voyage. In that time, they traded to R. de Nuna, about 40 leagues northward of S. Leone, but has no knowledge of the intermediate country, and 20 leagues to the southward of that river, in the R. Sherbro.

He once went three days journey inland, which he P. 146. supposes might be fifty miles from the head of the river or creek Caramanca. Believes he did not stay above two days. He never went so far at any other time, seldom above 3, 4, or 5 miles from the coast.

He has sometimes found all trade stopped, and the P. 147. depredations of European traders have been assigned by the natives as the cause, and he has, more than once or twice, made up breaches of this kind between the ships and the natives.

He believes several captains of slave-ships were honest, humane men, but has good reason to think they were not all so. The taking off slaves by force has been thought most frequent in the last voyages P. 148. of captains. He has often heard masters and officers express this opinion. Depredations and reprisals made to get them were so frequent, that the Europeans and Africans were in a spirit of mutual distrust: he does not mean that there were no depredations, except in their last voyage. Has known Liverpool and Bristol ships materially injured from the conduct of some ships, from the same ports, that had left the coast. It is a fact that some captains have committed depredations in their last voyage, who have not been known to have done it before.

He was, for most of his residence, in an abject P. 149. state of servitude and sickness. He knew the natives better, when a master to the same part.

He felt the trade very ineligible, but had no scruple of its lawfulness while engaged in it.

Witness examined,—James Morley, Gunner of the Medway.

1790.
Part II.
P. 149.
P. 150.

Made 6 voyages to Africa, the firſt in 1760, the laſt in 1776: ever ſince in the king's ſervice. Left the African trade from the ill uſage he himſelf received, and ſaw towards others. He continued in the trade from a promiſe of promotion, and to maintain his family. In the firſt ſhip, being then 9 or 10 years of age, he was a ſervant; alſo in the ſecond; in the third before the maſt; in the fourth gunner; in the fifth boatſwain and mate; in the ſixth mate.

Has been much on the coaſt, and far up the country. Has been, by computation, 3 or 400 miles up the river Nazareth, and about 200 miles up the river Gaboon (above Parrot's Iſland, p. 164.)

P. 151.

Has alſo been at Angola, Aſſenie, Cape Apollonia, Cape Coaſt, Anamaboe, and Old Calabar (at this laſt, 3 voyages—and at Commenda, Succundee, Dixcove, Amunda, Brandenburgh, and many other places, p. 164.)

Africa produces cotton, gold, rice, peppers, palm-oil, tobacco, and dye woods. He never was ricing on the coaſt, but has bought ſome of it off the river Siſters, and different places on the Windward Coaſt. This rice was brought alongſide in canoes, without any inquiry for it (in baſkets holding about 2 gallons, p. 167.)

The natives were always willing to do any ſervices, for which they had a proſpect of being paid immediately. He has had much intercourſe with

P. 152.

them, and apprehends they would raiſe produce, if made to ſee that they could get as much by it as by ſelling ſlaves. They traffic only in proviſions and ivory at their markets; alſo for ſlaves all through the country.

They

They treat their slaves with the greatest kindness, more so than our servants or slaves in the West Indies. They do not care to sell canoe-boys and house-servants, who raise provisions, fish, get pahn-oil, and palm-wine, make grass and other cloths, build houses, go in the canoes, and do the house business. Is convinced it is a common practice for them to set slaves to work, who are refused by the Europeans. In Old Calabar he saw a slave that was offered to his ship, at work in the plantation.

1790. Part II. P. 152.

P. 153.

He owns, with shame, that he has made the natives drunk, and has given an extra price for a good man or woman. He has seen this done by others. Captain Hildebrand paid an extraordinary price for one of the wives of a man whom he had made drunk, and who wished to redeem her next day, as did the person he (Mr. M.) bought the man of; but neither of them was given up. Supposes they would have given one-third more than their price to redeem them (knew of no other instance, p. 166.)

Most of the slaves, as far as he saw, were obtained by purchase. He knew and saw only one taken by fraud by the black traders. It was one that came down to get shell-fish, that he bought. Has been told by the natives at Calabar, (but never saw it, p. 165.) that they took slaves in what they call war, which he found was putting the villages in confusion, and catching them as they could. A man on board the ship he was in, shewed how he was taken at night by surprise, and said his wife and children were taken with him, but they were not in the same ship. Had reason to think, from the man's words, that they took the whole village, those that could not get away.

P. 154.

In Old Calabar, persons are sold for slaves, for adultery and theft. On pretence of adultery, he remembers a woman sold. He learnt that this was only a pretence from her own mouth, for she spake good English, and from the respect with which her husband, king Ephraim, treated her, when he came

on

1790. on board; whereas, in real cases of adultery, they
Part II. are very desperate.

He has seen children on board, without parents or relations.

P. 155. Off Taboo, two men came along-side in a canoe. One of them came up and sat on the netting, but would not come into the ship, on which the captain intoxicated him so with brandy and laudanum, that he fell in upon deck. (Does not know laudanum, but the captain ordered him to pour in laudanum, and he (Mr. M.) saw him pour out the liquid, which was of a very dark brown, p. 165.) The captain then ordered him to be put into the mens room, with a centry over him. The man in the canoe, after calling in vain for his companion, paddled off fast towards the shore. The captain fired several musket balls after him, which did not hit him. About 3 or 4 leagues farther down, 2 men came on board from another canoe. While they were on board, a drum was kept beating near the man who had been seized, to prevent his hearing them, or they him.

P. 156. When they came into Gaboon, in the Tom, captain Matthews; desired the mate to call himself captain, while he hid himself. Two of the chiefs sons coming on board, told the mate that he lied, and that he was not the captain: on this the captain came up the scuttle, laughing. The chiefs sons asked him what he had done with their sons, and the boys he had carried off, and told him in English, that if he came on shore there to trade, they would have his head. They then went into their canoe, and left the vessel, calling to him and making motions to the same purpose. Is not positive as to any other instance.

When at Furnandipo, in the Marcus tender-sloop, in the height of trading with the natives for provisions, a man stole a few strings of beads. Bishop, the master, striking him, the natives flew up to the wood. Bishop fired among them, and ordered the

boat's

boat's crew to do the same. A great shrieking was heard, and they immediately all disappeared. The boat's crew left the boat, and saw the track of blood for many yards; but they could never learn whether any of them were killed. Does not remember that any of the natives had offered violence to the boat's crew.

From Old-Town, Calabar, to the Duke's-Town, is 4 or 5 miles, by the creek; but by the mouth of Crofs River, 16 or 18 miles, or more. New-Town is a long way from the shipping. Before the towns parted, they always went by the creek.

When there has been a full purchase, the slaves are closely stowed; but, when a short purchase, and they have had mortality, they have more room. He has been employed in a full ship, in stowing them as close as he possibly could. In most ships he has been in, the men were in irons all the passage. In full ships, he has seen them in great perspirations, especially when rains obliged them to keep the gratings long covered. He has wiped them, and seen them wiped, in perspirations so violent, as to give reason to think, if they had been long kept so close, suffocation must have ensued; but this he never found. He has seen them under great difficulty of breathing. The women particularly, often get up on the beams, where the gratings are raised with bannisters, about 4 feet above the combings, to give air, but they are generally driven down, because they take the air from the rest.

He has known rice held in the mouths of seasick slaves, until they were almost strangled. He has seen the surgeon's mates force the pannikin between their teeth, and throw the medicine over them, so that not half of it went into their mouths, the poor wretches wallowing in their blood or excrements, hardly having life, and this with blows of the cat, d——ing them for sulky black b——. He declares he has known the doctor's mate report a slave dead, and have him thrown overboard, when he has

seen

1790. seen him struggle in the water; no one could imagine why, only to get clear of the trouble.
Part II.

P. 159. In his first voyage, in the Eagle Galley, 700 were taken on board; believes above 250 were lost. In his second voyage, in the Amelia, about 200, or more, were taken in, 18 or 20, more or less, were lost. In his fourth voyage, in the Tom, about 150 were taken in, 25, more or less, lost. In his fifth voyage, in the Venus, between 250 and 300 taken in, about 20 lost, but is not sure.

P. 160. Some slaves sold on board, most commonly on shore. He never saw them sold by scramble, except in his last voyage, in the Whim. Refuse slaves are sold by vendue. He has seen refuse slaves, that came out of the ship he was in, lying about in St. Kitt's, in a very bad condition, and apparently deserted. He has known the poorer people buy slaves at vendue, for a trifle, not thinking of the expence of cure; when they find the raising of them will cost a good deal, let them go about any where. He has been on an inquest at Jamaica, where, from the appearance of the body, the verdict was, "Died for want." Upon inquiry, the person suspected to be the owner, has denied that it was his slave.

Some seamen enter voluntarily, but knows others are kept by landlords, till in debt, when they offer them a Guineaman or gaol. One Sullivan, a landlord in Bristol, got 2 or 3 young fellows in debt, and forced them, in his hearing, to go on board the Guineaman he belonged to, or to gaol. He helped to carry them on board himself; cannot positively say this is a common practice.

The seamen in the Guineaman he sailed in, were generally treated with great rigour, and many with cruelty. Recollects many instances. Matthews, the chief mate in the Venus, would knock a man down

P. 161. for any frivolous thing, with a cat, a piece of wood, or a cook's axe, with which he once cut a man down the shoulder. In the Amelia, captain Dixon, the men were tied up, and had 4 or 5 dozen lashes at a time,

time, and then rubbing them with pickle, he told 1790.
them, "They should not stink, for he would salt
them well." He has heard him tell them so often. He
(Mr. Morley) when his cabin-boy, for accidentally
breaking a glass, was tied to the tiller by the hands,
flogged with a cat, and kept hanging some time. He
has seen great severity in all the Bristol vessels he has
been in; but capt. Butler, in the Whim, from Liverpool,
neither treated the slaves nor the men severely.
He has known him send the only bit of fresh
provisions he had from his table, to the sick slaves.

The seamens provisions were usually scanty. Have
no shelter. Has seen them lie and die upon deck.
In all his first 5 voyages, he has seen seamen sick and
ulcerated; for it was all to a sickly part of the coast
that he went. They are generally treated ill. He
has known men ask to have their wounds or ulcers
dressed; and has heard the doctor, with oaths, tell
them to take their dung and dress them. Never
knew the captain compel the doctor to do his duty;
nor does he know that the doctor made this answer
in the captain's hearing.    P. 162.

The seamen were paid in West India currency, in
every ship he was in. There are more deserters
from Guineamen, than from any West Indiaman he
has been in. He has frequently seen Guinea seamen
lying about the wharfs, &c. in almost all the islands,
with ulcerated legs, and other disorders, almost dead.
He has often relieved them.

In Jamaica, he saw a man hoisted up taught to a
crane on a wharf, with 3 or 4 fifty-sixes to his feet,
and flogged with a short whip, and the skin swelled
up in great lumps: it was not broke, but bruised.
The negro flogger then flogged him with ebony on
the same parts, until the blood ran from most of his
back. He was told the slave's crime was running
away; and that the ebony was used to let out the
bruised blood. Another time, he saw a woman
cruelly flogged at Kingston. He was told she was P. 163.
to pay her mistress so much a month, which she had
  Numb. 3.        I            not

1790. not done. He knows many such instances. In Ja-
Part II. maica, he once (and only once) saw marking irons
heated over the flame of rum, and applied to the
thick of the thigh of the slaves, as they came through
the barricado-door one by one.

Captain Briggs's chief mate, in Old Calabar river, lying in ambush to stop the natives coming down the creek, pursued Oruk Robin John, who, jumping on shore, shot the mate through the head.

Mr. Walker, master of a sloop, was on board the Jolly Prince, captain Lambert, when the king of Nazareth stabbed the captain at his own table, took the vessel, putting all the whites to death, except the cook, a boy, and he believes one man. Captain Punter, of the Prince of Wales brig, asking Walker why the king of Nazareth took this step? he said, " It was on account of the people that Matthews " had carried off from Gaboon and Cape Lopas, the " voyage before." Walker escaped, by knowing
P. 164. the language. The Jolly Prince belonged to the same owners as Matthews's ship.

He was sometimes a week, sometimes 2 or 3 days, on shore at Gaboon. He saw a great quantity of ivory there, which comes from inland, on the shoulders or heads of the negroes.

By the water-side about Gaboon, the country is flat or marshy in some places, but the farther up the river, the better the land. It runs so high in the back country, as to be seen a great way off. The country was never overflowed while he was there, and he never heard that it was.

P. 165. There are great quantities of cotton at Calabar and Gaboon, but no rice that ever he saw. Never saw any cotton exported from thence; but he has made pillows of it. It is very fine, but very short in the pod.

Sailors in the West Indies are called wharfingers, by seafaring people in general, because they have ulcerated legs, and are sickly, lying about the wharfs and private places. The sailors call them so where
.....ere

there are wharfs; but they call them beach horners, and other cant names, where there are no wharfs.

Very particular in most captains purchasing no slaves but such as appeared to be in good health.

They had always an hospital forward, before the men's room.

---

Witness examined—Capt. THO. BOLTON THOMPSON,

Of the Royal Navy.

He was second lieutenant of the Grampus in 1784, 1785, and 1786, and commanded the Nautilus in 1787, in carrying out the black poor to S. Leone, where he was from May to September.

The principal products are cotton, indigo, tobacco, sugar-canes, cam-wood, gums, cardamums, rice, ivory, and gold-dust.

Were the natives instructed and encouraged, he supposes they would cultivate those things. Several natives at S. Leone, assisted the blacks he carried out, in building their houses, at a small expense.

The natives did not appear inferior in capacity to other uncivilized people. On the contrary they appeared possessed of great quickness and cunning. Those of S. Leone appear harmless and inoffensive.

He has heard that the word " panyar," which is common on the coast, means kidnapping, or seizing of men.

From the many complaints which he received from them, he concludes that seamen are far from being well treated in the slave-ships. One Bowden swam from the Fisher, of Liverpool, captain Kendal, to the Nautilus, amidst a number of sharks, to claim his protection. Kendal wrote for the man, who refused to go, saying that his life would be endangered. He therefore kept him in the Nautilus till she was paid off. He was a diligent, willing, active seaman.

1790. seaman. Several of the crew of the Brothers of Liverpool, captain Clark, he thinks, swam towards the Nautilus, passing by; two only reached her, the rest, he believes, regained their own ship. The majority of the crew had, the day before, come on board the Nautilus, in a boat, to complain of ill usage: but he had returned them, with an officer to inquire into and redress their complaints. This was in July, 1787. He received many letters from seamen in slave-ships, complaining of ill usage, and desiring him to protect them, or take them on board.

Is inclined to think the seamen in ships trading in produce are not so ill used as those in slave-ships. Several of his own officers gave him the best accounts of the treatment in the Iris, a ship trading in wood, &c. and of the healthiness and good order of the ship. She was near him several weeks.

He should suppose the slave-trade is not a nursery for seamen, as those on board the slave-ships appear very sickly, from their being very much exposed to the sun, rains, and dews, in small craft. Thinks a trade in the produce of Africa would not be so unhealthy as the slave-trade. A crew may be kept as healthy in those parts of Africa he has been in as in any other tropical climate. Only one man was lost in the Nautilus, while there, and that was from neglect.

Thinks more are crowded in a slave-ship than can be carried with a due regard to their health or comfort. His ship was about 320 tons, and she had her full peace compliment, 100 men. It would have been impossible to stow 4 or 500 people in her, with a due regard to their health and comfort. It was as much as he could do to stow his 100 men, with any comfort; but, on his return, by the West Indies, being ordered to take in 70 or 80 invalids for England, the ship was much crowded.

Thinks the S. Leone settlers were landed at the most improper season, the beginning of the rains.

At Barbadoes he has seen several seamen begging, apparently

apparently very sickly and destitute. He believes 1790.
most of the Guinea seamen receive a great shock to Part II.
their constitutions.

In the West Indies, he has very often seen the
negroes backs bear indelible marks of the whip.

Believes there are several species of gum in and P. 172.
about S. Leone; but the principal is gum copal.
Has always understood there is a great demand for
gum copal here.

Each man has from 18 to 24 inches for his ham- P. 173.
mock, in a man of war, according to the room they
can spare.

Believes about 380 free negroes were sent to Sierra
Leone. Many more were embarked, but some got
ashore, and others died. Their behaviour was generally very bad: most of them were worthless,
lawless, and drunken. Some of them, he believes, P. 174.
were mechanicks; but most of them vagrants who
infested London. Thinks a colony may certainly be
established there, by people of a different character,
under proper laws, with every prospect of success, as
it is a very fine fertile country. The river is a good
port.

At sea little more than half a man of war's crew
are in their hammocks at a time, as they are generally
at watch and watch. Height between decks from
5 feet 4 or 5 inches, to 5 feet 10 inches.

He seldom or ever visited a Guineaman, as his
disgust always overcame his curiosity. Certainly no P. 175.
comparison can be formed between the situation of
seamen in a man of war and slaves in a Guineaman.

Cardamum is in great plenty in Africa. He has
seen some black pepper; red peppers of many species
in abundance, and, he has been told, wild nutmegs.
The island of St. Thomas abounds in wild cinnamon,
(which he cannot distinguish from cassia) but he
never saw any on the continent, though he thinks it
equally calculated to produce it. Wild grapes, tho'
not very palatable, are in plenty at S. Leone, and
he

1790. he planted some cuttings of Teneriffe vines, which throve very well.

---

Witness examined—Captain JOHN HILLS,

Of the Royal Navy.

P. 176. Was at Goree and the Gambia as commander of his Majesty's sloop Wasp, he thinks, in the end of 1781 and beginning of 1782. (In all near 6 months in Africa, p. 181.)

Knew at Dacard, Moriel, a high priest, very intelligent.

He saw the natives, in an evening, often go out, in war-dresses, as he found, to obtain slaves for the king of Damel, to be sold. Some pirates, who had obtained a slave improperly, brought him bound on board the Zephyr, to sell him to him. On his releasing him they desired he might stay till morning, to be carried to governor Wall; who would take him. Next morning the man jumped out of the canoe, and was rescued by the Dacard people.

He has seen them tied back to back in several
P. 177. huts. He was told by one person, that the king was very poor, not having received his usual presents, and that parties were sent to get slaves for him on that account.

At Dacard, where the ship watered, Capt. Ganna, received the king's dues. This Ganna brought the kidnapped man to him as aforesaid. Moriel, his brother, a respectable man, held this mode of seizing the natives, in high indignation. They were both the king of Damel's subjects, and chiefs of villages. (Understood Ganna was not a Maraboo, p. 180.)

The natives all go armed: he imagines for fear of being taken.

When in the river Gambia, wanting servants on board,

board, he expressed a wish for some volunteers. A black pilot in the boat, called two boys who were on shore, carrying baskets of shallots, and asked captain H. if they would do, in which case he would take them off, and bring them to him: this he declined. From the ease with which he did it, concludes this was customary. Black pilot said the merchantmen would not refuse such an offer.

1790. Part II. P. 178.

He was advised not to go ashore at Gambia, by the merchants there, for fear of being taken by the natives, who owed the English a grudge, for some injuries. A man at Gambia, who called himself a prince's brother, had been carried to the W. Indies, in an English ship, and was sent to Europe by the governor.

A boy, whom he bought from the merchants, had been carried in the night from his father's house, where a skirmish had happened, in which, he believes, he said, both his parents, but he well remembers one, were killed. The boy said many were killed, and some taken.

Several natives spoke very good French and English. He had a letter from a man at Gambia very well written in French. A man, whose child was to be buried, could not stand the shock, and requested to stay on board the Zephyr, till the ceremony was over, and he shewed much grief and emotion.

P. 179.

He was often applied to by the merchants (English, p. 180) for help, owing to deaths and sickness among their seamen. He did not lose a man in his own ship.

Never saw the women working in the fields; but has often seen the men raising provisions near Dacard. Has seen them dress their corn in a large hole, by cutting it to pieces with sharp instruments on staves. Has seen them working their common cloths in their looms.

He apprehends the boys (aforesaid) were free people

P. 180.

1790.
Part II.
ple from the pilot's mode of speaking, and from his winking, implying it was an illicit thing.

Was informed the person's brother who was brought to him bound, was a great man in the village he was taken from. He should apprehend no crime was alledged against him; because the next day he returned to his own village.

They always paid the king of Damel for wooding and watering. There was a fixed price for every boat landing.

P. 181. He attributes the healthiness of his crew in Africa to medical precautions, (which were used to guard against the noxious land-vapours, p. 181). Bark and Madeira wine were always given the men when they went on shore, and returned on board.

The natives in Damel appear very lazy and idle. In the Gambia, he had no opportunity of landing to see their industry. He does not think they could be very easily induced by any encouragement, to manufacture their produce so as to become articles of trade.

He had on board the Zephyr, on an average, about 90 men, which was her compliment. She was about 200 tons.

---

Witness examined—GEORGE BAILLIE, Esq.

P. 182. Resided 25 years in South Carolina and Georgia. Commenced merchant in Charleston in 1756, (p. 193.) afterwards planter in 1767, (p. 194.) and as Commissary General of Georgia. Settled there in 1762, (p. 197.)

Many vessels arrived while he resided at Charleston and Savannah, with slaves from Africa. He saw many of the crews of those ships who had squalid countenances, and ulcerated limbs.

Notice of the sale having been given some days before, the slaves were ranged in a close yard, a great gun fired, and buyers rushed violently in, and seized

seized the best looking slaves, afterwards picking and
culling them to their minds. They were immediately purchased and hurried out of the yard; so that,
in a few hours, only the refuse slaves remained;
whose health had suffered, generally, as he conceived,
from crowding and confined air on board, and who
were afterwards sold at a great under-price.

In America, the overseer roused the slaves and set
them to work in the morning. They did not work
for set hours, but by task-work, generally a rood of
land to each, when easily cultivated; if otherwise,
the overseer set the strongest to the hardest work,
and vice versa; and indeed it was usual to lessen the
piece of land considerably when uncommonly foul.
The negroes generally helped those who could not
finish so soon as the rest; so that they left the field
at once, pretty early in the afternoon when their
work ceased, and they were at perfect liberty for
the rest of the day. They had no other time but
Sunday, and a few holidays at Christmas. Sunday
was intirely at their own disposal.

Each man and woman slave had weekly a peck of
Indian corn or clean rice, each about 14lb. or a
bushel of potatoes, near 40lb. and the children, in
proportion to their age. (A peck of Indian corn
about 7½d a peck of rice 10d. a bushel of potatoes
from 8d. to 10d. p. 196.) Besides they had generally as much ground as they chose to cultivate, the
produce intirely at their own disposal.

Each man received, at the beginning of winter, a
coat, waistcoat, and breeches and boots of white
plains, also a milled worsted cap and a pair of strong
shoes. In summer they commonly have an Osnaburg's
shirt and trowsers. The women were clothed much
in the same way, except the boots. The children had
each a long warm gown down to the heels. They
had also every second year, a warm duffel blanket.

It was usual to have overseers to superintend every
plantation, and drivers under them. Generally from

1790.
Part II.

P. 183.

P. 184.

P. 185.

thirty-

1790.
Part II.

thirty-two to thirty-five workers were under one overseer and one driver.

In America, he has seen marks on them, but not very often, and seldom when they had humane masters. The drivers seldom or never whip the slaves through their day's work; because it was impossible to know, till towards the close of the day, whether a slave would or would not finish his task; and it was thought time enough to punish, when their neglect deserved it. He has very rarely seen them, in America, with clogs on their legs; but never with chains.

The rearing of children was very much attended to in America. Pregnant women did no work for a considerable time before delivery. Coarse child-bed linen was provided, and sufficient care taken of them when lying-in. The child was properly clothed,

P. 186. and taken care of. Believes they are raised in as great a proportion as children in Europe, when they are in healthy situations. Never heard of the tetanus in that country.

The chief produce was rice, indigo, and humber. Lands intended for rice, if swampy, are drained and banked to keep water from lodging on them. When perfectly dry, the rice is sown (about March 20th, p. 195.) in straight trenches, weeded as it grows, and, when about three feet high, and quite clean, the sluices are opened, and the water admitted about June 20th, which stands about a foot deep, till towards the first week in September, when it is ripe. After the ground becomes a little dry, it is cut and cocked up in the field. Having stood there some little time, it is stacked, in the barn-yard, like corn in Europe. It is thrashed like European grain, winnowed, put through wooden mills, to take off the external coat, and into mortars, worked by horses or water, to divest it of the inner skin. It is then sifted, and put up for exportation.

P. 187. In October or November 1777, he went to Jamaica and the Bahamas, having been forced from the continent

tinent by the disputes there. Was several months in 1790.
Jamaica, (viz. from about Dec. 1778 to February or March 1779, p. 198.)    Part II.

Having then had little to do in Jamaica, he went from curiosity to various estates, and to compare their management with that of the continent. (He crossed the island for the same reason, p 198.) He must confess, he differed in opinion with several planters in their way of working the slaves, as thinking it rather served to depress their spirits, and their general appearance was, by no means, favourable. He observed that they worked, almost from sun-rise to sun-set, he might say; (they had almost an hour for breakfast, and nearly two hours for dinner, p. 200) and that they were constantly followed by drivers, who forced the weak to keep up with the strong, as far as possible. Looking into the books of an estate (of Mr. Gray's, p. 199) under the direction of a friend, (Mr. Hugh Polson, who was rather attorney, he believes, than manager, p. 199) to his utter surprize, he saw that the negroes were turned out on Sunday as regularly as on any other day, to work in their own grounds: but it appeared that the produce was appropriated to the negroes subsistence, and not to their emolument, unless perhaps there was a surplus of food. How far that surplus was applied to their benefit, he is not perfectly clear.

He thinks he could perceive a considerable difference between the general appearance of the field and the town slaves; because the latter were much better fed and clothed, and not worked so hard. Believes that might be the reason.    P. 188.

The situation of married men-slaves on the continent was generally very comfortable, as they had a house and ground where they could raise many little necessaries; and they took great pleasure in raising their children, for whom they seemed to have the sincerest attachment. He must confess, he did not think the W. India slaves seemed to enjoy the same comfort,

1790.  comfort in that refpect; as he apprehended it was
Part.II. not fo much the wifh of planters there to increafe
flaves by births, as on the continent.

He has in companies in the Weft Indies (he does not think they were very ferious neither—it is a very invidious thing) heard them fay, that after giving a certain price for a negro, if he worked a certain time, there would be no great lofs fuftained by his death; but believes they are too humane to wifh a man to die. Does not think, that on the continent, any gentleman would have fuggefted fuch a matter. (Thefe matters paffed only in curfory converfation, probably at a table. Does not fay this opinion was general, by any means, p. 200.)

Except their not being fo much driven through the day, believes punifhments, on the continent, as fevere as in the Weft Indies.

P. 189.  Planters in America refided almoft entirely on their eftates; but, from what he could obferve, confiderable Jamaica planters moftly lived in Europe. It appeared to him, that the flaves of a refident proprietor had a chance of better treatment.

Several of his flaves took every ftep in their power to be taught to read. On Sundays many of them went regularly to church (or meetings, p. 197.) which he encouraged. In evenings they very often had a kind of regular worfhip, among themfelves. They bought fpelling-books, with their own money, and with the help of other negroes that could read, fome came to read tolerably.

When near a town, they regularly carried their produce to market. Some mafters bought it of them; or little veffels bartered with them for their produce, poultry, and pigs.

P. 190.  Has known feveral town-negroes buy their freedom; but the country ones never did, or could come at property enough to do it. Free negroes in America may hold every kind of perfonal property; but, he thinks not land. Is not very clear.

The

The negroes in summer were much healthier than in winter.

The field-negroes in Jamaica appeared worn down with extreme labour, and being constantly pressed upon, through the day, by the drivers.

He thinks the climate of Jamaica, in every respect, much more favourable to negroes than that of America, and hence they were subject to fewer disorders: is also of opinion, that many of their complaints arose from extreme fatigue, and that rest generally restored them, without medicine.

The negroes on the continent, in winter, were extremely subject to pleurisies and peripneumonies, and sometimes dysentery. In summer rarely so comparatively.

Jamaica families had considerably more domesticks than those of Europe.

He thinks negroes perfectly capable of learning any trade. Has known many, and some of his own slaves, who almost without instruction, became good common house carpenters and coopers. He bought an African lad who, without initruction, but just seeing carpenters work, and using tools at times, became so good a carpenter, that he could frame and build any common house, and also build boats for the estate. He has known many silversmiths, blacksmiths, taylors, and ship-carpenters. A mercantile house, of his acquaintance, had a number of black ship-carpenters and blacksmiths, with the superintendance of two or three whites, built ships of 400 tons, which were sent with rice to the Thames, and sold for above 3000l.

There might be some few worthless fellows among the negroes; but, upon the whole, they were always very willing to work.

He has seen many instances of very affectionate parents, and of their being possessed of every social idea. A slave of his, whose son was drowned, did not recover his spirits for many months. All his slaves shewed him a very firm attachment, and were
fully

1790. fully grateful for every favour. During the siege of Savannah, he and another had rice estates on Hutchinson's island opposite Savannah, where there was much grain and forage, to protect which, the commander ordered the slaves on the island to be armed, and sent several whites to lead them on. A French 34 gun frigate anchored to batter the town, and landed troops on the island, to destroy the barns. His slaves and others beat the French, who, he thinks, never made another attempt.

Is perfectly satisfied that the cultivation of cotton or coffee is much easier than that of sugar, but that of rice fully as laborious (p. 201.)

P. 193. He bought a man about 35 years old, seemingly very steady. While the other slaves were cheerfully reaping, he shewed him how manage the hook. He disappeared for several days, and at last he was discovered hanging to a tree, about which the birds hovered. As he had not been at all ill treated, and did not see the negroes at extremely hard work, he conceived he committed suicide, because he would not brook slavery. He was an imported African (p. 201.)

On almost every American estate there were great numbers of very thriving children, who soon became useful, and always made the best slaves.

A child, soon after birth, was valued in America at 5l. sterling.

Field-work on the continent was not held degrading to Mulattoes or free negroes, nor does he think it would in Jamaica. Both certainly worked in the field, for their own benefit, in America. Not positive whether they did so in Jamaica.

P. 194. He had various tracts of land, but planted from 120 to 130 acres of rice, chiefly on Hutchinson's island, where had between 200 and 300 acres of very
P. 195. valuable land, and about 40 working slaves. The land could produce any thing, and, at times, he planted (perhaps 40 acres of) indigo, with Indian corn, pease, &c. for the negroes.

In

In Georgia, light frosts usually set in about Oct. 1790. 25th, which generally checked vegetation. The greatest severity of winter seldom till Christmas; spring began about March 20th, when grain was sown. (The winter is about the same length in S. Carolina as in Georgia, p. 196.)  Part II.

In winter, the negroes threshed and prepared the rice, and a little before spring, repaired the banks.

£.110 Georgia currency, and 140 l. Jamaica currency respectively equal to 100l. sterling.

Before the American disputes, he never knew the least scarcity; but afterwards, when people were driven away, and much disturbed in planting, there was a considerable scarcity. P. 197.

Mr. Whitfield had grants of land for a house and a plantation. He erected an orphan-house, with collections chiefly from England, bought slaves, settled a plantation, and, with the produce, supported the house.

Does not think his residence in Jamaica was long enough to give him a complete idea of the system. He only speaks of such things as he saw. P. 201.

He has heard, and partly knows, that the Eboes are very high spirited, and do not brook slavery so well as several other Africans. P. 202.

He saw a small yellow Indian corn, on several estates, and believes it was for the horses, and perhaps the negroes; also some very large plantane-walks, he believes for the slaves' use.

As it was customary in America, for free negroes and Mulattoes to get leave to plant on parts of estates, or to rent a piece of land to plant, and as he can conceive this might be the case in Jamaica, he does not think such labour would be held degrading; yet it was not common for these people to work among field-slaves. Is clear they do not in America, but not so positive respecting Jamaica. P. 203.

His residence in Jamaica was not long: but must confess he did not think the negroes there so robust and good-looking, as in general in America. He does

1790.   does think himself so far acquainted with negroes that
Part II. the working them by task is far preferable to the W.
Indian mode of working them constantly. Really
believes the superiority in appearance just mentioned,
may be partly ascribed this different mode of working.

P. 204.   In the upper parts of Georgia and S. Carolina,
where grain or Indian corn was cultivated by the
plough, white men sometimes hired themselves as
servants.

---

Witness examined,—SIR GEORGE YOUNG,

P. 205.   A captain in the navy. Has been 4 voyages to
Africa, in 1767 and 1768—1771 and 1772. From
Cape Blanco to Cape Lopas, including every Eng-
lish settlement, and some Dutch.

His opinion (from information of natives and set-
lers) of the general modes of obtaining slaves on the
Coast of Africa, was, that the greater part were prisoners of war; part for crimes real or imputed; kidnapping; but the term there is panyer; and a fourth
mode was, the inhabitants of one village seizing
those of another weaker village, and selling them to
the ships.

When at Annamaboe, at Mr. Bruce's, a very great
merchant there, Mr. B. had 2 hostages, kings sons,
P. 206. for payment for arms, and all kinds of military stores,
which he had supplied to the 2 kings, who were at
war with each other, to procure slaves for at least 6
or 7 ships, then lying in the road; prisoners on both
sides were brought down to Mr. B. and sent to the
ships.

Believes, from two instances, that kidnapping was
frequently practised. One, that of a beautiful infant
boy, which, after trying to sell at all the different
trading ships, they came along side his (the Phœnix)
and threatened to toss it overboard, if no one would
buy

buy it, faying, they had panyar'd it with many other people, but could not fell it, though they had fold the others; he purchafed it for a quarter cafk of wine.

The fecond was, a captain of one of the Liverpool fhips had got, as a temporary miftrefs, a girl from king Tom, of Sierra Leone, and inftead of returning her on fhore at leaving the coaft, as is ufually done, he took her away with him. Of this, the king complained to him (Sir G. Young) very heavily, and begged him to apply to his brother George (meaning our king) to get her reftored to him. This, king Tom called buchra, or white man's panyaring.

The term panyaring, feemed to be a word generally ufed all along the coaft where he was, not only among the Englifh, but the Portuguefe and Dutch.

Has always heard, that the fovereign or chief of a diftrict, generally derives a certain profit from the fale of flaves.

Has heard many inftances of depredations on the Coaft of Africa, by European traders. For one; going into the river St. Andrew, and making a prefent as ufual to the king, of a cafe of gin, was obliged to drink a dram out of each, of 12 bottles; upon afking the reafon, the king faid it was ufual for traders (but did not fay whether black or white) to make ufe of poifon; but that he fhould not have obliged him to drink, if he had known the fhip had been a man of war, as he knew a man of war had no defign of panyaring.

The natives all down the coaft, were fearful of approaching the fhip, till convinced of its being a man of war, when they readily came on board.

Many negroes he met with, feemed to poffefs as ftrong natural fenfe as any fet of people whatever; their temper appeared to be very good-natured and civil, unlefs where they fufpected fome injury; are however naturally vindictive, and revenge the injury done.

Numb. 3.          L          He

1790. He verily believes, that the natives would cultivate the foil for natural productions, provided they had no other means of obtaining European commodities. He recollects some circumstances in proof of their industry. A number of people from the Bullam shore, came over to Sierra Leone, and offered their services to work, at a very low price; he accepted of a few (who worked very well) and might have had thousands of the same description. Further is of opinion, from observation, that Africa is capable of producing every thing of the East or West Indies, in equal perfection, with equal cultivation. Of spices, he met with two sorts of cardamoms, black pepper, same as in the East Indies; the bird pepper; Chili pepper, or Cayenne; also a species of ginger. Brought to England several plants of the cinnamon tree, from the island of St. Thomas, where it is in great abundance.

Has been several times on board a slave ship; they were all in a state of cleanliness; as clean indeed as their situation, with the number of men confined on board, would admit of. He attempted to go down the fore hatchway of one of them, but was deterred by the stench, which was intolerable, though there was then only 300 on board, and waited for 200 more. The men slaves were all chained, which he considered as a necessary precaution, as there was not quite 20 seamen on board at the time.

The African slave trade, not a nursery, rather a grave for seamen. Those of them which he saw on board the slave ships, complained of ill treatment, bad feeding, and cruel usage; all of them wanted to enter on board his ship. He asked some of them the reason why they were so treated, they answered, it was the practice of the owners and masters of the vessels to treat them so, that they might run away in the West Indies, and so forfeit their wages. It was likewise the custom for the seamen of every ship in sight, to come by their boats on board his ship; most of them quite naked, and threatening to turn pirates,

pirates, if the king's ship would not take them; they said openly, and is persuaded, if he had had a ship of the line to have manned, he could have done it in a very short time, for they would all have left ships. Though he took particular notice, he could never see a boy on board any of these ships; in every other trade, there are always boys on board.

Has heard many instances of sailors escaping to the woods; several he has received on board his ship from the woods, where they had no subsistance.

Has seen a great deal of very fine timber; in his opinion, useful for ship and house-building, as well as furniture; likewise dying woods of great variety; some of the wood he brought home, and turned into furniture. He is in possession of specimens of ebony, iron-wood, and other sorts, all very hard. When at Sierra Leone, he saw a vessel belonging to Mr. Pintard, built upon the rocks, of the woods of Sierra Leone.

Has been a great deal in the West Indies; at Barbadoes, Antigua, St. Kitt's, Dominica, Grenada, Guadaloupe, Martinique, Port Rico, and lastly at Jamaica, from the years 1761, to 1763. Has been since there several times in a man of war, and sometimes a passenger in a merchant ship.

Was twice in the Phœnix, at Barbadoes, Antigua, St. Kitt's, Dominica and Jamaica, in 1767, and 1768.

Farming, and the management of land, has in England been his amusement and pleasure, ever since the last peace. When in the West Indies, has remarked to the gentlemen there, the great want of the plough and spade; and considered the hoe as an implement much more laborious.

Never saw, or heard of task-work practised in any of the West India islands.

Has remarked very bad effects from the absence of the proprietors, and the estate and slaves being left under the direction of managers, which greatly lessens the value of West Indian estates; he will take upon him to say, to the amount of at least one-fifth part of the whole; for the overseers or managers, in a little time, always became rich, and frequently more so than their masters. It is also injurious to the slave, because he was made to work harder, than he is sure the owner would have allowed; their provisions were not so good; generally salt provision, sometimes dried fish, or stinking salt meat, which their masters, he is sure, would not have allowed; for he has the honour to be acquainted with some of them. He was informed by the merchants of Kingston, that it was not an uncommon practice for the overseers to buy sickly slaves at half price, or less, and charge them to their masters as prime healthy slaves; those frequently died, as it is said in the seasoning, which he considers as a farce altogether.

Understood, that purchasing African slaves was much the cheapest mode of keeping up the numbers; for, that the mother of a bred slave was taken from the field labour for 3 years; which labour was of more value than the cost of a prime slave, or new negro.

P. 212. The negroes work in gangs, and in regular rows, with hoes, with which they kept regular time in their work, the whole gang together, so that the weak were obliged to keep up with the more robust. For there were black drivers over them, with a whip called a cowskin, with which he supposes, if they had not kept up, they would have been punished.

Has been a great deal in the East Indies; never saw or heard of any labourers working in the field, under the whip of a driver there, or in America.

Recollects a particular instance of the high spirit of the negroes, which occurred at Accra. The governour had bought a slave (of a country, the natives of which, when enslaved, are always known to kill themselves) and was complaining to commodore Collingwood and him, that he had been cheated by the merchants, of whom he bought him; that he was a very fine fellow; asking whether they would not

go

go and see him, for that he had mortally wounded himself last night; when carried to him, they upbraided him with his rash conduct, by the interpreter, and his reply was, that no man of his country could live as a slave, but that he was very well inclined to serve the commodore in the man of war, but not as a slave; he died the next night.

The negro women on the coast of Africa, appeared to him as prolific, as any race of people he ever saw in any part of the world; the climate of the West Indies not less favourable to them than their own.

Was about 6 months on the coast of Africa each time. The crew of the ship he commanded, amounted to 100, of which lost 2, who were sickly when they went out, and 1 boy by an accident.

The stock of slaves might be kept up, or increased, without importations from Africa. At first indeed, the deficiencies would be felt for a few, perhaps 20 years; but after a while, they would double their numbers, as he sees no physical cause to prevent a black man and woman being equally prolific in the West Indies, as in Africa.

The land of Africa is mostly cultivated by the men; the women sometimes set fire to the grass, but that is very little; the men turn up the ground with pointed sticks, having no European implements there that he saw.

In the West Indies, he resided longer on shore at a time in Jamaica, than any other island; once so long as 6 weeks: never above a week on shore at any other island. At Jamaica, lived for above 3 weeks at Mr. Prevost's, Old Harbour; and Mr. Thomas's, Sixteen Mile Walk, about 3 weeks more; both sugar estates.

In the arguments which he held with the planters, respecting the superiority of the plough and spade over the hoe, was never able to make a proselyte.

Under the present system, the slave trade is necessary to the cultivation of the West Indies; but if
the

1790.
Part II. the breeding of the negroes were promoted there, it would be unneceffary. His reafons for thinking that due attention is not paid by the planters to the rearing of children, are, that when he was upon the above-mentioned, and fome other eftates, he found no encouragement given the blacks to marry; that they cohabited promifcuoufly, and that the women generally mifcarried, as he was told by Mr. Prevoft and Mr. Thomas, from their hard field labour; and that it was a rare thing for a negrefs employed in field labour, to have a live child.

At the ifland of Cuba, after the capture of the Havanna, he affociated with the Spanifh planters, and found they made it a ferious point to marry their negroes, wherever they could, to make them Chriftians, and to keep them regularly together: they had them chriftened, and gave them little rewards, and according to the number of children they produced and reared; and the men ufed to boaft of their being Chriftians, and wear a crofs about their necks; though he inquired all he could, he remarked nothing of the kind done in Jamaica.

P. 215. The planters reafons againft the ufe of the plough were, the hardnefs of the ground, the negroes ignorance, and that it had ever been the practice to make ufe of the hoe; fuch was the fubftance of their argument, which he thinks was faying nothing.

It feemed to be the univerfal fyftem, to fupply their eftates with African negroes, rather than be at the trouble of breeding.

Conceives thofe parts of Dominica, and the other iflands ceded by France (by the peace of 1763) yet in woods and uncleared, cannot be cleared, without the purchafe of negroes from fome part or other.

The cultivation of the Weft India iflands, to the extent of which they are capable, certainly will increafe the trade and navigation of Great Britain: was
P. 216. informed there is a great deal of land fit for cultivation ftill uncleared in Jamaica.

Does

Does not think, that the loss of seamen by the unfavourable circumstances of the slave trade, can be put in competition with the increased number of seamen that must be consequent upon the increased cultivation of the islands; but at the same time he must observe, that the loss of seamen in the African slave trade, as now carried on, is annually greater than the increase in the West India trade.

From the observations he was able to make at Mr. Prevost's estate, he could not discover any distinction made between the weak and strong; but they were in gangs most certainly.

Where, in the Privy Council Report, he is stated to have said, that he could not get the men to work for him, he meant, of some particular parts of the coast, not in general. And where, in the same report, he is stated to have said, that the field labours are usually performed by women, as to what part of the coast he meant to refer that assertion, says to no part whatever; for he never saw the women do any thing but carry the corn home, and set fire to the stubble of last year.

Is of opinion, that by shewing the natives of Africa how to cultivate the land, it would call for the labour of ten times the number that are now transported to the West Indies as slaves; and require a greater quantity of shipping and seamen in the commerce, for the natural productions of that country, without any greater inconvenience in point of health to the seamen, than in the present West India trade.

And believes, if the slave trade were abolished, and every proper regulation adopted, to encourage the breeding of negroes in the West Indies, the stock of negroes would gradually increase, so as to be adequate to the clearing and cultivation of all the islands, to the full extent of which they are capable.

The regulations which he conceives to be still wanting, are, that marriage should be encouraged; that the man and woman should have a hut to themselves; that the woman should be taken wholly from field

1790.
Part II.

field labour, and only put to such as she is capable of, as a woman bearing children. The man should be allowed one day in a week to work for himself and family; a reward should be given to the woman, who had, and should rear, the greatest number of children. Under these regulations, he conceives, in the course of 20 years, their present numbers may be doubled, and the trade in slaves from Africa, totally unnecessary.

P. 218. Is not competent to judge, how many additional negroes are now wanted, to clear and cultivate the present uncleared lands in the British islands. Does not know the specific number of negroes in each of these islands; nor the specific quantity of lands now uncleared and uncultivated; has not been in the West Indies since 1772.

The principle upon which he fixes the period of 20 years, for the purpose above-mentioned, is, the circumstance of the Americans doubling their numbers in less than 20 years.

---

Witness examined—ANTHONY PANTALEO HOW, Esq.

P. 219. Was in Africa in 1785 and 1786, chiefly on the Gold Coast, in the Grampus man of war, employed by government as a botanist. When at Secundee, some order came from Cape Coast Castle; the same
P. 220. afternoon several parties went out armed, and returned the same night with a quantity of slaves, which were put into the repository of the factory. Next morning saw people who came to see the prisoners, and requested Mr. Marsh the resident to release some of their children and relations. Some were released, part sent off to C. Coast Castle. Had every reason to believe they were obtained unfairly, as they came at an unseasonable time of the night, and from their parents and friends crying, and begging their release. Had been told as much from Mr. Marsh, who said,

he

Cannot speak from his own personal knowledge as to the conduct of planters and their slaves in the other islands mentioned. The negroes over which Mr. Macvie presided, seemed in a much more comfortable state than any he had seen in the W. Indies. He seemed a father to his slaves. Had seen negroes whipped on the wharfs in Jamaica on Monday mornings. The mode was to make fast their hands to the hook of a crane, and their feet to a weight or two. The crane was then hove up to stretch their hands, and prevent them from moving, while flogged by a black man. Their backs afterwards prickled with a small bush. Does not recollect the number of lashes, or know whether these punishments were inflicted by judicial sentence, or the private order of the master. In Jamaica, has seen one or two of the distressed seamen called wharfingers carried by the blacks to a burying-place near Spring Path, the blacks themselves telling him "It was poor Buchra man." Believes the blacks performed this office of their own accord.

1790. Part II.

P. 244.

P. 245.

At Tobago has known the surf to run so high for two or three days together, that they could not land or take off goods.

The instrument with which negroes are whipped, is generally called a cow-skin; a piece of cow or bullock's hide twisted or plaited together, which, when dry, becomes exceeding hard.

He recollected seeing once a sailor in a man of war receive three dozen with the boatswain's cat, at the gangway, and only once being on deck when a man was flogged from ship to ship, his hands and feet are tied to prevent his moving. In this instance he fainted, but cannot describe other particulars. Believes all hands are turned upon deck to see the punishment as the man comes alongside. His back receives it.

P. 246.

Always understood that the usual punishment of negroes on the wharfs at Kingston on Monday morning, were for crimes of the preceding week. Never understood

1790. understood it was by order of the magistrates, but by
Part II. direction of their masters or mistresses. Never saw negroes punished on plantations in Jamaica. Heard there is at Kingston a jumper, a man who punishes the negroes, and is paid for it, but of no such person on the estates. Knows not by whom this jumper is employed, but only that he was employed to whip the negroes.

---

Witness Examined—Rev. THOMAS GWYNN REES.

P. 247. Went to the W. Indies as Chaplain in the Princess Amelia. Arrived at Barbadoes end of 1782. Made observations on the situation of slaves, in consequence of being informed in England how they were treated. Had opportunities by going ashore almost daily, and visiting such plantations as were within four or five miles of Bridge-Town. The negroes appeared generally to be in a very bad state. It struck him with the impression that they were not in general well fed. The clothing of the slaves was a small rag to cover their nakedness. Some had breeches or trowsers.
P. 248. Their lodging, in small huts covered with cane leaves to appearance. Their furniture consisted of stools or benches. Saw no beds or bedding in the houses he was in. They slept on a kind of board raised a little from the ground, and some on the ground. Saw three or four gangs or more at different times, working on the plantations. The first he saw, were working with hoes or mattocks in their hands, with a negro driver after them with a whip, all in a row making small holes to put corn in. A driver attended each gang, whom he observed more than once to use his whip on the negroes at work. One of the women appeared pregnant, and rather behind the rest. He called to her to come on, and going back, struck her with the whip up towards the shoulders. Saw three working with iron collars in one gang, and one with a piece of chain to his leg. Asked a pregnant slave whether

did not mind how they got them, for he purchased them fairly. Cannot tell whether this practice subsisted before; but when he has gone into the woods, has met 30 or 40 natives, who fled always at his appearance although they were armed. Mr. Marsh said, they were afraid of his taking them prisoners.

Concludes the slave-trade obstructs industry and civilization of the Africans. Has been at almost all English settlements, and found the culture always in a higher degree there where was less slave-trade, and vice versa. Had been about 50 miles inland from Secundee, and about 15 or 16 from Apolonia, and found the inland every where well cultivated, and hardly any where on the shore. Most cultivation at Winnebah, Accra, and Goree. Beautiful cotton and indigo plantations at Goree. Saw no European commodities in the interiour parts; is sure no European spirits were to be had there. The inhabitants there remarkably industrious, also hospitable and obliging. A village of several hundred houses on the Lake of Appolonia, whence in the rainy season they supply the sea coast with vegetables, grain, palm-wine, &c. Thinks they have but little capacity in regard to manufactures, but quick in learning languages. No manufactures among them except at Goree, where they weave cloth, and have almost abolished the slave-trade in the part now belonging to the French.

Abreast of Cape le Hou, several canoes came along side of the Grampus, desired her colours might be hoisted. Finding her an English man of war, they came on board without hesitation, which otherwise they would not have done (see p. 225.) Reason alledged, that an English Guinea trader, a fortnight before, had taken off six canoes with men who came to trade with provisions. The next day about 10 leagues off, several canoes approached, but finding it was a man of war, retreated. On coming to Appolonia were told by Mr. Buchanan, the resident there, that a Guineaman (belonging to one Griffiths, a notorious kidnapper) was in that latitude, the cap-

1790.
Part II.

P. 221.

P. 222.

Numb. 3. M tain

1790.  tain brought on shore, tied to a tree, and flogged for
Part II. four days, in revenge for a depredation which another
had committed: thus accounting for the retreat of
the canoes on finding the Grampus a ship of war, and
fearing retaliation of the punishment.

Four children of the captives brought in to Secundee, sent in the same canoe with himself to C. Coast Castle.

The slaves kept in the Factories chained day and night, and driven to the sea side twice a day to be washed. In the factory saw different kinds of iron
P. 223. chains, also an instrument of wood, which Mr. Marsh informed him was thrust into a man's mouth, to prevent him from crying out when transported at night along the country. From their mild behaviour to their attendants, in the inland country, concludes they had no domestick slaves; on the sea side this behaviour very different.

The natural productions of Africa consist of cotton in abundance, indigo of a fine quality, various dye roots and woods, yams, sweet potatoes, rice, millet, pulse, oranges, limes, bananas, plantanes, cocoa-nuts, palm-trees, yielding wine and oil, black pepper, grains of paradise, cinnamon, cardamoms, assafœtida, cabinet-woods, and timber-trees. Of the latter, a species of the Ficktonia grandis, considered
P. 224. as the most eligible for ship-building, the worm neither touching nor the iron corroding it; grows in plenty at Appolonia, Secundee, and wherever he had been. Has specimens of most. Has no doubt but spices in general, and all other tropical productions might be cultivated with success there. The soil and climate adapted to produce the sandal wood. Has seen indigo at Appolonia in its raw state, and
P. 225. also manufactured, but not manufacturing. Also cotton growing in great abundance, but knows not that any or either of these two articles were exported.

Was on the coast shortly after the rains, when the indigo began to decay, in November, December, and January. At places, at Appolonia and Winnebah,
the

the furf runs high in thefe months. It is eafy to
land a ton or two of goods; only performed by the
inhabitants in canoes built on purpofe: though at
Appolonia thefe pretty frequently overfet, feldom any
thing is loft in the furf.

Cinnamon plants at St. Thomas, at the fea fide, about 20 feet high; from what he heard grew inland to a higher fize; thofe on the fea fide he confidered only as fhrubs. He faw a number of them, and from the appearance of the bark brought down, concludes there muſt be a great quantity inland. The cinnamon and caſſia tree of different genera; the one belongs to the clafs Laurus, the other the Caffia; their genera not quite eftablifhed. Of the laurus, the leaf oblong, nerved, fhining, fimple. Of the caffia, the leaves are bipennate; different from the laurus, and not unlike the mimofa or fenfitive plant. Is not pofitive that it is the fame cinnamon which grows in India, but the bark, leaves, and whole ſtructure of the tree, the fame as thofe brought from thence to Kew gardens. Had never been at Ceylon, but had feen the tree both at Bombay and Cambay in private gardens, brought as prefents from Ceylon. The African caffia not unlike that he had feen in Eaſt Indies.

The foil on the Gold coaſt, within reach of the furf, every where fandy (Goree iflands alfo fandy) in the reſt of the fettlements he had been at, a heavy loom or clay: every where fertile. As far as eight or ten miles inland, various woods produced, ufed in dying, feveral of which are exported.

At Winnebah and Accra rocky; alfo about Appolonia within three miles of the coaſt, but the inlands 10 or 12 miles from the fhore, very well cultivated with rice, yams, fweet potatoes, indigo, and cotton; are fertile, and plentifully watered.

Within 5 miles up the country from Sccundee, it is mountainous and uncultivated; the roads therefore very bad; in parts about five feet broad, but where the country is cultivated, in fome parts they are cut

1790. through the woods from 15 to 20 feet broad. Understood from Messrs. Buchanan and Marsh, that produce was brought down in the rainy season in canoes.

Knows of no navigable rivers on the Gold Coast, except one at Accra, only navigable for small boats and canoes. The Lake at Appolonia runs inland about 20 miles. Has seen the produce, as far as the Lake extends at Appolonia, brought in small canoes, rowed by a single woman, but never saw them carry any thing in a basket.

Griffiths, the notorious kidnapper, was a white man and slave-trader, between Cape Le Hou and Appolonia. Understood from Captain Thompson (who offered him a reward of 100l. if he could catch him) that he was a native of England; but had no knowledge of him himself. Knows neither name of ship or captain, who was flogged for four days by the natives, but understood she was an English slave-trader from Liverpool. Witness is a Polander, left Africa 15th February, 1786. Afterwards went with Capt. Thompson in the Nautilus, commissioned by this government on a private expedition. After his return, stayed several months in London, and was again commissioned to go to the inland countries of the E. Indies, from whence he returned 19th of August last, and has been in England ever since.

Slave-trade on Gold Coast mostly carried on in neighbourhood of Cape Le Hou, Secundee, Commenda, and Anamaboe. Has a quantity of indigo given him by the chief of the village, near Appolonia, who told him it was manufactured there, but had never himself seen it manufacturing. Never understood manufactured indigo was imported into that country as an article of trade.

1790.
Part I.

Witness examined,—Mr. NINIAN JEFFERYS.

Mr. Ninian Jefferys, master in the Royal Navy, superintending ships in ordinary at Portsmouth, was at Jamaica in 1773, Tobago 1774, Jamaica 1775, Grenada 1776, Tortola 1779, Barbadoes and St. Lucia (in the navy) 1782, Antigua and St. Kitt's 1783, and at Jamaica a few days in 1784. In Jamaica in 1773 and 75, and at Tobago in 1774, had several opportunities, being employed as second mate in landing goods and taking off sugars from the islands, chiefly at Tobago. Observed the field-negroes at work with one or two white men looking after them, and a black man or two, called drivers, constantly cracking the whip over them, and sometimes lashing them, which he thought very oppressive; sometimes a white man whipping them. Had frequent opportunities of observing the plantation-slaves in his visits to Jamaica. The greater part of them had marks of the whip, particularly the back. Says, they must have been the effect of severer punishments than he ever saw inflicted in a man of war, which last are not in the least to be compared with them. Saw wheals on their backs which no time can erase, never any of the kind at a man of war's gangway. Has seen slaves with their ears cut off, and understood it was done by or by order of their masters, though never saw it done; also some with one of their hands cut off, which he understood was for lifting it against or striking a white man (believes by the laws of the island, p. 239.) Has seen negroes sick or past their labour, apparently neglected and destitute. At Tobago, more than once, at an outhouse in a very miserable situation. In Jamaica, and about Kingston, has frequently seen negroes apparently past their labour, and in a diseased condition lying in the streets and roads. Observed a very great difference between the domestick and plantation-slaves; considered the former as a nuisance

P. 231

P. 232

nuisance from their numbers, as generally over well fed, and saucy; the plantation slaves, as a poor depressed part of the human race. Has frequently seen women with sucking infants working with the rest of the gang. Their lodging were little huts, with clayed walls, and the roof covered with cane trash. Does not recollect any bedding. The black tradesmen, fishermen, boatmen, free negroes, and mulattoes, seemed in general to be in a much better condition than the plantation negroes. Appeared to him that no comparison could be formed between the situation of the labouring poor of this country and the plantation slaves; who are treated in many respects like cattle. Has seen slaves branded with initials. Has ever understood the picking of grass to be oppressive, as encroaching on the hours of rest; and the most common cause of their desertion is ill treatment. Has seen them at work with logs of wood fastened to their legs; in the stocks; also with an iron collar round their necks, with a perpendicular hook on each side projecting from the upper part of the head, and understood for running away.

In conversations respecting the most desirable qualifications of managers or overseers, always understood he was considered the best manager who sent home the most sugar. At these conversations, white persons from the estates have been present, but does not recollect whether they were the managers.

Always considered the negroes as good mothers; as to their feelings and capacities, he never considered them, being young when among them. Knew an astonishing instance of high spirit and greatness of mind: was present at the execution of 7 slaves in Tobago in 1774, whose right arms were chopped off; they were then dragged to seven stakes, and a fire of trash and dry wood being lighted about them, they were burnt to death. Does not recollect hearing one of them murmur, or their doing any thing which indicated fear. One of them, named Chubb, had been taken that morning, and was executed in

the

the evening. Witness stood close by him when his arm was cut of; he stretched it out on the block, and pulled up his sleeve with more coolness than he (the witness) should have done to be let blood; would not be dragged, but walking to the stake, turned about and addressing himself to the witness, said "Buchra, you see me now, but to-morrow I shall be like that," kicking up the dust with his foot. Two other negroes were present at this execution, and shewed no marks of dismay. One of these, named Sampson, was hung alive in chains the next morning, and so lived (to the best of witness's recollection) seven days; believes the other was sent to the mines in South America. A stronger instance of human fortitude he never saw.

Observed a much greater number of children among the domestic or free negroes, in proportion, than among the field negroes.

Saw numbers of seamen, who came on shore from the Guinea ships in the W. Indies, in and about Kingston, in a very distressed state, ulcerated, apparently in want, and lying about on the wharfs, known by the name of wharfingers; has seen them in a dying state. Believes not usual for king's ships to take such seamen on board, especially in time of peace; lest they should bring contagious distempers with them. Believes they were not able to do the duty of a merchantman. Never saw instances of seamen discharged from other trades lying about in a similar situation. Thinks the slave trade is by no means a nursery for seamen, and that the West India trade is not in any degree so destructive to the health and lives of the seamen, though not so much a nursery as other trades.

Was about four months in Jamaica, in 1773: was then aged about 19 years. Resided on board the ship he belonged to; was on three or four plantations; but not more than a day and a night at a time. Was about 4 months in 1774 at Tobago, chiefly residing on board ship, though some time at a friend's house in the country, not a sugar plantation. Was at Jamaica,

1. maica, as second mate, about four months in 1775,
II. residing mostly on ship-board, and sometimes a day
or two together on shore at Kingston where the ship
loaded. Was not then, at above two or three sugar
plantations, nor above a night or two at a time.
Received sugars at water side.

39. What he said respecting the mode of working negroes, relates to Tobago only, where the greater part of the plantation negroes were marked with the whip.

Travelled through a great part of Tobago, never continuing but two or three nights on one estate, besides that of his friend, which was not a sugar estate.

Believes the field slaves to be more useful to the owner than the domestic ones. Cannot account for so many of the latter being kept, and better fed. The conversation on the qualifications of a manager were held at Kingston, and on board the ship he belonged to; and the doctrine beforementioned, supported by gentlemen about Kingston, and white men from the estates, who he did not conceive to be planters.

40. The crimes for which the men were burnt at Tobago in 1774, were murder, and destroying the property on the estate.

There may be an hospital at Kingston in Jamaica, for the reception of sailors and transient poor, but he never saw it.

42. Had been near a week at a time on Little Courland estate, the proprietor, or chief gentleman whereof was Stuart Macvie, Esq.; and frequently spent a night in the boiling-house of different estates, waiting for sugar being carted down. Saw no punishments inflicted at Mr. Macvie's. Does not particularly know, but believes about 200 negroes on that estate. Recollects no regular punishments; except of those men who suffered death, as he believes, by the sentence of the law. It was in Kingston market, in

43. Jamaica, where he saw negroes with their ears cut off, and understood it was done by their masters, or their orders. In the year 1784, witness had not frequent opportunities of making observations in that island.

Cannot

whether she was forced to work like the rest, and she said, Yes. Saw sucking infants in baskets on the ground, just by where the women were at work, and one of the latter suckling her infant. Recollects in a sugar mill a young girl between 20 and 30 years old, chained to a large block, within reach of the mill, which she fed with sugar cane. She said she was to be chained there a twelvemonth, of which two months had elapsed, for running away from her master, who had used her badly, and that she was obliged to sleep where she was, on the ground, having very little but cane juice to sustain her; which was confirmed by a slave present. Says that about half a mile from Bridge-Town, he heard the groans of a person at a small distance. On inquiring of her, she told him that she had been flogged for running away, to such a degree that she could hardly move. Saw the marks. Her left side appeared to be in a mortifying state, almost covered with worms. On her saying she could eat if she had victuals, he sent for some to the town. On his return in a few hours, saw her again. Repeating his visit a day or two afterwards, was informed she was dead, and carried away to be buried. The observation made by him and Mr. Vivian, the purser of the Princess Amelia, (then in his company) was, whoever inflicted that punishment would have done a kindness to have killed her.

Supposes they remained on the station a fortnight or three weeks afterwards. On shore every day, but did not hear of any public inquiry respecting the transaction. In saying that he saw 3 or 4 gangs or more at different times, he meant that number every time he went on shore. A great many more in the whole.

Often saw negroes returning from their work with bundles of grass; one of them said it was for his Master's cattle, and that, if he did not procure it, he should be flogged; thinks picking grass must make a considerable addition to their labour, and to the length of time they were employed, as in the parts

1790. he saw grafs did not appear to be in plenty. The
Part II. whipping the negroes while at work, by the driver,
was a common practice. Thinks it impoffible to
P. 252. walk in the ftreets or roads about Bridge Town without feeing fome of the negroes, apparently in great diftrefs, fome with the leprofy, fome enfeebled thro' age, and others who have loft their limbs, begging.

Obferved very frequently the marks of former fevere whippings on the backs of the plantation flaves. Has often feen feamen flogged on board a man of war, particularly in running the gauntlet, which is a violent flogging; but did not obferve marks of equal feverity on their bodies. Obferved marks of former floggings on feamens backs, but the wounds did not appear fo deep, nor the wheals fo high above the fkin, nor were the fcars fo long as on the flaves.

Has feen the negro-dance, obferved a difference in the dancers, fome better dreffed than others; was informed the well-dreffed were domeftic fervants, and the others field flaves. In different companies, the well-dreffed appeared better in their countenances and in fpirits.

P. 253. The negroes appeared to be as reafonable as any other beings whatever (confidering their education). Thinks no comparifon can be drawn between the ftate of plantation flaves, and that of the labouring poor in England.

Was between two and three months at St. Lucia, where the condition of plantation flaves feemed much the fame as in Barbadoes.

P. 254. Had no idea from what he heard in England before he left it, that the ftate of flaves in the W. Indies, was fo bad as he found it to be.

Remembers a converfation at Mr. Prettyjohn's, on the difference between breeding and buying flaves, in which having afked if they had not enough born without fending to Africa for them, and if population was encouraged; Mr. P, anfwered, they could not encourage it more than they did, as it was not worth while.

Does

Does not recollect his mentioning any particular means that had been used to encourage population. 1790. Part II.

Was at Barbadoes about five or six weeks. Don't recollect the names of the proprietors of any sugar estates in Barbadoes. Slept once or twice on shore, about four miles from Bridge-Town, but don't remember the name of the planter: thinks it was on a sugar estate: a boiling house on it. Supposes he was not on 20 sugar estates. Knows not how many of them within four or five miles of Bridge-Town; nor how the lands in its vicinity are divided; the chief he saw were in corn and cane plots, and very little potatoes or cassada. Made very little inquiry respecting the food of plantation-slaves. Was told by one of them that it was chiefly of corn and cane juice. Respecting their clothing, huts, and manner of sleeping, his knowledge was got from his own observation. Intended to be better informed by Mr. Prettyjohn, but their sudden departure prevented it. Mr. P. he thinks is both merchant and planter, and that he was generally at Bridge-Town while they were there. Dined twice or thrice, or oftner with him. The first time with Admiral Hughes a week or nine days after their arrival. P. 255. P. 256.

Had conversation with him about ploughing the ground for corn; he said it had been tried, but would not answer. Did not talk to him of using the plough in the cultivation of sugar, thinking it impracticable, the canes being put down in holes. Mr. P. appeared to be an ingenuous sensible man, whose opinion would be taken as soon as any body's. Was no otherwise acquainted with the Rev. Dr. Wharton, than by probably having dined with him at a public-house.

Never asked the name of the proprietor of the plantation on which he saw a woman chained to a block, feeding the mill, as it might have prejudiced him against one who in other respects might be valuable. Thinks if it would deter others from similar usage, the perpetrator of said cruelty ought to be published to the world. Did not mention it to Mr. Prettyjohn P. 257.

but

1790. but on board the ship. Three or four of them were
Part II. together when it happened.

P. 178. Does not recollect to whom the woman said she belonged, whom he found to have been so punished. She was found from half a mile to a mile from Bridge-Town. Thinks he did not tell Mr. Prettyjohn of it, and whether to others, does not recollect. The reason he did not promote her receiving that medical assistance which seemed necessary, was a hope that her master would soon take care of her, and they did not care to interfere a-

P. 258. bout his slaves. Witness resides at Ilchester in Somersetshire, and is not a beneficed clergyman. Asked if he has heard of persons suffering in England for the death of a servant by cruel usage, and has observed in Great-Britain, miserably diseased white persons lying about, apparently neglected, with sores and ulcers exposed to naked view; begging relief, and a nuisance to the public: answers, he has. Never saw a slave punished on a plantation in the W. Indies, but by 2 or 3 licks of the driver. All the poor in England have a parish to go to, which is obliged to maintain them when incapable of work. Their parish furnishes medicine when they are sick, and their labour

P. 259. keeps them from starving. The usual wages pr. week where witness resides, of labouring men, is generally 6s. but less in winter. Is of opinion that a labouring man with a wife and 2 or 3 children and their assistance, although unassisted by the parish, can support himself with the necessaries of life.

Thinks it was in January when he saw the woman chained to a block in the mill, and that they were cut-

P. 260. ting canes in Barbadoes when he was there. Asked whether, when the woman said she was to continue feeding the mill a twelve month, witness thought she must be mistaken, as she could not have canes all the year to feed it; answers, he thought she must.

Holes for corn made with the hoe, small and not very deep. Thinks not much difference between that labour, and reaping corn in England. The pregnant woman before-mentioned, had a hoe in her hand: thinks

thinks he was told she was making holes for corn. 1790. Has seen pregnant women reaping corn in Wales, but thinks not in England.

Thinks it would have been more for the safety of the woman he found in the situation before-described to have communicated it to the owner or overseer of the estate she belonged to, but as a stranger, did not choose to interfere. Did not know how far off she lived; nor, as many must have seen her, whether her master was not informed of it.

Most of the negroes had a little rag to cover their nakedness; some, breeches or trowsers. Could see evident marks of whipping on their backs, and on the breech of those who had only rags to cover them. The women have short coats.

His being suddenly called away, prevented his obtaining that accurate information of the condition and treatment of slaves which he intended. Should have made more inquiry, thinking that those he saw who had been punished, might have been guilty of worse crimes than they acknowledged themseves to have committed. Thinks that two or three that he casually asked whether they ever went to church, answered, No, or very seldom. Does not recollect to have ever had or heard any conversation about any attempts made by the masters to promote their religious improvement. Remembers asking a driver how he could strike a person so hard as he did, and that the answer imported, if he did not beat him, he would not work. Does not recollect the particular objections to the use of the plough in the culture of corn, but thought there was not grass enough on the the island to maintain the cattle, as those he saw were generally very poor. Has known the plough used in a soil wherein there was abundance of large stones, and an extremely uneven surface. As at Stapleton, Wiuterborn, Long-Brady, &c; in Dorsetshire, where there are flints; and at Newport in Wales, where are stones under ground, and the plough can scarce go its length without meeting one. Never saw labourers in Britain working

1790. working under the whip of a driver, but has seen
Part II. them beat for not working.

Thinks that of green provender, they give the cane tops, as well as grafs to the cattle. Knows not whether cattle are fed with potatoe vines, and Indian and Guinea corn. Were ufed to give Guinea corn leaves to cattle on board. Suppofes he was on fhore a fcore
P. 264. of times at Barbadoes.

---

Witnefs examined—Mr. THOMAS WOOLRICH.

Was in the Weft Indies from 1753 to 1773; but in the interim took two or three trips to England, and two to North America; was in a mercantile line chiefly in Tortola; but alfo, occafionally at Barbadoes, Antigua, and St. Kitts. On his firft arrival at Tortola, faw much feverity ufed upon negroe flaves, though their fituation was more tolerable than afterwards. At that time their number not being near fo great, they were allowed fufficient provifion ground, which fome years afterwards being abridged, had a tendency to a want of food for their fupport;
P. 265. as the ifland was more and more cleared, more was converted into cane land; the number of negroes increafed, their grounds were more divided, or were given them in fmaller lots; as the number increafed their punifhments became more fevere. Had many opportunities of feeing field-flaves at work. Lived fix or feven years in the houfe of a principal planter. On leffening the flaves provifion ground, food was very feldom imported from abroad; there was no certainty or dependence on it.

Had heard planters comparing the number of negroes at prior dates, with the then number, and they fignified their increafe by births without importation; there was reckoned a general increafe upon the whole, through the ifland. At that time the planters were altogether in good credit with the merchants;

merchants; none known to be involved in debts to the merchants in the island or in England. Being a merchant he had many opportunities of knowing their situations; their payments were very punctual; had great opportunities of knowing the produce of most estates; their expences moderate at that time; seldom under the necessity of purchasing provisions for their slaves. The planters he thinks then wholly resided on their own plantations in that island. The chief articles of produce then were Sugar, Cotton, and Rum. But Cotton-planting diminishing, as that of Sugar increased, not near so much Cotton was made the latter part of his time there. Planting of Sugars is more laborious to the slaves; in some instances it proved more profitable to the owners, but in general otherwise. About three or four years after his arrival there, some Guinea ships came down with cargoes of slaves; the planters in general bought: this induced many to turn out cotton and plant canes, which is more laborious. Many of the new negroes often die in seasoning, and Guinea ships coming down time after time, the planters bought to supply their places. This continuing, many planters got much involved in debt by purchasing slaves on credit, and were obliged to mortgage their estates and slaves to merchants in England. Has never known a planter who thus mortgaged pay off the debt. Some in consequence have been obliged to have them sold by auction much under value, and the English merchant has suffered in his debt. Has known some of these estates sold, where the owners have become overseers upon them. During the latter part of his stay in Tortola, many field-negroes had small lots to plant provision upon, where it could be afforded, but supposes it was not general. Some planters allowed them Saturday afternoons, except in crop, to raise provisions; many also who had land worked it on Sundays, obliged thereto by the owner or overseer. Very difficult to judge of the

1790.  
Part II.  
P. 266.

P. 267.

Numb. 3.      O      increase

1790. increase of negroes, by births, in Tortola, in the latter period of his stay there; but in that period they did not increase in the proportion they did on his first arrival, when fewer in number, and more moderately used. Droughts are common in all those islands; sometimes great and long; and a cause of scarcity whereby the negroes suffer greatly, near to a famine; and slaves have pined away and died, as food could not be procured. Never saw a gang of negroes that appeared to him any thing like sufficiently fed; their appearance sufficiently proves their situation. A sight of a few gangs of the field-negroes would convince more fully than his description by any number of words. Slaves frequently run away from their masters. It is to be attributed to severe usage for trivial faults. With respect to their emaciated appearance, speaks as to every other island he had been in: has seen it more in Antigua than in Tortola. During the whole of his stay at Tortola, the clothing of the field negroes was very trifling; the men, generally a pair of trowsers; the women, a peticoat, made of coarse Osnaburghs, given them once a year in general by their owners; some do not give so much. Apprehends the field-negroes in general do not cost their masters half a crown per head per annum in clothing. Their houses are small square huts, built with poles, and thatched at the top and sides with a kind of Bamboo; built by the negroes for themselves: the field-negroes lie on the ground, in the middle of the huts, with a small fire generally before them; have no bedding; some obtain a board or mat to lie on before the fire; a few of the head negroes have cabbins of boards, raised from the floor, but no bedding, except some who have a coarse blanket. The usual punishments of plantation-slaves according to the nature of their crimes; of a runaway, it is exceeding severe; four negroes to take hold of each arm and leg, and lay him on the ground, when the chief whipper lays upon their bare back 40, 50, 60, or more lashes, just at the pleasure of the owner or overseer. Has seen

seen negroes whipped, when the firſt ſtroke has made the blood ſpout out immediately. There are other ways of correction very barbarous; ſuch as ſetting upon a picket, which is ſtanding on one foot upon a ſharp ſtick; alſo the thumb-ſcrews, which give intolerable pain. It is very common to ſee marks of whippings on the perſons of the ſlaves, ſome with their backs an undiſtinguiſhed maſs of lumps, holes, and furrows, by frequent whippings; moſt of the field-negroes are marked by the whip; all that he had ſeen, work under the whip, which the drivers carry for their correction, and of which they are continually in dread. It is made generally of plaited cowſkin, with thick ſtrong laſhes; a formidable inſtrument in one of the overſeers hands, who would take the ſkin off a horſe's back with one of them; has ſeen them lay its marks into a deal board. Knows not of any protection ſlaves had from the ill uſage of their maſters. A negro ran away from a planter with whom he was well acquainted; the overſeer having orders to take him dead or alive, a while after found him in one of his huts, faſt aſleep, in the day time, and ſhot him through the body. The negro jumping up, ſaid, "What, you kill me "aſleep," and dropt dead immediately. The overſeer took off his head and carried it to his owner. Knew another inſtance in the ſame iſland: a planter offended with his waiting man, a mulatto, ſtepped ſuddenly to his gun, on which the man ran off, but his maſter ſhot him through the head with a ſingle ball. Mentioned another inſtance, a manager of an eſtate in Tortola, whoſe owner did not reſide on the iſland, ſitting at dinner, in ſudden reſentment, ran his cook, a negroe woman, through the body, and ſhe died immediately. The negroes were called in to take her away and bury her. All the white people in the iſland were acquainted with theſe facts, which happened when he was in it, and which none doubted: neither of theſe offenders were ever called to an account, nor were they at all ſhunned or conſidered

1790.
Part II.

P. 270.

1790. sidered in disgrace. Had several times seen slaves
Part II. working in the fields, in chains; the most striking
instance of it was in Antigua, where a considerable
gang were working in one chain. Had seen another
gang or two carrying down sugars from the mountainous parts of that island, upon their heads in tubs,
P. 271. baskets or bags, heavy laden. Their appearance was
shocking, from the scantiness of cloathing, their apparent great want of food, and other instances of
severe usage. It was noticed by some gentlemen
who also saw them, and seemed to express themselves
in terms denoting resentment at such severity; but it
is too common.

In all the islands, so far as he has seen, it is usual
to turn the field negroes out to their work as soon as
the light well appears, and they are not discharged
from their drivers or overseers until the close of the
evening, or dark. They have time to eat their food
in the morning, and also at noon; but their usual
hours, or other particulars of rest, he cannot speak
to. When discharged from field labour, they have
generally to pull grass for their master's horses and
cattle. By the time this is done, it is dark. If
picking grass be reckoned as a part of their day
labour, it lengthens the day; if as an addition to it,
it is a great hardship. When grass is plenty, it is
no harder work than field labour, but in droughts it
is scarce; and if they fail in their quantity, they are
often punished. Are compelled to do this business
P. 272. as duly as any part of the day's labour. Thinks
that pregnant women (field slaves) had some little
indulgencies, but it is customary for them to work
in the field, till near their time. The whip occasionally used upon them, but not so severely as on
the men, that he ever observed.

The "seasoning of negroes," not any disease or
distemper. Always understood the new negroes
deaths to be occasioned by being put to hard labour
soon after being landed, and from the scarcity of
food, and want of almost every other necessary.
Knew

Knew many instances of this seasoning being extremely fatal to slaves. Some planters, who purchased new negroes, told him they have lost one-third of the number, or more, in the first year of the seasoning. Never saw a cargo of slaves, but what had sick or refuse negroes, more or less, which sold at a lower price; probably for cotton planters, an easier business than that of the cane.

Negro slaves, attached to a plantation, besides field slaves, are house carpenters, coopers, and masons. The treatment of these generally better than of field slaves, they have more certain allowance of provisions. Many of the female domestics are in a pretty good situation: their labour is more moderate, and they have more food and cloathing. Heard but of few instances of suicide among the Creole slaves; but of a good many among Africans. The principal instance: A planter purchased six men slaves out of a Guinea ship, and put them on a small island to plant cotton. They had a white man with them as overseer, who left them of a Saturday night. There were no white inhabitants on the island. On the Monday following the overseer returned, when he found all the six hanging near together in the woods. Had often inquired of the most sensible negroes what could be the cause of such actions, and the answer was, " That they would rather die, than live in the situation they were in."

Not able to say particularly what a tradesman slave and a field slave could earn for themselves. Many field slaves have it not in their power to earn any thing exclusive of their master's work. Some few raise fowls, and some few pigs, and sell them: but their number is very few. The black tradesmen in Tortola have very seldom any jobs to do on a Sunday, which is the only day allowed for themselves. The intellect of the negroes are various, as among other people. Some that are brought up amongst the white people, of as good abilities as are common amongst mankind, considering their situation, and want

1790. want of education. Had obferved the young negroes
Part II. learn trades as readily as whites. Many are ingenious
workmen. Knows of no exceptions to their poffeff-
ing the focial affections as ftrongly as whites, more
particularly the Creoles. Apprehends their natural
affection for their children and relatives, is as great
P. 275. as elfewhere. No kind of religion amonft the negroes
of Tortola. The Creoles have a certain belief in a
Supreme Being. The Africans, at firft coming,
fpeak no language but their own; but he never knew
one that could exprefs himfelf, but allowed of a
Supreme Being. If the word of a flave is difputed,
he will frequently lift up his hands, and fay, God
above knows what they affert to be true. After the
arrival of African negroes in Tortola, they are generally kept a few days before they are put to field
labour. Never knew any who were not put to labour
a week after they were purchafed. Knew but one
or two planters who branded their flaves. Never
faw the operation.

Droughts generally affect all kinds of vegetation,
and hurt the provifions. Some kinds are lefs injured
by them than others, and it is faid yams leaft.

The lower orders of people in this country cannot
be compared with the general condition of flaves.
The fituation of thefe is very lamentable, (would
not wifh to ufe any word to exaggerate) but it can-
P. 276. not be defcribed to the full to the underftanding of
thofe who have never feen it. Never knew any
planter or owner of a gang of flaves that ufed them
as well as either a good or bad mafter ufes his fervants in England. Hard labour, with the want of
neceffaries of life, wages, or cloathing, are fufficient
to make their condition much harder than the loweft
degree of fervants in England. Certainly the mafter's intereft to treat his flaves well, as the contrary
never fails to bring lofs and embarraffment on their
owners. Believes it is from want of wifdom that
they are treated ill. Apprehends the mafters of
flaves become morofe and cruel by being ufed to that

kind

kind of business, and that it considerably hurts the morals of the white people.

Since he left Tortola, by means of correspondence, or seeing some person from the island, (which is generally every year) he has been informed of its state from year to year, to the present time. The last information represented the planters to be in very distressed circumstances. Divers of their estates, mortgaged in England, had been sold at public vendue, upon very low terms, because few were able to pay for them; and the general credit so low with the planters, that but few could obtain the necessaries they want from the stores kept there, by reason of the debts to English merchants. It has been his opininion for many years, that the unnecessary purchasing of African slaves, has been the main cause of their embarrassments, and the accumulation of their debts. Many new negroes dying soon after imported, the planters are induced to buy again upon credit, by which their debts have been increased with the English merchants.

Has asked many African slaves how they were brought into that situation—amongst others a waiting boy he had, who told him, that he and his sister being catched together in the field, tending some corn, were both carried away. Men slaves had told him they were surprized, and made prisoners of by the enemy, in the night, in their own houses or village: others, that they were prisoners of war.

Amongst different planters there are different usages of their slaves. Some feed and treat them better than others. Fully believes the circumstances of the owners have a great effect in that case. The slaves of those who are much in debt, are generally more severely and worse treated, than slaves of such as are in easy circumstances.

The planter, with whom he resided 6 or 7 years, was named John Pickering, whose house was on his plantation, and he had none in town. Lodged there that

1790.
Part II.
〰〰

P. 280.

P. 281.

P. 282.

that space of time, but was never so long at one time in Tortola, but a longer space at two different periods.

The lands in Tortola, which used to be planted in cotton, could not have been cultivated for sugar in so short a time, without the importation of slaves from Africa. Apprehends the planting of sugar would require a larger body of negroes than the cotton planters generally have. There never has been any cotton planted in those parts of the island where the sugar-cane is planted. As to comparing the planting of cotton and sugar by equal quantities of land, is not a judge of the difference of labour. Cotton is planted upon the poorest parts, upon rocky and steep places, mostly where canes are not planted. No regular plantations of cotton but upon keys and rocky hills. When he first went there, he thinks more than one-half was in its native woods. The best parts were in the hands of different proprietors, who cleared small parts of it from year to year, whereby they enlarged their sugar plantations, and made new ones.

During the whole of his residence in Tortola, a court of justice was held the first Monday in three or four months of the year, by the governor and six magistrates, but no assembly: though the island was not under the same settled administration of justice that prevailed in the other islands, justice was administered in as good and regular order, as in any of the others before mentioned.

The wood lands, by clearing of which the sugar estates were increased from 10 or 12 to 50 or 60, could not have been in so short a time if there had been no importation. Is very certain the event has been greatly to the loss and embarrassment of the planters, owing to the bad management and hard usage of the slaves; and that 7-8ths of the planters would have been in much better circumstances, if they had not bought any negroes during the time of his

his residence there, but had used those they had with humanity and care.

Water brackish and scarce in Tortola.

Never resided on any other sugar plantation than J. Pickering's. Thinks a pair of trowsers and a shirt are quite sufficient cloathing for a working negro in the field; and that a petticoat and jacket for a woman is an equivalent. Cannot say that a shirt is absolutely necessary, but it appears beneficial, and is what they would chuse. Has never known those who had one on, to pull it off, when at work in the field.

When he settled in the Road Town, his family consisted of a clerk and two apprentices in his store, and occasionally three, four, or five black domestics. Sometimes fowls or vegetables were to be bought from the negroes, but very rarely. The supply of these articles in the stores was very small. Generally used salted beef and pork. Sometimes dried pease from America. Fresh meat dear and scarce through the island. Beef and mutton, killed by the planters, at times to be bought. A good supply of fish at times, and always at a reasonable price.

Heard of a great number of wrecks of ships upon the island or reefs of Annigado, but was never there: also that a Spanish ship was wrecked a year a two before he went to Tortola, and that before his arrival lieutenant-general Fleming, the commander in chief of the Leeward Islands, came down from St. Kitts, to demand and secure for the right owners, the money saved from that wreck. Was told that some delivered to him what they got of it, and that others delivered none, but never heard of any being brought to justice upon that account.

Has been two or three times in Barbadoes, but never above two weeks at a time; and then did not reside on any sugar plantation.

Has been four, five, or six times at Antigua: believes the longest was three or four weeks, but did not reside on any sugar estate there.

Numb. 3. P Had

1790.  Had been only once, a very short time, in St.
Part II. Kitts, and not on any sugar estate.

P. 287.  Kept one horse, while resident in the Road Town at Tortola. The grass for him was bought from negroes who sometimes brought it to the road for sale, in the evening. It was their own property, and generally paid for with tobacco, salt herrings, or coarse linens. In crop time their horses were fed from cane tops, which were had for fetching. Apprehends such of the other merchants in Road Town as had no estates of their own, supplied their horses in the same way. Computes the grass bought for his horse every night when the negroes came, to have cost two bits, or about 11d. sterling, but without oats thinks two bits worth would have been insufficient. Grass picking in the evening on plantations, continues in crop time and all the year.

P. 288.  Never saw any cane tops carried home for planter's horses or stock; the draft mules at the mill live entirely upon them during crop time. They are a nourishing food for mules, who altogether live on them; and for horses also. Does not know whether horned cattle, sheep, and goats, eat them or not. Negroes in a plantation who have a hog to feed, have what quantity they please to take for that purpose. The pork fed on them reckoned the best. They had generally, he thinks, the skimmings of the boiling of sugar. Cannot say if that skimming is allowed or not by their masters; thinks some prime negroes would not be debarred of it, as it seemed not to be fit for any other use. Knows of no negro being flogged for feeding his hogs with it. J. Pickering had a distillery for rum on his plantation. Apprehends the skimmings of the sugar-coppers are not a main ingredient used in the distil-houses, for setting of liquor in the casks for making of rum. Molasses is the main and principal ingredient; but thinks skimmings are also always used with the molasses for setting casks for distilling.

P. 289.  He traded at Tortola, in most kinds of manufactured

tured goods; also in Irish provisions; sometimes in American cargoes of flour, bread, and other articles; but no corn. Has sold Osnaburghs, checks, and other coarse linens, &c. to the negroes. Has frequently imported and sold salt herrings from Ireland; never any cod or mackrel, that he recollects; sold the salted herrings to the planters; for the slaves in crop time were generally employed at hard work the whole 6 days of the week. They are a perishable commodity, and he thinks will not keep good a whole year in that island. Knows no instance of great scarcity of Irish salt provisions, since he kept a store in the road. There was a scarcity of flour and bread, but not much to distress the white people. There was never, to his knowledge, any certain supply of provisions, suitable for the negroes, at all times of the year. There was, more frequently, no necessary food for them to be bought at the merchant's stores. Never had any concern in planting, or as proprietor of any plantation at Tortola, or elsewhere. Never had more than 4 or 5 slaves at one time. One of them came to England with him, the others were left at the store with a partner. During his stay in Tortola, there was no complaint that white people could not obtain legal redress for injuries they might have received. The inhabitants were sensible there was not in the island a sufficient authority to bring capital offenders to trial and punishment, without a special commission from the governor general. While he was there, a murder was committed by one white person upon another. The murderer was tried, in consequence of a commission from the governor general, by a jury, who acquitted him. Redress was to be had on complaints of smaller offences, from the governor and council. White mechanics or tradesmen pursued their occupations in Tortola, throughout the day, as in other countries. Did not serve on the jury; is one of the people called Quakers. In speaking of Tortola, he also included the Virgin Islands.

1790.
Part II.

P. 290.

P. 291.

P 2       Witness

Witness examined,—HENRY HEW DALRYMPLE, Esq.

1790.
Part II.
P. 291.
P. 292.
Was lieutenant in the 75th regiment, in garrison at Goree, and on various parts of the coast, from May to the end of September, 1779. Made it his business to inquire as to the mode of obtaining slaves; had his information from French mulattoes and natives, particularly the Maraboo of Dacard, a sensible and intelligent man. Inhabitants of Goree respectable. He was weekly on the continent, with a view of knowing the situation of the country, and modes of procuring slaves, because he held slaves himself in the West Indies, and wished to ascertain that matter beyond doubt. In consequence, was informed that the great droves (called caffillas, or caravans) of slaves brought from inland, by way of Galam, to Senegal and Gambia, were prisoners of war. Those sold to vessels at Goree, and near it, were procured either

P. 293. by the grand pillage, the lesser pillage, or by robbery of individuals. The grand pillage is executed by the king's soldiers, from 3 or 400, to 2 or 3000, who attack and set fire to a village, and seize the inhabitants as they can. The smaller parties generally lie in wait about the villages, and take off all they can surprize; which is also done by individuals, who do not belong to the king, but are private robbers. These sell their prey on the coast, where it is well known no questions, as to the means of obtaining it, are asked.

It seemed to be universally believed on the coast, that their wars are undertaken for the purpose of procuring slaves. Whenever he asked the negroes in the West Indies (who had been brought in those caffillas, or droves) how they had been made prisoners, they generally told him, had been thus taken by surprize, either at night in their villages, straggling from their huts (particularly the women) or when

cultivating

cultivating their fields. He does not say no wars arise in Africa, but from a desire of making slaves; but that this, from answers received, appeared to be the general cause. Every body on the coast reported that these wars were seldom of more than 8 or 10 days continuance; that seldom, in the most decisive actions, the number of prisoners or killed, amounted to more than 20 or 30, and that it is principally on the coast marauding expeditions are found. Kidnapping is so notorious, that he never heard any person, French or native, deny it there. Two men, while he was at Goree, offered a person, a messenger from Senegal to Rufisco, for sale, to the garrison. They did not deny he was a free man, but rather boasted of what they had done, in making themselves masters of him. Witness indisposed, withdrew. On a subsequent day, desired to explain the former part of his evidence, having been so ill when he delivered it: said, that as to the marauding expeditions, information from slaves in the West Indies, tended to convince him, they were procured in that manner in the interior of Africa also. Many were brought to Goree while he was there, but seldom more than 3 or 4 together, and oftner only one. He understood it common for European traders to advance goods to chiefs, to induce them to seize on their subjects, or neighbours. Not one of the mulatto traders at Goree, ever thought of denying it. These depredations are also practised by the Moors; saw many slaves in Africa, who told him they were taken by them; 3 of these, one of them a woman, cried very much, and seemed to be in great distress; the two others more reconciled to their fate. All crimes in the parts of Africa he was in, were punished with slavery. At Goree, where most inhabitants are mulattoes, slaves are common; but on the continent there are but few, and these are treated so well, eating and working with their masters, that they are not distinguishable from free men. Never saw any whip or instrument of torture used there; nor did he believe, on

inquiry,

1790. inquiry, that slaves there were used with severity.
Part II. They believe in witchcraft.

Frauds are often practised on the natives, by European merchants. He has heard mulatto merchants, and European captains, boast of it.

While at Goree, a ship attempted to sail out of the bay with a number of negroes, without paying for them; and this was the reason given for their orders to fire on her, and bring her to. From what he saw and heard, he has no doubt but the thing is common.

P. 297. The productions of the part of Africa he was in, are cotton of 3 kinds, indigo, dyes of different kinds, spices, sugar canes, tobacco, millet of 2 kinds, ebony, and different kinds of cabinet wood. The sugar canes were thought, by judges, to be superior to any produced in the West Indies. The cotton grows spontaneously almost every where, though sometimes cultivated; is of a remarkable fine staple, and as he was told by Mr. Oswald, an African merchant, is esteemed, by the English merchants, far superior to any that comes from the West Indies. The indigo is likewise of a better quality than what grows in our islands; it is reckoned equal to that of Guatimala. He has reserved specimens of these articles. They have beside, at Goree, a root which dyes a beautiful scarlet, and its leaves a bright yellow or orange. The soil and climate seem both extremely favourable for the growth of spices. Cardamoms are found in great perfection near Cape Verd.

As far as he could judge, in natural capacity the negroes are equal to any people whatever: and in temper and disposition (of which, from being constantly among them, he had, he believes, as many opportunities of judging, as any Englishman on the coast) they appeared to be humane, hospitable, and well disposed. The country well cultivated, and from the general disposition of the natives to labour, he is convinced, that had they a proper market for their produce, they would be as industrious as any Europeans.

Europeans. He remarked, that where there was little or no trade for slaves, they were most industrious. They manufacture cotton cloths, almost equal in the workmanship, to those of Europe; they work in gold, silver and iron, remarkably neat; also in wood, and make saddles, bow-cases, scabbards, gris-gris, and other things of leather, with great neatness.

Was much and often in the country among the natives; and having learned (from La Brue and other writers) that it was a common practice for their kings to seize their subjects and sell them as slaves for European goods, he wished to know whether the report was founded in fact.

When he was on board the Atalanta sloop of war, they fell in with a ship from Gambia, the crew of which had all died but the captain, whose name was Heatly, and the mate. On going aboard he found the captain lying on deck upon a mattress, and the mate appeared in bad health.

He was on his passage to the W. Indies in a slave vessel two months, during which the slaves were exceedingly unhappy, made many attempts to rise: not succeeding, they begged to be permitted to throw themselves overboard, and perpetually regretted their own country.

He was three times in the W. Indies; in 1773, at Grenada six months; in 1779 and 1780, at Antigua, Barbadoes, Tobago, St. Lucia, and St. Christophers; and in 1788 and 1789, at Grenada, Coriacou, St. Vincents, and Tobago.

General treatment of the negroes was very cruel. He lived near the market-place of St. George's, at Grenada, where negroes were flogged every day by the particular orders of their masters; they were tied down upon the ground, every stroke brought blood; and very often took out a piece of the flesh. Saw them often in chains, thus marked. A French planter sent for a surgeon to cut off the leg of a negroe, who had run away. On the surgeon's refusing

*1790. Part II.*

*P. 298.*

*P. 299.*

1790.  fusing to do it, the planter took an iron bar and broke
Part II. the leg in pieces, and then the surgeon cut it off.
This planter did many such acts of cruelty, and all with impunity. It did not appear to be the public
P. 300. opinion that any punishment was due to him, for tho' it was generally known, he was equally well received in society afterwards as before.

Walked into the country at Grenada, almost daily. Many of the field-negroes bore the marks of the whip on their bodies, and several worked in the fields in chains. Whip is made of a thong of cow's hide, about half an inch in breadth, with large knots on it in several places. The day after his arrival at Antigua, he saw three or four old negroes, reduced to skin and bone, digging in the dunghills, in the streets, for food: and was told by themselves and others, that they had been turned off by their owners, who could not afford to keep them. This he under-
P. 301. stood was no uncommon practice. As he was perpetually removing from place to place with the fleet and army, in 1779, and 1780, he had then but little opportunity of seeing the treatment of the negroes in the plantations. In Grenada, the plantation slaves generally worked (out of crop-time) from day-light to dark. On some plantations he has known them called out long before day-light; they generally have an hour allowed them for breakfast, and two for dinner. When last at Grenada, he lived in the country, about 15 or 16 months; and observed that slaves are generally sent to pick grafs after the field-labour, which continues till sun-set is over. A certain quantity is required, and if they do not produce it they are punished; though it is often very scarce and brought from a great distance. In crop-time they are obliged to work as long as they can, which is as long as they can keep awake or stand on their legs. Sometimes they fall asleep through excess of fatigue when their arms are caught in the mill and torn off. He
P. 302. saw several who had lost their arms in that way.

Except one or two holidays a year, he did not understand

understand they had any time allotted them for their own amusement or repose: for on Sundays they labour more than on any other days of the week; it being then that they exert themselves in procuring supplies of food for their own sustenance, and therefore are not attended by the driver. At other times every gang is attended by one or more, who make frequent use of the whip, without distinction of sex. He believes, that in general, their food is neither sufficient in quantity nor good in quality; though the domestic are better fed than the field-negroes. On the fortifications, where their labour is of the severest kind, they had only seven pounds of bread and four of salt-fish per week. They carried bricks, lime, and large planks, from the shore to Richmond Hill, about a mile and an half, and were often scarcely able to move under their burthens.

Is not positive if these slaves were paid for by government or by the island.

Believes it depends entirely on disposition and ability of masters whether they are well or ill fed. In Grenada they were differently fed at different times. He dined at the house of a gentleman, who said his grass field had been plundered the night before, by certain negroes, some of whom he could have taken and punished, but refrained, because he knew their allowance so small that without robbing they could not have existed; but only speaks to this particular instance. The place was near town, where grass sells at a great price. It was the general opinion, that it was more profitable to import slaves and work them out, than to breed them. Believes they are not considered as protected by law; for negroes were often treated cruelly, and even murder had been committed, not only with impunity, but without its being supposed the perpetrators could be punished on that account. At Grenada, in the town of St. George, a mason, named Chambers, killed a negroe, in the middle of the day (he thinks in the church-yard) and no notice was taken of it. The

1790. present chief judge of Grenada (who has permitted
Part II. him to use his name on this occasion) assured him it
was true. Another instance was of a planter who
flogged his driver to death, and even boasted of it to
the person from whom witness had the account.
(Does not exactly know the time this happened,
but it was before the year 1773, when he heard
P. 305. of it from the Chief Justice, p. 316.) Another
was that of the French planter who broke his
negroe's leg in order to prevail on the surgeon to
cut it off. And in June last, he saw a negress
brought to St. George's to have her finger cut off:
she had committed a fault, and ran away to avoid
punishment; but being taken, her master suspended
her by the hands, flogged and cut her cruelly on the
back, belly, breast and thighs, and then left her suspended till her fingers mortified: in this state witness saw
her at Dr. Gilpin's, but no notice was taken of the
fact, though it happened months after the new act
for the protection of slaves was passed. Another
negress who, though a young woman, had no teeth,
informed him that her mistress, had with her own
hands pulled them out, and given her a severe flogging besides, the marks of which she then bore.
This relation was confirmed by several town's people
of whom he inquired concerning it.

He was in Grenada, 1788, when the act was passed, entitled, " An Act for the better protection and
" promoting the increase and population of slaves."
P. 306. The principal objection, and which he repeatedly
heard, to its passing was, that it might make the
slaves believe, that the authority of their masters was
lessened: but otherwise, many thought it would be
of little use, as it was a law made by themselves,
against themselves, and to be executed by themselves: they observed besides, that such laws were
unnecessary for the protection of negroes who were
treated well; and that others had so many opportunities of evading the law, (the evidence of negroes
not being admitted) that it would be of no use.
The

The members of the legiflature were not all planters. Some of them were flave merchants and ftore keepers, in the town of St. George. At the time of paffing faid act, the propofal in the British parliament for the abolition of the flave trade was a matter of general difcuffion in the ifland: and he believes was a principal reafon for paffing it. For report faid, that the agent for the ifland had mentioned in a letter, that unlefs they made laws themfelves for the protection of flaves, the Britifh parliament would. This letter he never faw, tho' he fought it; and as a proprietor in the ifland thought he had a right to read the agent's letters. He, however, often heard it urged as an argument that the act fhould pafs. He believes it will prove ineffectual: becaufe, as no negro evidence is admitted, thofe who abufe them will ftill do it with impunity; and people who live on terms of intimacy, would diflike the idea of becoming fpies and informers againft each other. — P. 307.

Believes the chaftity of the wives of flaves is not protected by law: and has never heard that there was any punifhment for its violation. That fometimes female flaves are offered by the mafters to their vifitors; and has known compulfion ufed to oblige fuch to fubmit to proftitution.

Does not fay, that flaves never become poffeffed of much property; but he never knew an inftance; nor can he conceive how they can have time for it. Neither did he ever know of field flaves having expenfive feafts. A negro woman, who became unfitted for labour by difeafe, was turned off by the truftees of his father's eftate. She fubfifted by charity in the town of St. George. — P. 308.

The tetanus, or locked jaw, was formerly very fatal to negro children; but there are now means of treating the mothers and children, which render it lefs fo.

Field flaves did not appear to him cheerful or happy.

1790. happy. There are frequent instances of slaves destroying themselves.
Part II.

Has a landed estate in Grenada, but it is not cultivated. Part of it has been.

P. 309. His personal observations on the coast of Africa extend to part of the kingdom of Cajore, which is opposite Goree, to the country north and south for some leagues; and to about eight or ten miles inland from the shore. Within that distance indigo is manufactured fit for use; and cloths dyed with it. Never saw the process. The manufactures he mentioned in gold, silver, iron, and other materials, are

P. 310. the work of both negroes and Moors. He saw but few Moors in the country about Cape Verd, and those were strangers; and none at Goree, or in any other parts where he had been. He thinks, as the negroes are remarkably industrious, they might, with proper encouragement, be brought to cultivate the different productions of that part of the coast to a much greater extent than they do at present: for where there was a demand for any article or produce, he observed they were remarkably industrious.

In 1773, went to Grenada on a visit to his father. He was then 22 years of age; and Mr. Leyburne then governor of the island. He then staid 6 months, mostly in town; but was sometimes in the country, when he made frequent visits to different plantations; but in both town and country saw many instances of cruel treatment. Some of the punishments inflicted might be by order of the magistrates; but many, he was informed, were ordered by the masters: and he knows, that by the laws of the island, they have such a power; for there is an act, passed Oct. 18. 1784, for regulating the fees of the clerk of the market, and authorising him to take 18d. for every slave he shall flog, whether it be ordered by

P. 312. the magistrate or owner. These were generally belonging to people in town.

Does not remember the name of the French planter, who treated his negroes so barbarously, nor precisely the year: but was informed of it by several;

ral; and believes many Grenada gentlemen now in England have heard the story. Has seen this man in the best society of the island oftener than once, after the story was generally known. It was spoken of as a thing notorious, and believed. Does not know whether or not such atrocious acts are considered by the better sort of people as worthy of investigation or punishment. Would willingly believe they are, by such, disapproved of; but never heard that there had been any attempt to punish this offender.

He went, in the slave ship mentioned, to the island of Antigua; was there about three weeks, in the year 1779: from thence to Barbadoes: was there a fortnight or three weeks, and thence to St. Kitt's; where he staid about the same time. In these islands he was mostly in the towns.

His own affairs drew him to Grenada, 1788. At the death of his father he inherited his slaves; but the estate being in possession of the mortgagee, he can give no account of the manner of providing for his own slaves; but he understands the planters in Grenada allow their slaves salt provisions and flour, which are brought from England and America. Many of them distribute these, exclusive of the ground provisions, regularly every week, some of them daily: and at times corn of various sorts either in grain or meal; but many others do not.

The inhabitants of the towns in Grenada are furnished with grass and other green provender for their horses, by plantation slaves in the neighbourhood, who, he believes, sometimes receive to their own use the money or other commodities they get in return: but that is sometimes sold for the account of their masters. The planters do not commonly dispose of their grass; but sometimes sell milk and greens. He is uncertain whether they cultivate grass to sell, or for their cattle.

He frequently conversed with the present chief justice of Grenada, who told him the fact already mentioned,

1790. mentioned, in his own house; and thinks he said it
Part II. was committed in the year 1768.

P. 316. Being asked if he, or any other person, ever informed the chief justice of the cruel treatment received by the negro girl whom he saw at Dr. Gilpin's, said, he inquired after some time whether any notice had been taken of it, and did not find there had. He did not himself inform the chief justice, nor does he know whether or not he was informed of it. At the time it happened, he was preparing to leave the island, and believed as it was known to so many people, that the chief justice must have been informed of it by somebody; but he did not know that it passed unnoticed, till he was just setting

P. 317. out for Europe, after which he never saw the chief justice.

Recollects a clause, or clauses, in the law, for the protection of slaves, whereby three persons, freeholders in each parish, are appointed guardians for carrying it into execution; and their testimony declared to be competent in all cases necessary thereto: but is of opinion, that while a slave's evidence is not admitted in a court of law, they can be of very little or no service to him. Slaves, however, would not be without remedy in every instance: but thinks such as are disposed to treat their negroes ill, may find ways of evading these laws. Laws for the protection of the negroes, and feeding them, had been before passed; but it was found necessary, notwithstanding, to make a new act. That dated 10th Dec. 1766, for the allowance of provision grounds to slaves, directs the appointment of four freeholders by the justices of each parish, to inspect the grounds, and see that there was a sufficient quantity of provisions: yet the preamble to the last act seems to imply that this former one had not been sufficiently attended to.

He believes it common for plantation slaves in Grenada, to bring to market, and particularly on
318. Sundays, various articles of fruit and vegetables, poultry,

poultry, pork, kids, and goats, their own property, and raised by themselves.

Supposes it cost him two shillings a day each to maintain his horses in grass and other green provender, and that grass is more less picked the year round: that the provisions of the slaves on the fortifications at Grenada were only the allowance made by government, of 7lb. of bread and 4 of salt fish per week each, without any ground provisions from masters; but of this is not certain. The rations necessary for their support in this service, he apprehends, were ascertained by the commander in chief; and the quantity of their labour by managers and overseers, no European officer being so competent to judge of either as the W. Indians themselves. A white or a black man was sent by the owner with his slaves, to take care of them; and supposes a person was set over the whole by the commander in chief to see that they did their duty. Does not remember any soldiers were employed to work on the fortifications; or whether the excess of labour, in carrying burthens as before mentioned, was to be ascribed to the person appointed on the part of the king, or those sent to take care of the slaves by the planters. He believes there is an act of assembly, constituting a joint committee of the council and assembly, to see to this service of the slaves and their food: but that nevertheless those employed by the committee can ill treat the slaves in many respects, without its coming to their knowledge.

Says he might have put his estate under cultivation by getting slaves from the house Backhouse and Tarleton in Grenada; but knowing when in Africa, how happy the negroes were there, and the unjustifiable means of enslaving them, their cruel usage on ship-board and in the West Indies, he could not, consistent with his ideas of right, purchase any slaves, especially as he did not intend to remain on the plantation himself.

He

1790.  He has seen many diseased and disabled seamen in
Part.II. the town of St. George, and on inquiry found they
had belonged to Guinea ships which had left them
there.

Could not say it was likely any planter would be
desirous of interfering very actively, to remedy the
smaller abuses practised by white people on their negroes; nor what Mr. Bruce's method was of curing
the tetanus; but Mr. B. assured him, from the time
he adopted it (which he thinks was two years before)
he had lost none, or but one or two children. He
thinks one part of his method was, to give the women immediately before the labour, a large airy
room.

Does not pretend to say that all slaves in Grenada are ill used, but believes that bad usage is too
general. Some he knew who treated their slaves
well.

P. 322.  As to happy state of negroes in their own country, he can speak positively only of that part of the
coast where has been, which might be rather less than
40 miles extent.

His plantation he purchased from Mr. Townsend,
the treasurer of Grenada, who was trustee of his father's estate. It lies in the parish of St. David, and
about seven or eight miles from George's Town. It
P. 323. was cultivated in cocoa and provisions, and consists
of about 250 acres. At present it is uncultivated,
and no slaves belong to it.

On inquiry of chief justice, he mentioned one instance of a white man being brought to trial, and
hanged for the murder of a slave; but said, he believed if this murderer had been a man of good character, or had had friends or money to pay for the
slave, he would not have been brought to trial. He
was of a very bad character, and had been obliged to
leave Barbadoes on that account. At Grenada he had
been a bailiff's follower, and from his rigour in exe-
P. 324. cuting his office, and bad character, was particularly
obnoxious

obnoxious to the inhabitants of the town of St. 1790.
George. Part II.
He had been at St. Vincent's and Calliaqua, and
had converfed with the Yellow Caribs, but not with
the Black; the latter he fuppofes a mixture of the
Yellow Caribbs and fome negroes caft away on the
ifland. The Caribbs had no other clothing than a
clout or girdle about the middle, and no fhoes; but
all, as far as he can recollect, were armed with cut-
laffes. The black Caribbs attended the market of P. 325.
Kingfton with tobacco and other articles, which the
women carried. The fugar eftates which he faw under cultivation in St. Vincent's were chiefly border-
ing on the fea coaft.
The white man who was hanged for murder he
thinks was named Bachus Prefton.

Witnefs Examined—Rev. ROB. BOUCHER NICHOLLS,
Dean of Middleham, in Yorkfhire,

Was born in Barbadoes; refided there fome years P. 326.
in his youth, and two after he was of age, from 1768
to 1770, when in holy orders. While there was enabled to judge of the fituation both of field and houfe
flaves: for his uncle, with whom he lived four years,
had a fugar eftate. Several others whom he vifited
were concerned in eftates; and in his laft refidence
there, he himfelf refided on a very large eftate, and
obferved the management both of that and furround-
ing eftates. The fituation of flaves with refpect to
food and treatment, he thinks cannot be comprehend-
ed under any one general defcription, fome being well
fed and taken care of both in ficknefs and health, and
others much neglected and feverely treated. The
latter fo impreffed his mind, that he faid to a perfon
largely concerned in the management of flaves, 'This
people will find a Mofes;' which perfon lately remind-
ed him of the words. Never read the laws of Bar- P. 327.
badoes, but underftood flaves were not protected by
Numb. 3.         R              them;

1790. them; that murders by owners were punished by fine. Part II. But if not by owner, then he received the value of the negro from the murderer, and the fine was paid into the exchequer, at the suit of the Attorney-General. He never understood that where negroes were stinted or ill used, legal redress had ever been applied for, or could be obtained; what legal provision for it there is, cannot say. Knew often, where the master's regard of his own interest did not prevail, with respect to using his slaves well, and giving sufficient food, &c.

P. 328. Among the rest, that of one M'Mahon, whose severity was generally mentioned, (and always with detestation, p. 338.) had destroyed more negroes, than the value of the additional crops, produced by their extra labour. So that though in eight years he paid off a considerable debt, he was said to have destroyed more negroes than the amount of it. Also recollects where slaves were reduced to a general state of debility and discontent, from a want of necessaries while they were urged to their accustomed labour: so that he heard it observed that the manager of a particular estate, " for a long cane would produce a dead negro." On the other hand, he could mention many instances, where humanity, and a regard to interest joined in providing well for them; particularly that of Dr. Mapp, whose estate was in the most flourishing condition, both in respect to the number of negroes by natural increase, and the success of his plantation.

The treatment of slaves appeared to depend wholly on the persons who had the management of them. Sir Hanson Berney's estate was managed by his brother, humanely and judiciously; he believes without any punishment, and that the estate was productive. Has often heard a relation of his who had the care of several large estates, declare, that he would willingly submit to have the power of punishment taken from him, if he might allow sufficient rewards for good behaviour and labour. One estate in particular he conducted for two years; during which, (though the

Witness

Witnefs vifited him almoft daily) no inftance of pu- 1790.
nifhment had occurred. And yet he declared, when Part II.
he took the management of that eftate upon him,
though there was hardly a place on the backs of the
labouring negroes free from the mark of the lafh, it
had not been fuccefsful to the owner in point of crops.

Says, effects of owners embarraffed fituation on P. 329.
flaves, is pufhing them beyond their ftrength, and leaving them without their ufual allowance of provifions, or any thing as a fubftitute, for a week or two;
this was confirmed to him by the manager of a gentleman fo circumftanced. This manager alfo told
him that the fame perfon, as well as feveral others,
either abridged or withheld in crop time, the ftated
allowance given at other times.

Ufual inftruments of punifhing negroes were the
thong-whip, chains on the legs, irons on the neck,
and confinement in the dungeon. In cafes of enor-
mous crimes, they were gibbetted alive in chains:
but he never faw but two inftances of the latter. The
punifhnent of whipping is fevere, cutting deep into
the flefh, and leaving marks which are vifible a long
time; fometimes to old age. The flaves always work P. 330.
under a driver, with a thong whip plaited.

The rights of marriage as among the negroes, he
believes, are not protected in the fmalleft degree, either by law or cuftom; but the chaftity of the women intirely liable to invafion by the manager, or
other white perfons.

Natural capacity and difpofition of negroes, apprehends to be juft the fame as thofe of the whites. He
grounds his opinion on many inftances. One of a
negro woman purchafed from a flave fhip, and given
to him by his father. She appeared at firft as dull
and fullen as any negro he ever faw; but on inftruc-
tion, became quite the reverfe, and of her own accord
defired to be made a Chriftian.

She afterwards was his domeftic fervant, and by
her fidelity to her hufband, and her good behaviour in
all refpects, manifefted a good underftanding, and the

1790. best disposition. He observed in many negroes in the
Part II. northern provinces of America, the same improvement where equal care was taken. He remembers a
Phillis Wheatley in Boston, an African slave, who in
less than three years, learned the English language,
and wrote elegant English verse, which has been published.

He has seen other instances of their ingenuity in
arts and letters. Among others, an elegant chair,
which a negro of Jamaica carved with a knife only.

Their disposition is in general affectionate where
well treated, which he thinks would easily lead to
piety, if they were in the way of improvement.

Several in Barbadoes, who had attended the church,
expressed to him a wish to become Christians. Many
are so in the Northern provinces of America; but
knows not of many in Barbadoes, who were instructed
or baptized.

They were generally regarded by persons of principle and education among the whites, as unfortunate
men entitled to compassion and good treatment; but
the bulk of the whites considered them as beings of
an inferior species.

P. 331. His father had a boy who said he was the son of a
prince in Africa, and taken away forcibly. He afterwards knew a negro woman, who alledged that her
father was a king in Africa, and as she could find
none her equals in Barbadoes, she would neither eat
nor converse with any of the other negroes. This her
mistress declared had been the case for 20 years.

Apprehends the slaves frequently robbed the provision grounds of the neighbouring plantations: to
prevent which, armed watchmen are therefore set;
and he has heard of negroes brought home wounded.

P. 332. Some persons allow their negroes all Sunday, besides
5 or 6 holidays in the year, and sometimes a Saturday
afternoon, during the time of holing. Others allowed less vacation, requiring, on Sundays, meat for the
cattle, to be gathered twice in the day; and often in
the

the crop, continue the boiling of the sugar till late on Saturday night.

In one instance recollects it to have been protracted till sun-rise, on Sunday morning; and the care afterwards of setting up the sugar jars, must require several hours. The slaves had commonly no other day than Sunday, (except as above) to cultivate their own grounds.

The criterion of a manager's merit in general, he apprehends to be the production of large crops.

The quantum of ground allowed the field negroes for raising provisions, does not admit their frequently possessing any considerable property. It is not likely they can spare much of the produce for sale. Sometimes they possess a pig and two or three fowls; and if they have also a few plantain trees, these may be a means of supplying them with knives, iron pots, and such other conveniencies, as the master does not allow.

Cannot positively say they never have expensive treats, but the utmost he ever heard of was, that sometimes, when a negro married, he has provided a pig for his friends. Never understood that the dances were attended with treats; and believes if their entertainments had been expensive, he should have heard of them. The principal feasts they ever give, as he understands, are after the funerals of their friends, when they scatter some provisions on the grave, and eat the rest themselves, with a view of holding a communion with the deceased.

He does not recollect any instances of the Creole negroes destroying themselves, but remembers five or six such instances of African negroes, immediately after they were purchased.

He knew very few free negroes. One of them was wife to a Mulatto slave, on Sir Hanson Berney's estate. She was very industrious in the care of her family, and in raising poultry to sell, with the profits of which she paid for the schooling and cloathing of her children, which she was encouraged to do, as knowing

1790. knowing they would be free. They were baptized,
Part II. and the whole family fo orderly, that he never heard
any mifbehaviour attributed to them. The hufband
ferved in feveral capacities on the eftate, was very
fkilful in the care of the fick, and remarkably
honeft. Having met with reward and indulgence,
by his own and his wife's induftry, it was faid he
amaffed 100l. fterling, which he offered for his freedom;
but it was refufed, his mafter not being willing
to part with him at any price. What relates to his
own and wife's behaviour, the witnefs knew from his
own obfervation.

The only other inftance of a free negro, in his
knowledge, was of a Joe Rachell, in Bridge Town.
He was a merchant, had large and extenfive concerns,
and was fo much efteemed for his honefty,
that he was commonly admitted to the company and
converfation of merchants and planters.

The fituation of domeftic flaves, was not by any
means as comfortable as that of the correfpondent
rank of people in this country, though preferable to
that of field negroes. The indulgence given domefticks
here, is withheld from the flaves, and thefe are
liable to corporal punifhment. In the country domeftic
flaves are commonly corrected by the driver,
and in town a man was employed, who went from
houfe to houfe for that purpofe, who was called
the Jumper. Neither does he think the ftate of field
flaves will bear any comparifon with that of the labouring
poor in this country; becaufe of the feverity
of the heats, which are little varied by the feafons,
becaufe the intermiffions from labour are lefs frequent,
and the food lefs fubftantial than in England;
and becaufe they are perpetually fubject not only to
arbitrary punifhment from the chief overfeer, but
from the book-keepers and drivers, who follow them
conftantly at their work with the lafh, correct them
before an excufe can be heard, and often vent their
own refentments upon them, under the plea of punifhing
them for negligence.

The

The white people called Tenants, who serve in the militia for a small allotment of land, commonly work in their grounds with the negroes, if they have any; or if not, cultivate them by their own labour. These usually raise provisions, but not canes. Many whites in Barbadoes exercise handicraft trades; such as carpenters, joiners, masons, copper-smiths, black-smiths, shoemakers, &c. and also some of the poorer whites spin cotton for the lamps in the boiling houses. Whites are also employed in the coasting vessels, and as fishermen.

1790. Part II.

In respect to stocks of slaves, kept up by the births only, understood from Dr. Mapp's son, that the stock on the estate to which he had just succeeded, had increased so much, that there was a redundance sufficient, nearly, to stock another estate. Another instance which came within his own observation, was of slaves, the property of the Rev. Mr. Carter, who increased considerably; they cultivated his glebe, and he annually planted canes, which were manufactured into sugar at an adjoining estate. His own brother informed him, that his negroes had doubled their number by natural increase in twenty years; and he believed they were generally employed in common field business, as other negroes. He had heard of several others of his acquaintance, who had kept up their stocks by the natural increase, without purchase. In conversation with judicious planters, he understood it to be their opinion, that the rearing of slaves on the estates, depended much on the managers.

P. 335.

Remembers to have seen two Guinea sailors, who were lame, begging in the country, at the house of a person who had relieved many such, by extracting the Guinea-worm, and healing sores contracted in that service.

Cannot say what difference a long residence of the blacks in the islands might occasion, as to their happiness, as he did not himself make a long residence; he however remembers both to have seen and heard,
that

1790. that those newly imported, were often dejected,
Part II. emaciated, and incapable of work, so as even to
resist all attempts to console and administer nourishment to them.

P. 336. Never saw the act of branding; has seen marks, but does not remember how they arose, nor whether they were made in Africa, on board ship, or elsewhere. Were not many.

Never heard of any nation of negroes prone to suicide in their own country. Besides the five mentioned, who destroyed themselves the day after they were purchased, he remembers to have heard of a slave who destroyed himself, sometime after he was purchased, supposed from dejection, and certainly not from ill treatment.

P. 337. Does not know by what law the pecuniary punishments, annexed to the murder of a slave, are imposed. He supposes it to be by an act of the island, because the laws of this country inflict a different punishment for murder. When a law is passed in the island, he apprehends it is immediately sent to be presented to the King in council, and is valid unless negatived within three years, without any distinct approbation of the law being expressed.

P. 339. While in Barbadoes, many particulars mentioned by him, which fell not within his own personal knowledge, he had from his father and brother, who resided near him. They at different times had the care of slaves, to the amount of between 1000 and 2000, and knew the state of the whole island; some particulars had been communicated to him by letters, and most of the information since, he had from a person then in England. Has conversed and corresponded with another gentleman of some distinction, a proprietor of estates and slaves in Barbadoes, and has been in both countries, within the last 10 years, but absent from Barbadoes about five years. Has understood from himself and some disinterested persons, that the management on his plantation since his absence, fence, has not been prejudicial to the flaves in point of treatment and provifion in the fmalleft degree.

He lived much with his father and uncle who were humane men; recollects but one inftance of correction of a negro by either of them, and that was for breaking open a ftore, and ftealing a pipe of wine, for this he thinks the culprit received 24 lafhes.

During his laft refidence on the ifland, he avoided feeing the punifhment of flaves, yet recollects feeing them with irons upon the feet and neck, and once to have heard a tremendous punifhment adminiftered, which he did not fee; it was for running away, and confifted of 60 lafhes on the breech with a thick whip. A perfon in the fervice of the owner, who ordered that correction, told him that the flave was compelled to run away by harfh treatment; and another who faw the punifhment, that the whip had made incifions large enough for the finger to be laid in.

The flave was afterwards fent to the dungeon. This he thinks the fevereft chaftifement he can recollect.

Correction with the whip was generally on the back, on all parts of which, it was common to fee very large wheals (the remains of lafhes). On fudden provocation believes the blows to be on the back; in formal punifhments on the breech.

Does not remember an inftance of property acquired by any negro flave, beyond that of Tom Perryman, the mulatto already mentioned. Believes they have indulgencies, but to what extent is uncertain. On further recollection remembers another flave, of the fame Sir Hanfon Berney, who was employed to carry the rum of the eftate to market and fell it, and to make bargains for fmall fupplies, with the traders in town; for which he had fome indulgence allowed him, and lived comfortably upon it; but whether he had acquired any property or not, the witnefs is uncertain. This man he believes had alfo a free woman for his wife.

1790.   Speaks only to what he knew; and does not sup-
Part II. pose that his want of a more extensive knowledge of
the subject, is to criminate other gentlemen, many of
whom possessed principles of honour and humanity,
though he could not see a detail of their estates.

P. 341.   Cannot however think himself entitled to say what
encouragement was generally given to negroes of the
above description; or, from the sentiment then formed, and ever since possessed (setting aside on one hand
particular instances of great severity, and on the
other hand particular instances of great humanity)
that treatment altogether humane and proper, was
the lot of such as he had either observed or heard of.

Has repeatedly seen negroes, at the negro-market,
in Bridge-Town, on Sundays, selling several different
articles of vegetables, and poultry, sometimes pig-
meat; but of other meat but little, as they never keep
the larger cattle. Goats are much discouraged, and
the pigs necessarily confined, lest they should injure
the canes. Whatever returns the negoes obtain, he
believes are allowed to themselves.

He resides between his two livings at Middleham
in Yorkshire, and Stony Stanton in Leicestershire.
One farmer of Leicestershire informed him, that he
gave 10l. a year and board to his waggoner. Another, that he gave 9l. a year and board to his day-
P. 342. labourer. In Stony Stanton parish, a day labourer
in agriculture had 6s. per week, and a load of coals
brought 17 miles from the pits free of expense. In
all other maters he found himself, except in harvest
time, when he was allowed provisions. In Yorkshire
he believes labour is rather dearer. About Middleham he gave 14d. a day for labour in the garden,
from between seven and eight in the morning to five
in the afternoon.

In Leicestershire the average wages of labouring
men in the farming business, who find themselves,
and contract to serve the year through, he understands is 6s. per week. The food of such he cannot
specify, but as it is a cheese country, supposes that
cheese

cheese enters largely into their diet, with wheaten and rye, and sometimes barley bread. They use some but not much oatmeal, and fresh butcher's meat on Sundays, of which they commonly make broth; also beans in summer; bread with hog's lard instead of butter; meal fried with lard, sliced apples, and small pieces of bacon, if they have any, and potatoes. This is a general description of the fare of such labourers.

Besides the 6s. wages, such a labourer has sometimes aids from his wife's spinning, knitting, and other work, by which they earn from 3d to 6d. per day; also from corn-gleanings, which are sometimes considerable; besides the relief which he obtains during harvest, in more substantial living. Some of them have a little bit of garden ground, others hire land and keep a cow, or have the priviledge of a common. In Stony Stanton the bulk of the labouring inhabitants are employed in the manufacturing of stocking. From the means thus stated they generally are enabled to furnish themselves and families, with necessary food, and defray the expense of house rent, clothing, medical assistance, and other incidental charges. He instances a widow left with two children, who never had so much after her widowhood, and yet maintained, and brought them up to be industrious members of the community, and parents of families, without assistance from the parish: and another day-labourer, who had uniformly lived with comfort, and brought up an useful family. Several other instances are adduced to shew, that a sober man with an industrious family, is capable of maintaining them, as a day-labourer only. In Yorkshire prizes have been given away to some such, who have brought up large families, with no other assistance than their own labour. In the instance above mentioned of the woman and children, the woman spun worsted, and assured the witness, who attended her when dying, that in order to keep her family from the parish, she sat up to spin through the whole of two or three nights

1790.
Part II.

P. 343.

P. 344.

1790. nights in the week. In the other instance of the day-
Part II. labourer, his wife was dead at the time mentioned,
but he brought up two sons in the stocking trade,
one of which living with him earns 9s. per week;
the daughter is industrious, and appears very decent.
In visiting the father when sick, she was sometimes
spinning, at others knitting, or nursing her father.

P. 346. So far as he observed, where the slaves in Barbadoes were under judicious and humane masters, they
were well fed, clothed, lodged, taken care of in sickness, and treated with moderation and lenity. He
considers liberty as the first comfort of life, as well
as an unalienable right; that the want of it lessens
the comforts of life, and is a source of continual regret, by cutting off the hope of bettering one's condition, as in the case of Tom Perryman, before-mentioned, &c. To shew that this is not mere speculation, he could give instances in England, of agricul-
tural labourers, rising into situations that enabled
them to marry with a fortune of £500, and provide
well for, and educate their children, at grammar and
boarding schools.

P. 347. Does not believe, that negroes are not so susceptible of the sentiment of liberty, as the free peasants
in England: for the several rebellions engaged in by
the negroes, and especially the 2 great rebellions,
mentioned by Long, in his History of Jamaica, sufficiently prove the contrary.

He conceives diet and accommodations of the labouring peasantry here, more substantial than that
of the negroes, and is confirmed in that opinion, by
the large size, health, and long life, of many of them
in Yorkshire, particularly at West Whitton, where,
out of about 500 inhabitants, there is a large proportion of peasantry, answering the above description in all points; and in the parish of Bolton, adjoining, there is scarcely a day labourer, who does not
keep a cow. Does not say this representation holds
universally, but thinks it unfair in forming a comparison, between the negroes in the West Indies, and
peasantry

peasantry of Britain, to take a part of the one which 1790. is best treated, to compare with the whole of the latter, among which, though there are many in comfortable circumstances, yet there are many others extremely distressed for the subsistence of themselves and families. But if he was to judge from his own P. 348. observation (setting aside liberty on the one hand, and cruelty on the other) he should prefer the condition of a peasant in England, believing it, if even with equal labour, to be much preferable.

Stated allowance of food to negroes in Barbadoes, under what is called good management, was, 9 pints of Guinea, or India corn, and 1 pound, 1½ or 2 pound of salt fish, or from 4 to 6 herrings per week. This was the species of provision in most instances, that fell within his observation throughout the year. There was sometimes a variation, by allowing yams or eddoes, or pidgeon peas, the growth of the island, in lieu of the corn: but does not recollect that oatmeal, meal of wheat, or rye, were ever offered as a substitute: nor that there was a sufficient growth of cassada, to answer that purpose. Biscuit, flour and oatmeal, have been allowed in sickness, and particularly in fluxes; but rarely in health. On some estates the weekly allowance was equal to 12 pints of corn, and 6 herrings, to field negroes; but to women not working in the field, and children, it was much short; and also to those past labour. Some humane masters have continued the usual allowance to negroes past labour, and this was noted as very humane.

The above-mentioned articles of food, vary in the P. 349. degree of nutrition they afford; Guinea and India corn are less nutritious than wheat or barley. When India corn happens to be heated in the hold of the ship, it creates disorders. Eddoes are the most nutritious and wholesome article of food in the islands: yams are less so. Potatoes and pidgeon peas are wholesome, but the latter have a very thick coat. Salted herrings, with other salt fish, often suffer by
the

1790.
Part II.

the voyage, and are often in a broken, unwholesome state. Salt beef and pork are seldom given, but when other provisions fail, or as a great indulgence, in small quantities; sometimes in a bad, and sometimes a good state, as they happen to come to market. He never knew them given as a part of the stated allowance.

The negroes frequent the Sunday markets in Bridge Town, with pidgeon peas, Guinea corn, eddoes, potatoes, and whatever other native provisions of the island they can spare, which they sell, or commute for other species of provisions. The hucksters often give them, at a disadvantage to the negroes, small loaves of wheaten bread for corn; for instance, a small half-penny loaf for a pint of Guinea corn; and sometimes they sell their provisions to obtain rum, and other matters, which they think necessary to their convenience. This exchange is often made when the negro, tired of his labour, has not time or inclination, to grind the corn, or fetch water, and procure fuel to boil it for use.

P. 354. It struck him, to speak generally, that negro mothers commonly went into the field too early after their delivery, taking their children, while yet very tender, with them; that the milk of the mother became feverish with labour, and the heat of the sun too powerful for the child, which was commonly exposed in a basket, and in rainy weather unsheltered. He understood that this was so generally the practice, that some humane gentlemen, resident in England many years since, gave directions to their overseers, to observe a contrary practice.

He never heard that M'Mahon, already mentioned, ever suffered any other ill consequence from his severity to his negroes, than the loss consequent thereon.

P. 355. Again, not having any right to their children, is a discomfort necessarily resulting from the constitution of human nature; and especially as those children, if females, may be subjected to the brutal lusts of their superiors, without remedy from law. being obliged to labour at the will of another; being unprotected by laws, and enduring punishment at the caprice of another, are certainly inconveniencies, which necessarily arise out of slavery itself, and prevent a fair comparison being made between a slave and a free man.

The 1790. Part II.

P. 356.

---

Witness examined,—HENRY ELLISON, Gunner of the Resistance Man of War.

He thinks his first voyage was in 1759, to Gambia; was in the slave trade till about 1770; was pressed in 1771; was 3 voyages to Gambia, 1 to Benin, 1 to Old Calabar, 2 to New Calabar, and 1 to Isle de Los.

P. 361.

A native, called captain Lemma, came on board their ship to receive his customs; he saw a canoe in shore, with 3 people in it (an old man, a young man, and a woman) he ordered one of his canoes to take this canoe, which they did, and brought the people on board, and Mr. Wilson's chief mate bought the young man and woman, the other being too old, was refused. Lemma ordered the old man into the canoe, his head was chopped off, and immediately thrown overboard. Lemma had many war canoes; some had 6 or 8 swivels; he brought about 10 when he received his customs; he seemed to be feared by the rest of the natives. Mr. E. did not see a canoe out on the river while he was there, except this, and if they had known he had been out, they would not have come. He discovered by signs, that the old man killed, was the 2 negroes father, and that they were brought there by force; could not conceive Lemma had any right to sell them, they were not his subjects. Lemma staid about 10 days near their ship; he was on board every day to get his customs, and eat and drink.

P. 362.

P. 363.

He

1790.
Part II.

He never remembers any slaves brought on board with marks of wounds. Does not remember any other instance of slaves being obtained by fraud or force.

He has known many boys and girls, in every ship he has been in, without parents and near relations. He speaks the Mandingoa, and has often conversed with slaves that spoke it, who all said they had been stolen and sold.

He has often known slaves brought on board in the night in the Gambia; supposes they were afraid to be seen in the day; he has assisted in fetching canoe boys on board in the night. It is common, when their masters want goods, or for trifling offences, these boys are brought on board. We fetch them in our own boats from their masters houses, when asleep in the night, for fear they should escape; supposes they could not know they were to be sold, or they would have made their escape; he has known their master call them out of the canoe to bring him something, and when on board, immediately put in irons.

P. 364.

He never saw these canoe-boys ill treated; has seen them eating and drinking in the same house with their masters, and sometimes with them.

He knew 2 slaves taken from Furnandipo while there, by the Dobson's boat of Liverpool, and carried to Old Calabar, where the ship lay. He went for yams a few days after, and fired, as a signal to the natives, to bring them; seeing some of them peep through the bushes, wondered why they would not come to the boat; he swam on shore, some came round him; an old man made signs a ship's boat had stole a man and woman; he was soon surrounded by numbers, who presented darts to him, signifying, they would kill him if the man and woman were not brought back. The people in the boat fired some shot, when they all ran into the woods; they left a goat and some yams, which they put into the boat, and staid to see if they would return, but they did not.

P. 365.

not. He went to Calabar and told his captain they could get no yams, from two people being stole; captain Briggs told the captain of the Dobson, there would be no more trade if he did not deliver up the people, which he did; when the natives saw them, they loaded the boat with yams, goats, fowls, honey and palm wine; they would take nothing for them. They had the man and woman delivered to them, whom they carried away in their arms.

The Dobson did not stay above eight, ten, or twelve days. That was the last trip her boat was to make when they carried off the two slaves.

When they were laying at Yanamaroo in Gambia, slaves were brought down. The traders raised the price. Captains would not give it, but thought to compel them by firing upon the town. They fired red hot shot from the ship, and set several houses on fire. All the ships, seven or eight, fired.

They often took children and relations as pawns for goods. They carried off two in the Briton, captain Wilson, who were much dejected. All the slaves he saw brought on board were very much dejected. He never saw the women otherwise than modest and decent.

He has seen both men and women work in the fields.

He has seen slaves faint away in ships from heat and stench.

They were always much crouded. Had two tier of people on one deck. One on platform. They were much crouded in the Nightingale, a small snow, about 170 tons. Purchased 270 slaves. Thirty boys messed and slept in long-boat all the Middle Passage. No room below.

The Briton, 230 or 240 tons. Much crouded. Purchased 375 slaves.

Thinks only buried 6 or 7 in the Nightingale, were remarkably healthy. They buried near 200 in the Briton. Last man brought on board had the small-pox. Doctor told Mr. Wilson it was the

Numb. 3. T small-pox,

1790. small-pox, who would not believe it, but said he
Part II. would keep him, as he was a fine man. It soon
broke out amongst the slaves. He has seen the platform one continued scab. Hauled up 8 or 10 slaves dead of a morning. The flesh and skin peeled off their wrists when taken hold of, being intirely mortified.

They buried in the Nightingale's second voyage about 150, chiefly of fevers and flux. They had 250 when they left the coast.

P. 368. Men slaves generally fettered on board vessels he sailed in, being two and two shackled together. When brought on deck, a chain is reeved through a ring on the shackle on their legs, and locked abaft the barricado. They are chained on both sides the deck. They are made dance every day; sometimes are willing to dance, sometimes compelled by the cat.

Has known in the Middle Passage, in rains, slaves confined below for some time. He has frequently seen them faint through heat, the steam coming through the gratings like a furnace. Has been obliged to get on deck, lest they would die in the rooms.

Never saw wind sails used in any vessel. Never saw slaves treated ill in any ships but the Briton and Nightingale.

Has known Mr. Wilson order eight or ten up at a time, for making a little noise in the night, tie them up to the booms, flog them severely with a wire cat, and afterwards clap the thumb-screws upon them, leaving them in that state till morning. He has seen their thumbs mortify, fevers ensue, and death.

The women making a little noise over head while the captain was dining, he came out, and with a wire cat began to flog away among them: 6 jumped overboard, 5 of which were drowned. The other he ordered to be ducked at the crotchet-yard-arm:
she

she was led up and down a dozen times, he believes. She died, he thinks, next day.

1790.
Part II.
P. 369.

The Nightingale was lying in New Calabar river, when the slaves rose on board the Africa. They were quelled, and about eight or ten picked out as the ringleaders, for punishment: they were tied to a spare mast, and the people of the Africa, with the boat's crew of the Nightingale, took spell and spell at flogging them, till they all were tired; yet they were so stubborn they never cried out. Captain Carter came on board, and ordered some cooks tormentors and tongs to be made red hot, and with his own hands burnt their bare breech in a most dreadful manner.

Slaves often refuse their victuals; when they do, they are flogged till they eat.

Women are whipped or beaten, but not so very often as men In the Nightingale, on the passage, a woman disobliged the second mate one day, who gave her a cut or two with a small cat he had in his hand: she flew at him with great rage, but he pushed her from him, giving her three or four smart strokes with the cat. Finding she could not have her revenge of him, she sprung two or three feet on the deck, and dropped down dead. Was thrown overboard about half an hour after, and torn to pieces by the sharks.

The chief mate and boatswain have charge of the men; the second mate and gunner, if there is one, of the women; each having constantly a cat in their hand.

Slaves, at the time of their dancing, always sing to some tune or other in their own way; has often heard them sing mournful tunes in the night.

P. 370.

Besides the instance given of slaves rising, they attempted it in the Upton, but it came to no head, (a few, though women, had got out of irons).

As to the situation of seamen in different ships he has been in, respecting food, lodging, and general treatment:—The allowance was small in all the ships, especially in the Middle Passage; were always

1790. at allowance outward and homeward. In the Middle
Part II. Paſſage, were obliged to fetch a gun-barrel from the
top-maſt-head when they wanted to drink, and to
carry it back without permitting another to uſe it
at the time: has often been drier before he came
down again, than when he firſt went up; but durſt
not bring the barrel down a ſecond time till ſome
other had uſed it: the ſick ſo long as they were able
were obliged to do ſo; remembers one who had
bad ulcerated legs, when he had got half way up,
the main ſhrouds, was ſo weak he could get no further; he and another went and helped him down
again, and begged of the doctor to give him a little
decoction, which at firſt he refuſed, but afterwards
gave him a ſmall pannikin full. The man died in
a day or two after, (p. 372.)

Never was in a ſhip in which the ſeamen had a
place to put their heads in below, but were obliged
to lie upon deck in all weathers.

P. 370. The ſeamen he ſaw worſe uſed, were thoſe in the
Briton and in the Nightingale: they had nothing
elſe but bad treatment in thoſe two ſhips from the
firſt of the voyage to the laſt. (p. 371.)

On board the Briton was a boy whom Wilſon the
chief mate was always a beating. One morning in the
paſſage out, he had not got the tea-kettle boiled in
time for his breakfaſt; when it was brought, he told
him he would ſeverely flog him after breakfaſt; for
P. 371. fear, the boy went into the lee fore chains: when W.
came from the cabin, and called for Paddy, (the
name he went by, being an iriſh boy) he would not
come, but remained in the fore chains; on which W.
went forward, and attempted to haul him in; when
the boy jumped overboard, and was drowned.

Another time, on the middle paſſage, Wilſon ordered one James Alliſon, (a man he had been continually beating for every trifle) to go into the women's room to ſcrape it; he ſaid he was not able, for
he was very unwell; but W. obliged him to go down;
he did not however begin to ſcrape; which W. ob-
ſerving,

serving, asked why he did not work, and was answered as before, that he was not able, on which he threw a handspike at him, which struck him in the breast, and he dropt down to appearance dead; he recovered a little, but died next day.

In the Nightingale, on the passage, the gunner was on the barricado with a musket, as a centry, while the slaves were going down; happening to look aft, he was asked by captain why he did not look forward at the slaves, said, "That he could willingly turn the musket, and blow his brains out:" but did not think the captain heard him. When the slaves were down, the captain caused him to be tied up, and flogged very severely. He died in two or three days after.

As to the seamen leaving their ships, on the coast of Africa; the boatswain and five of the crew of the Phœnix of Bristol, Cap. Bishop, made their escape in the yawl, but were taken up by the natives. When the captain heard it, he ordered them to be kept ashore, at Forgé, a small town at the mouth of Calabar river, chained by the necks, legs, and hands, and to have each a plantain a day only. The boatswain, who had been a ship-mate of the witness's, and a very good seaman, died raving mad in his chains; the other five also died in their chains.

As to the the motives which induce seamen to enter on board Guinea ships, believes they are compelled by want; by getting in debt to their landlords, when they must go on board a Guineaman, or to gaol. (p. 375.). Landlords are sure of getting paid by the advance-money the sailor has to receive on entering into the Guinea employ, if no other way. (p. 377.)

As to his opinion, which is most advantageous to the country, to become a sailor or go to gaol—to become a sailor, he should suppose. (p. 377.

Has been in many W. India islands, Barbadoes and Jamaica in particular; where he has often seen Guinea sailors lying on the wharfs, and under the cranes almost at the point of death, with large ulcers upon their

1790.
Part II.

P. 373.

their legs and feet, and in a starving state; and he has often carried them provisions from his ship. Has also seen the negroes carrying them when dead to Spring Path, and burying them. Believes they had, all whom he saw, left their ships from bad usage, without wages. It is commonly the case. Many told him they got no pay, but were glad to get ashore. He knew them to have belonged to Guineamen, because he knew, and had sailed with some of them, and others told him so. Never saw any belonging to other ships than Guineamen in that state.

Was almost daily on shore, for eighteen months, at Kingston, where he has seen six or seven slaves whipped of a morning, by a man they called Johnny Jumper; their backs much cut, and the blood running down. Saw also a woman at Dominica hung up by the wrists, on a stage (erected to punish negroes on) her feet two feet from the stage, and thus severely flogged with a cow-skin, by her mistress's order, it was said, for running away.

As to appearance of field and town-slaves, the last are always better dressed, and look better; the other look very poor and were always badly clothed; much marked with the whip.

They often bring down sugar and rum from the country to be shipped; when aboard they would beg and pray for a bit of biscuit and beef, which they are very thankful for, (p. 374).

On Sundays they generally bring some little trifle or other from the country to sell, such as oranges, plantanes, &c. to the value of half a bit, a bit, or two bits each; does not remember ever seeing them have any pigs or kids to sell. As to their being so well protected by laws, as to be able to sell these articles unmolested and for their own use; does not think there is any law for them; has seen their things taken by the sailors and then beat for asking their money; they would run crying through the street, and even follow them down to the boats, but they got neither the things nor their money (p. 375).

Has

Has been many voyages to Virginia and Maryland, and has often gone through the tobacco plantations while the slaves were at work.

1790. Part II.

Looked much better than those in the W. Indies; were much better clothed, and not so hard worked, having seldom seen a driver over them with his whip; they generally work by themselves; has seen them at their victuals often, in their houses, and they seemed to have plenty.

P. 374.

Has seen the slaves on board when sold in the W. Indies, very much distressed at the prospect of separation.

P. 375.

Was fifteen or sixteen years old when he went first to Africa; his first voyages were to Gambia. Talked the Mundingo tongue pretty well; understood but little of the other negro languages; does not recollect how old he was when told by the slaves that they were all stolen, but they commonly told him so in every voyage he has been, in the best manner they could make themselves understood. His highest birth on board a Guineaman was that of gunner.

P. 376.

Has been in the king's service since 1771; first station there, quarter gunner: has been gunner in the Resistance since June 1784 (p. 377.)

The canoes on the coast of Africa are rowed by slaves. Masters often sell their canoe boys. Such canoe boys as have been sold, he believed to have been slaves to those who sold them. Captain Lemma lived a good way up Benin River: the people whom he seized in the canoes, lived at a little fishing town at the mouth of the river, subject he believes to the to the king of Benin: he was very much feared by the natives of that part: cannot say whether he was at war with the king of Benin from his taking away his subjects.

Lemma was generally considered as a pirate, (p. 377).

The natives know very well, that if pawns are not redeemed before the ship sails, they will be carried off.

Witness

1790.
Part II.

Witnefs examined—JOHN MARSHALL.

P. 377. Has made about 19 voyages, chiefly to the Gold Coaſt. Never knew Africans go to war, to procure flaves to the ſhips. On the contrary, when wars have happened, it has been of the utmoſt prejudice to the ſhipping.

P. 378. Was at Annamaboe, when the king of Aſhantee made war againſt the Fantees, which ſo totally ſtopt the trade, that he lay ſixteen months there, before he was fully ſlaved. The Aſhantees failed of conquering the Fantee country. The Fantees, on the contrary, took many Aſhantees priſoners; moſt of whom would have been ſold, and ſome put to death, but for Mr. Brew, who propoſed to the king of Aſhantee the redemption of thoſe priſoners, which he gladly acceded to. Thinks kidnapping impoſſible. Is certain the governors of forts could not with impunity ſeize and ſell the natives; they are themſelves too much in their power to attempt it: never knew governors give any ſuch orders. Knows it is impracticable.

P. 379. Has been frequently at Cape la Hou; never knew or heard of natives carried from thence fraudulently. Natives come on board as freely as a boat would board a ſhip in the Thames.

On the Gold Coaſt the cultivation is very trifling: that for corn (which is very rude) is ſuch, that there is no certainty of ſupply there; in the Bight of Guinea, at Bonny, the only cultivation he knew was of yams. Is certain, that in Africa they know nothing of the manufacture of indigo, for both indigo and blue are carried from Europe, for the uſe of the gentlemen in the forts: and you cannot pleaſe a female better than by giving her a little of either, with which they paint themſelves.

Never failed in the night from Africa; it is the cuſtom to ſail in the morning, to have the land-winds:

winds: from Bonny it is impoſſible to fail in the night, the river is too dangerous.

1792. Part II.

He is not at preſent concerned in the African trade, either as captain or merchant.

He took on board the Elizabeth, one of the ſhips which he commanded, 546 ſlaves; was peculiarly unfortunate in the loſs of ſlaves and crew; had at one period ſmall-pox, meaſles, flux and fever on board; whereby he loſt 158 ſlaves; a greater loſs than in any 6 of his voyages together. Loſt alſo 22 out of 52 ſeamen; 45 of which Engliſh, and 7 Spaniards. The latter loſs was chiefly owing to intemperance; they were not to be controuled.

P. 380.

P. 381.

Is confident the king of Aſhantee's motives for war upon the Fantees, was to conquer their country, as he has often heard from the king's brother and nephew, who were hoſtages with Mr. Brew; could not ſuppoſe he had any view to ſlaves in making war on the Fantees, having no means of conveying them to the ſea but through their country.

Slaves ſold to the Europeans, come under the following deſcription; ſome are born ſlaves, a few taken in war, others forfeit their liberty by crimes, and many ſold for witchcraft; by ſuch means ſlaves are obtained in general, at leaſt, the natives ſay ſo, for in his various voyages he has often converſed with them on the ſubject. Of the ſlaves bought on the Gold Coaſt, one third may be inhabitants of the coaſt, the reſt are Aſhantees and Duncoes, who both ſpeak the Fantee language.

P. 382.

Believes, the perſons ſold for witchcraft, undergo a previous trial, though it is ſecreted from the Europeans.

In his voyages in the Alfred, he had very few boys and girls: in purchaſing ſlaves they generally go by height, and he made a point (it was indeed his orders) not to buy any under 4 feet 4 inches: on his laſt voyage he was allowed to buy them as low as 4 feet: ſuppoſes he might have had from 40 to 60 of that deſcription.

Numb. 3.        U        Where

1790.    Where our settlements or forts are, they are tole-
Part II. rably civilized, from their intercourse with the Eu-
ropeans, at other towns they are not so much so. Their natural abilities he thinks much inferior to the people of other countries; and believes they know nothing of morality.

P. 383.   Having said that kidnapping by the natives is impossible: his reason for it is, because it could not be done secretly, nor with impunity. It must be found out, either in conveying them to the water side to be shipped, or certainly after they were put on board; from the free intercourse the traders have with the ships, it is impossible for a person so taken to be concealed long: he speaks here positively, as he never knew an instance of the kind. And should such a thing be done by the first person in the country, restitution, in his opinion, is the least punishment which would follow; does not believe persons are ever unjustly accused with a view to be sold.

Believes that slaves are sometimes sold by their owners through the necessities of the owner. That
P. 384. they have a right to do so, he apprehends, because he has known it publickly done. One of the traders with his ship, sold him two of his houshold slaves.

The crimes which subject convicts to be sold, he believes, are principally, theft, incontinence, and others perhaps, which he cannot speak to.

He was never faather than three miles up the country on the Gold Coast.

Inhabitants did not appear to decrease in number; that this should be the case, notwithstanding the large drains continually made by the European traders, he can account for no other way than by the prevalence of polygamy.

Believes the treatment of seamen in the slave trade to be as in other voyages: as there are men of different dispositions in the African trade, as well as others, their treatment will vary accordingly.

Having said, " That they know nothing about
" the manufacture of indigo in Africa," he referred particularly to the Gold coast.

Has purchased rice on the Windward Coast, and corn on the Gold Coast; but the supply at either place was so uncertain, that he never depended much upon it, but generally carried most of his provisions from England.

1790.
Part II.
P. 385.

Believes, Europeans never inquire the right persons have to dispose of slaves; as it is taken for granted they have the right.

---

### Mr. George Millar, Gunner of His Majesty's Ship Pegase.

Has been in Africa; his last voyage to Old Calabar in 1767, in the ship Canterbury, Capt. Parke.

P. 385.

Says, a quarrel happened between the people of Old and New Town, which prevented the ships lying in Calabar River from being slaved. Believes in June 1767, Capt. Parke came one evening to witness, and told him that the two towns so quarrelling would meet on board the different ships, and ordered him to hand up some swords.

Next day several canoes, as Parke had before advertised him, came from both of the towns on board the Canterbury, witness's own ship, and one of the persons so coming on board, brought a letter, which he gave Parke, immediately on the receipt of which he, P. took a hanger, and attacked one of the Old Town people then on board, cutting him immediately on the head, arms, &c. The man fled, ran down the steps leading to the cabin, and P. still following him with the hanger, darted into the boys room. Witness is sure this circumstance can never be effaced from his memory. From this room he was, however, brought up by means of a rope, when P. renewed his attack as before on the man, who, making for the entering port, leaped overboard.

P. 386.

This being concluded, P. left his own ship to go on board some of the other ships then lying in the river.

1790. river. Soon after he was gone, a boy belonging to witness's ship, came and informed witness, that he had difcovered a man concealed behind the medicine cheft. Witnefs went and found the man. He was the perfon before mentioned to have brought a letter on board. On being difcovered by witnefs he begged for mercy, intreating that he might not be delivered up to the people of New Town. He was brought on the quarter deck, where were fome of the New Town people, who would have killed him had they not been prevented. The man was then ironed and conducted into the room of the men flaves.

Soon after the captain returned, and brought with him a New Town trader, named Willy Honefty. On coming on board he was informed of what had happened in his abfence; believes, in the hearing of Willy Honefty, who immediately exclaimed, " Cap-
" tain, if you will give me that man to cut cutty
" head, I will give you the beft man in my canoe,
" and you fhall be flaved the firft fhip." The captain upon this looked into Willy Honefty's canoe, picked his man, and delivered the other in his ftead, when his head was immediately ftruck off in witnefs's fight.

Believes fome other cruelties befides this particular act was done, becaufe he faw blood on the ftarboard fide of the mizen maft, though he does not recollect feeing any bodies from whence the blood might come; and others in the other fhips, becaufe he heard feveral mufkets or piftols fired from them at the fame time. This affair might laft ten minutes. Remembers a four pounder fired at a canoe, but knows not if any damage was done.

P. 387. In the voyage a fickly flave got through the neceffary, and in fwimming bore herfelf higher upon the water than he had ever feen any perfon: the circumftance being told the captain, he faid, " Damn
" her, let her go, fhe is not worth picking up," or fomething to that purpofe.

Recollects

Recollects a woman slave being brought on board, 1790, who refused any sustenance, neither would she speak; she was then ordered the thumb-screws, and suspended in the mizen rigging, and every attempt made with the cat and those instruments they have generally on board; but all to no purpose. She died three or four days afterwards. He was told by some of the women slaves, that she said the night before she died, she was going to her friends.

The death of 180 in the voyage above mentioned was mostly by the flux, brought on he believes by their being so much crowded in the ship: he had himself the care of the men slaves, and when stowed, there was not room to put down the point of a stick. The ship might be between 500 and 600 tons. The apartments for the slaves were very disagreeable, it could not be otherwise, being so much crowded; but they were kept as clean as possible. The men were generally fettered. The slaves appeared generally dejected when brought on board.

They were frequently made to dance, or jump up and down in their irons; if unwilling, they were frequently compelled to do it by the cat.

Recollects no instances of frauds practised on the natives.

The seamen, in the African ships in which he sailed, were very well treated.

Part II.

P. 333.

P. 389.

End of No. 3.—Part II. 1790.

# Number IV.

---

# ABRIDGMENT

OF THE

# MINUTES OF THE EVIDENCE,

TAKEN BEFORE A

*COMMITTEE OF THE WHOLE HOUSE,*

TO WHOM IT WAS REFERRED TO CONSIDER OF THE

SLAVE-TRADE,

1791.

OF THE

MINUTES OF THE EVIDENCE,

TAKEN BEFORE A

SELECT COMMITTEE OF THE WHOLE HOUSE,

TO WHOM IT WAS REFERRED TO CONSIDER OF THE

SLAVE-TRADE, 1790.

NUMBER IV.

Witness Examined,—RICHARD STOREY.

Mr. Richard Storey, lieutenant in the Royal Navy, P. 3. having been from 1766 to 1770, on every part of the coast from S. Leone to the river Sabon, declares, That slaves are generally obtained by merauding parties, from one village to another in the night. He has also known canoes come from a distance and carry off numbers in the night. P. 4.
In 1769, Captain Paterson, of a Liverpool ship, lying off Briftol Town, set two villages at variance, and bought prisoners, (near a dozen) from both sides. While resident at Briftol Town, on the W. Coast, for three months, he was in many villages, but did not hear of any persons being carried off; on other parts of the coast he has.
Has gone into the interiour country between the P. 5. Baffau and the river Sefters; and all the nations there go armed from the fear of merauding parties: there

Numb. 4.    A    were

1791. were no wild beasts to alarm them; and the people there have informed him, that they have obtained their slaves by war; these merauding parties are considered by them as war.

    He was twice in danger from these parties himself. In 1767 he was put into a trading long-boat of the ship; about this time a merauding party from Grand Sesters had come in canoes and attacked Grand Cora in the night, and taken off 12 or 14 of the inhabitants; soon after which, having in his boat a native of Grand Sesters, the people of Grand Cora came to the boat in the river Sesters, and told the mate they had a slave to sell, on which he went ashore with them, leaving only Mr. Storey, a boy, and the black man in the boat. In about four hours after, a canoe came on board the boat, with the four men that the mate had gone with, saying, the mate was in another canoe in sight; and taking him off his guard, two of them seized him, while the other two got the black man overboard. Mr. Storey freed himself, and drove the two men overboard: the mate lay all this time on shore tied neck and heels, which confinement was occasioned by his refusing either to give up the native of Grand Sesters, or pay them the price of a slave in goods. This black man had before told of this expedition of his countrymen against Grand Cora, and often declared himself afraid to go on shore for that reason; he never gave it to be understood that there was a war at the time between Grand Sesters and Grand Cora; the only reason he assigned for the expedition was, that his own countrymen were poor. It was impossible that there could be any existing wars between these two people, as they are 20 leagues asunder; and those of Grand Cora, not having canoes to carry more than two or three men, never go to sea but to fish: the canoes of Grand Sesters carry 12 or 14 men, and with these go merauding among their neighbours. He has seen them at sea out of sight of land in the day, and taking the opportunity of night to land where they pleased.

P. 6.

P. 7.

It

It is his opinion that the natives are often fraudulently caried off by the Europeans: he has been told by them, that they have loſt their friends at different times, and ſuppoſed them taken by European ſhips going along the coaſt. He has himſelf taken up canoes, which were challenged by the natives, who ſuppoſed the men in them had been taken off the day before by a Dutchman.

That the natives retaliate ſuch injuries is proved from the following facts: When lying to an anchor in his boat between the river Seſters and Settra Crue, a Dutch ſhip running down the coaſt ſent her longboat to where he was, to buy vegetables, &c. When come to an anchor, a number of canoes came about the two boats, and one of the head men of the place wiſhed him to go away, as they waited to take the Dutch boat and kill the crew. As a reaſon, they told him that a Dutch ſhip ſome days before had taken four men belonging to the place.

Afterwards, in 1768, being driven by contrary winds, in a coaſting ſhip in which he was a paſſenger into the river Angra, as there appeared a proſpect of trade, they ſtaid there. The ſecond day, two canoes with 12 or 14 men each came on board with two men bound, to ſell. Having agreed for one of them he went down for irons to put him into; but in coming up again was ſeized, with the maſter of the boat and another white man, whoſe throats were immediately cut. He got clear of thoſe who ſeized him, but could not get upon deck. Half an hour after, being covered with wounds, and weak with the loſs of blood, he propoſed to give up both boat and cargo if ſuffered to go to Gaboon, to which they agreed, and then helping him up on deck they ſtripped him naked, put him into a canoe, and took him on ſhore to their town. The reaſon they gave for this was, that a ſhip from Liverpool (name forgotten, the captain's name Lambert) had ſome time before taken a canoe full of their townſmen and carried her away. He heard the ſame thing afterwards at Gaboon.

1791.  He has been at Old Calabar, where slaves are brought down the river in war canoes, carrying upwards of 50 men armed, and a three or four pounder in the bow.

P. 9.  Captain Jeremiah Smith, in the London, in 1766, having a dispute with the natives of Newtown Old Calabar concerning the stated price which he was to give for slaves, for several days stopped every canoe coming down the creek from Newtown, and also fired several guns indiscriminately over the woods into the town till he brought them to his own terms.

He looks upon the natives of the Windward Coast to be in general a hospitable friendly people, always willing to sell what they have, and also to give the best provisions the country affords. The men in general are very active and industrious, and chiefly employed in fishing, and trade with the Europeans; the women chiefly in cultivating rice and other vegetables. Old men also taken by merauding parties, and not saleable, they are put into their plantations; and to this employment he believes that slaves refused by the Europeans as too old for service are commonly destined, having seen many such at this work.

On the Rice Coast, great quanities of rice are sold to the Europeans, the natives in parties of eight or ten bring it from the interiour country, three or four

P. 10.  days journey; he has known them take back salt and other European goods in return, and has every reason to believe, that if there was nobody to purchase slaves, they would turn themselves to cultivate their ground, and raise rice, &c. to purchase European goods. The quality of African rice is far superiour to that of Carolina, bearing one-fourth more water.

The natives carry on their heads from 40 to 60 ℔; has heard from them they go more than a month's journey inland with various articles from the coast, and has seen parties of more than 20 together men and women employed in carrying them.

In every thing they deal in, Europeans defraud the natives, adulterate spirits with water, and then heat it with pepper, and such guns have been sold to them, that he has seen many with their barrels burst and thrown away; he has also seen several natives without fingers and thumbs, blown off, as they said, by the bursting of these guns.

He has been in the West Indies, and has there at St. Christopher's, and part of Grenada, seen surfs as high, and higher than in Africa. At Madras in the East Indies much higher, for a longer time than on the Windward Coast, where there is no place (except where sometimes for a day or two the surf is too high,) boats are not continually loading in most places in Africa, some rocks or points of land break the surf, which is not the case in the clear and open coast of Coromandel. Goods are landed every where along the coast; has seen them sometimes wet, but never lost. They do not use the same expedients here for loading and unloading boats that are used in the West Indies.

In his first voyage to Old Calabar the slaves attempted to rise, but did not succeed. In the year 1769, a Liverpool ship between Cape Mount and Mesurade, had every person killed by an insurrection, except one boy.

In the ships he sailed in, the men slaves were always kept in irons during the Middle Passage.

In the Regus, first ship he had sailed in, provisions were plenty. In the second, the Tyger of Whitehaven, the seamen in ten days after sailing were put to an allowance of 4 lb. of bread per week, and half a pound of beef or pork per day, which was the whole fare for nine months; he has but little complaint to make of ill usage against the ships in which he sailed.

Think the slave trade very unhealthy in the rivers, but not on the open coast; they buried 14 out of 32 the first voyage in Calabar river; and in the Tyger in nine months, five or six out of 28. In three voyages

1791. voyages to Virginia they buried one man; in five Baltic voyages not one; in one to the southern whale fishery none; and in two Mediterranean none. Of the three Virginia voyages, the first was 11 months; the other two about seven months each. The number of men in each 16. The southern whale fishing voyage was of 11 months.

P. 13. In the Tyger the bread was tolerable, the beef and pork so salted that in boiling they shrunk to half this weight. Having once in this vessel, when handing rice to the slaves taken a handful for his own use, he was unmercifully beaten with a rope; he has known others who had done the same thing through hunger, treated for it in the same manner.

As an instance of similar ill treatment in other slave ships, he says, that lying in the Tyger at Bassau, he heard the sailors of three different ships complain heavily of their provision, as being bad, and insufficient in quantity; these were, the Lancashire Witch, Captain Coil; the Lilly, Captain Scragham; and the Violet, Browne, notorious all for bad provisions

P. 14. and ill usage; he has seen the sailors of each unmercifully beaten for the most trifling offences; knocked down with handspikes, or any other thing that came in the Captain's or officers way that took offence at the men. One man he saw in the Lancashire Witch confined for some trifle, with an iron collar on his right leg and arm shackled, and then chained to a ring-bolt on the deck, where he remained a considerable time in this condition without any other allowance but bread and water.

---

### Witness Examined,—JAMES TOWNE.

P. 15. Mr. James Towne, carpenter of His Majesty's ship Syren, made a voyage 1760 to the Isles de Los on board the Peggy, Captain Cuthbert Davis, about 140 or 150 tons; and another in 1767 to Grand Cape

Cape Mount, in the Sally, Captain George Evans, 1791. above 200 tons. The firſt voyage he remained between ſeven and eight months on the coaſt, then a boy; the ſecond as carpenter, ſtaid more than ſix months. He was moſtly on ſhore three months together in the firſt voyage; in the ſecond, for five or ſix weeks at a time. Repeated ill treatment was the occaſion of his being ſo long on ſhore, for having gone in the trading ſhallop, he run away; he went into the back country among the inhabitants for ſome time to conceal himſelf, and was up the rivers and inland together, upwards of between 300 and 400 miles.

The natural productions of Africa are rice and yams in abundance, plantanes, bananas, and all other tropical fruits; plenty of camwood and elephants teeth; ſome tobacco, cultivated by natives who had been in England, but not yet ſkilfully cured. Great quantities of ſugar-cane, long pepper; a bark like cinnamon; cotton in abundance, and often beautifully manufactured into cloth; a fine blue dye; beautiful woods for cabinet-makers; wax, ivory, palm-oil, palm-wine, and Indian corn.

The natives are hoſpitable and kind, and capable of learning quicker than white men. They differ as our own people in character, thoſe on the coaſt learn to be roguiſh; inland they are innocent. The intercourſe with Europeans has improved them in roguery, to plunder and ſteal, and pick up one another to ſell.

Slaves in Africa were never ill uſed by their own P. 16. people, but when bought by white traders they were uſed rather worſe there than when on board.

He has ſeen both men and women cultivating the lands, but not often the women.

When a ſhip arrives ſhe makes preſents to the traders, to encourage them to bring any perſon down to ſell as a ſlave, and they often pledge their own relations till they procure the ſlaves wanted. The black kings have told him, that they go to war on
purpoſe

1791. purpose to get slaves, and he has seen the prisoners, (the men bound, the women and children loose) delivered up to the white traders, or driven in gangs of two or three hundred for sale to the water side. He has known them go in gangs merauding and catching all they could. In the Galenas river he knew an instance of four blacks who took a man that had been to sell one or more slaves, plundered and stripped him naked, and brought him to the trading shallop and sold him. The people on board did not understand his language, nor imagine why he seemed so cast down as they all are, but king Battou coming on board and knowing the man, inquired the cause of his being there as a slave; he related the circumstance; a guard of grumettas, with some of Towne's people, were sent after the blacks to take them, but did not succeed. They could not make the man eat, not even by flogging; they then put him irons, and in a little time he died. He believes the slaves sometimes become so for crimes, as murder, theft, and adultery; the the last, if properly proved, is often punished with death.

P. 17. He has repeatedly heard both from the accused and accusers themselves, and he believes it common on the coast, to impute crimes falsely for the sake of having the accused person sold. One instance of a woman sold by her husband for adultery, and whom he himself brought off to the boat, and from her lamentations, and by her declaration, that she knew not what she was accused of, he thinks he has reason for imagining the crime imputed falsely. Mr. Murray, formerly of Bance island, Mr. Wood, his partner; Mr. Jenkins and Mr. Power, being to the windward of Bance Island, all told him that it was not an uncommon thing to bring on palavers to make slaves, and he believes it from the information of the slaves afterwards when brought down the country and put on board the ships.

Slaves are brought from the country very distant from the coast. The king of Barra has informed him,

him, that on the arrival of a ship he has gone 300 or 400 miles up the country with his guard, and driven down 200 or 300 slaves to the sea side. From Marraba, king of the Mundingoes, he has heard that they had marched them out of the country more than 700 miles, that they had gone wood ranging to pick up every one they met with, whom they stripped naked, and if men, bound; but if women, brought down loose; this he had from themselves, and also that they often went to war with the Ballam nation on purpose to get slaves. They boasted that they should soon have a fine parcel for the shallops, and the success often answered.

He was once present with part of the crew at an expedition undertaken by the whites for the purpose of seizing negroes, and joined by other boats to receive those they could catch. To prevent all alarm, they bound their mouths with oakum and handkerchiefs; one woman shrieked, and the men turned out in defence. He had then five tied in the boat, and the other boats were in readiness to take in what more they could get; all his party were armed, and the men of the town pursued them with first a scattering, and at length a general fire, and several of the men belonging to the boats, he has reason to believe, were killed, wounded, or taken, as he never heard of them afterwards. He was wounded himself. What became of the other boats, he knows not; for he knew nothing of the expedition, until ordered to take command of the boat, which though then he thought it a sport, he was afterwards sorry for having done. The slaves he had taken, were sold at Charleston, South Carolina. The natives had not previously committed any hostilities against any of the ships, whose boats were concerned in this transaction; they owed goods to the captain, for which he resolved to obtain slaves at any rate. He has had several shipmates, who have themselves told him, they have been concerned in similar transactions, and

1791.  have made a boast of it, and who have been wounded also.

  The Europeans endeavour to cheat the natives; they adulterate their liquors, and in buying and selling use different weights, to which they give the same appearance, by casing a stone and a piece of

P. 19.  lead alike in brass; he kept such himself, and used them in dealing for wax, teeth, &c. by order of his commanding officer, whom he has also repeatedly seen do it himself.

  The natives brought to the coast appear not to come on board willingly; on the contrary, they come down with a guard, and are forced into the boats.

  When on board, they are always fettered with leg shackles and handcuffs, two and two, right and left. They lie in a crowded and cramped state, having neither their length nor breadth, in a space by no means sufficient for their health; and such is their suffocated state below, that he has known them go down well, and in the morning be brought up dead. When they come on deck, they are all in a dew sweat, from the tarpawlings being laid over the gratings in bad weather. The height between decks in the Peggy (tonnage 140 or 150, see p. 15 at the top) was about 4 feet, and in the Sally, 4 feet 4 or 5. The Peggy took on board about 230 negroes; the boys room only had a platform: between 50 and 60

P. 20.  of the cargo died. There were 25 seamen, he does not recollect above 6 or 7 dying.

  The Sally (better than 200 tons, p. 15, at top) had platforms in boys and womens rooms, and the aft part of mens. The cargo was nearly 400, of whom about 60 died. The crew consisted of 40 men, of whom above 30 died. They were forced to get men from other ships on the coast; out of 6 mates, not 1 lived.

  Something better than a pint of water, after they are fed, served at twice, was the daily allowance of a slave; and after being fed in the afternoon, the boatswain taking one, and the mate the other side of the deck, they are made to dance, and flogged with a cat

cat if they do not. In fine weather they are brought on deck between eight and nine in the morning, and put down again at four, there to remain until next day. He has known them refuse their food in consequence of being confined; ill treated, to induce them to eat; they are flogged, and put into irons separately; both their hands handcuffed, both legs shackled, a collar round their neck, with a chain, and often the thumb-screw applied, to take the stubbornness out of them. This was his task, and sometimes, from their ill treatment, they attempted to jump overboard; at others, have gone mad, and died in that situation. They often fall sick, sometimes owing to their crowded state, but mostly to grief, for being carried away from their country and friends, which being very well acquainted with their language, he knows from frequent inquiries into the circumstances of their grievous complaints. He has known them attempt to rise on board, and on inquiry into the cause, has been asked what business we had to carry them from their country; they had wives and children they wanted to be with. To check them, they are put singly into irons and flogged. He has known women with infants on board, two particularly, who, when their infants died, grieved after them, and died themselves. Guinea captains seldom buy women with children. Has heard the slaves singing, but their songs were lamentations. A slave kidnapped or sold, contrary to the custom of the country, to the ships, cannot complain to the black traders on board, for these traders never see the main deck, nor even speak to the women abaft, left they might make signals to rise. When canoes come to the ship, no slave on the main deck can look over the ship's side; two officers stand with cats to prevent them, and this prevents their seeking release. A barricado of great strength, cuts off all intercourse between persons on the main deck and those in the after part of the ship; the women and the men thus cannot see one another.

1791.

P. 21.

P. 21.
P. 22.

When

1791.

P. 23.

When sick, in the vessels he sailed in, the negroes were put forward, which was considered the ship's hospital; and though sometimes medicines are given, and sometimes forced down, they are in general but indifferently attended, so that they often die in their own filth. They are seldom long sick before they die. Never saw one sea sick. Small attention, confinement below, and the situation of being slaves, he supposes the cause of this rapid death of the sick. He looks on their dying as partly due to want of attention; in one instance there was no surgeon on board.

P. 24.

Mr. Towne has been in the West Indies; at Barbadoes for near a year, in 1779 and 1780; in Antigua for about 15 months, in 1780 and 1781; for 2 months at St. Kitt's, in 1781; and a little while in Jamaica, in 1782. He was in many plantations at Barbadoes, particularly Mr. Gibson's and Mr. Bishop's; on Mr. Tyrrel's and Sir John Laforey's, at Antigua, and on shore at St. Kitts and Jamaica. Slaves are sold in the West Indies sometimes by vendue, sometimes in lots; those of the vessels in which he was, were sold to the best bidder, and sometimes in lots; he never heard of any care taken to prevent the separation of relations and friends. Refuse slaves are such as are sickly from any cause; they are often kept on board to fatten them for sale, but if they do not recover, they are sold then to any body, some even so low as a guinea.

P. 25.

The slaves in the West Indies work from four in the morning, till very late in the evening; if they come but a moment after their time, they are flogged with whips by the drivers, to whom they must come ready stripped for their punishment, to save time. Some, though lame, are obliged to work; if they complain, they are called lazy, and flogged by the driver. Has seen slaves laid down and stretched out to four stakes in the ground, and so receiving 40 or 50 lashes. He has seen them swang up to a crane, with weights at their feet to stretch them, so as to

enlarge

enlarge the wounds of the whip; men and women 1791. alike. After flogging, they bring ebony switches, full of thorns, and with these flog them again, to let out the bruised blood. To encrease the severity, they use a manner of whipping, which they call crossing. They then pickle them, to keep flies from blowing, and maggots from breeding in their wounds. A jumper who goes from house to house for employment, inflicts these punishments at Bridgetown, Barbadoes, and St. John's, Antigua. In the plantations, a black called the boatswain of the plantation inflicts them, under the manager's direction. The marks of former whippings he has also observ- P. 26. ed in a large proportion of the plantation slaves; there are in general scarce any without a number of them. They are nearly as large as a man's finger above the skin.

Mr. Bishop told him, that in his plantation, at Speight's Town, in Barbadoes, they had not bought a Guinea negro for upwards of 40 years, and that by good usage there were a great many more now there than then. Mr. Bishop told him, the encrease was due to more having been born, than had died on his estate. Knows of no encouragement given to the marriage of slaves.

Seamen are procured at Liverpool for the slave ships, by merchants clerks, who intoxicate them in publick houses, and so get them on board. The publicans also get them in their debt, and if they refuse a Guineaman, send them to gaol; the Guinea P. 27. captains are then informed, that if they want men, they may have so many, for paying these debts; and if then they agree to go, they are sent on board, and never suffered to come out of the ship again; if not, they remain in a gaol on a very scanty allowance; has known many instances himself.

On board the vessels in which he sailed, seamen were treated with the greatest inhumanity, in the Peggy, captain Davis; for instance, they were so soon as when round the rock of Liverpool, brought to an
allowance

1791. allowance of four pound of bread per week; their chests were staved and burnt, and themselves turned out from lying below. If any murmured, they were inhumanely beaten with any thing that came in the way, or flogged, both legs put in irons, and chained abaft to the pumps, and there made to work points and gaskets. The captain, as he passed by, repeatedly kicked them, and if offended at any thing they said, immediately called for a stick to beat them, and put their necks in an iron collar, with a chain. On the coast of Guinea, if not released before their arrival, they were made to row in boats back and forward, or any duty, in all their irons, and the chain locked to the boat, and at night, when returned to the ship, they were locked fast to the open deck, exposed to the heavy rain and dews, without any thing to lie on, or cover them. This was a common practice, but he adds, that not any of them died in this situation.

P. 28. On board the Sally also, where the ill treatment was general, one of the seamen had both his legs in irons, a collar on his neck, and was chained to the boat for three months, and when he complained, was often beaten most inhumanly, by both the captain and other officers. He grew at length too weak to sit and row. He was then taken on board the ship, and made to pick oakum, with only three pound of bread per week, and one-half pound of salt beef per day; his legs remained in irons, but the collar was taken off the latter part of the time. One evening, on the Middle Passage, coming aft to beg for something to eat, or he should die, the captain inhumanly beat him, and then ordered him to go forward and die and be damned; the man died that night.

One Edward Hilton also, being out in the boat watering, complained of being long without meat or drink, on which the boatswain beat and cut his head with the tiller. When he came on board all bloody, and was telling his story to Mr. Towne, the mate (by the captain's order) with the surgeon and boatswain,

swain, came forward, and beat him with canes (which they call serving out grog) the surgeon's cane struck his eye, which mortified, and was totally lost. His legs, when unable to stand, were then put in irons, and next morning he was sent in his irons, on the same duty in the boat, to which he was locked with a chain, until he was unable to remain any longer; he was then taken on board, and still in irons, laid forwards, and by the surgeon's advice, his allowance was stopped. Hilton lying before the mast almost dead, and Mr. Towne having received orders to go in the shallop to Jack River, when under weigh, the commander of the shallop was ordered to bring to, to take Hilton in, and to leave him on shore any where; he died early next morning. Two brothers, William and John Walker, were equally ill used.

1791.

P. 29.

The general provisions of the crew were three pound of bread per week, and half a pound of salt beef per day. Water they had from the gun barrel, lashed to the topmast cross-trees, which every one was to take down for himself; he was himself punished for giving the barrel to another half way up.

Captain Colly, on board the Hare Snow, (as he heard from the people of the ship at different times) killed his carpenter, carpenter's mate, cook, and another man, and when the crew complained of these murders in Virginia, they were not redressed, but sent on board, or threatened with the cowskin, 39 lashes, the general punishment of Guinea seamen, who are supposed to offend. He has seen many ships, and always found the same treatment as in his own.

Captain Scrogham, of the Lilly Snow, instead of complying with the request of a sick man, who came aft for something to eat, ordered him to be immediately stripped, and seized to the main shrouds, with his feet clear of the deck; he then stripped him himself to the shirt, and flogged him several times with a cat, the man still hanging by his hands; when tired, he called on his officers to flog, but they refused,

P. 30.

1791. refused, on which he made the men slaves come off the main deck, and flog him until he was dead. The ship was then along-side the wharf of Charleston, South Carolina, where some of the crew coming on shore with the surgeon and mate, who was the captain's brother, reported the murder; the corpse being brought on shore next morning, Mr. Towne and many others, stopped and examined it, and had a coroner's inquest, which brought in a verdict of wilful murder, through the evidence of the surgeon and the captain's own brother. Lord Charles Montague, the Governor, sent officers on board to take, and confine the captain in gaol, which was accordingly done, but for want of evidence he was afterwards acquitted.

He has seen sailors apparently diseased and disabled, wandering about in the West Indies, with sore legs, which is common in Guineamen, emaciated; he has known them turned ashore by the captains, and lie upon the beach and the wharfs, where many have died, as he has seen. They are called wharfingers; none chuse to employ them for their wretched appearance, and thus they are left destitute of support. He was himself thus left on shore, without money or friends, at Charleston, South Carolina, with two others, who died. That these sailors came from the slave ships he knows, from having inquired; but without inquiry, they are easy to know, from the abject state of their appearance.

P. 31. He has repeatedly known Guinea sailors jump overboard, and even from ships he belonged to, on the Guinea coast, where sharks abounded. Some have succeeded in getting away, but on the offer of a large reward, which was afterwards charged against their wages, have been brought back by the natives, and immediately punished inhumanly with irons, collar and chain, and locked as before to the boat, to row on the duties of the ship during the captain's pleasure, with a very scanty allowance; he has never known

known sailors jump overboard from any other than 1791. Guinea ships.

From the ill treatment he has seen, and the loss of such numbers on board, both the ships he belonged to, and was acquainted with, it is not his opinion that the African trade is a nursery for seamen. He knows that the treatment of sailors in the West India trade, is not similar to that in the African; they are not so hard worked; they live and lie well, and are always taken great care of by the captains.

He assigns as a reason, for staving and burning the P. 32. seamens chests, that it was done to clear the ships for slaves; their contents, which were wearing apparel, if no bag was found to put them in, were often thrown overboard. The seamen's bedding, as well as their chests, was thrown upon the deck, and none suffered to lie below but the captain and the mate; if caught below to sleep, they were severely punished. This was the case of the ships he sailed in, both during the outward and Middle Passage.

The reason of his being left on shore at Charleston was, the fear of returning to captain Evans, after having been refused to be taken on board by a king's ship, to which he, and the two others, had applied for in vain; redress of grievances against captain Evans.

Being asked whether he meant to assert, that what he has said concerning West India punishments, was the general practice, or only, that he has himself seen the circumstances he has related, he answers, That he only meant to speak to such things as he was an eye-witness to, a number of times.

---

Witness examined—Mr. CLAXTON.

Mr. Claxton sailed in the Garland, Capt. Forbes, for Africa in 1788, as surgeon's mate, and there on

1791. the Bonny Coast commenced surgeon to the Young Hero brig, Capt. Molyneux.

P. 33. They had 250 slaves, of whom 132 died, chiefly of the flux; so crowded that they could only lie on their sides, if they did otherwise, it created quarrels among them: they stowed so close, that he could not go among them with his shoes without danger of hurting them. This crowded state aggravated their sufferings when ill, and tended to increase the disorder. It was impossible to treat them with the necessary accommodations. The steerage and boys room insufficient to receive the sick, so greatly did the disorder prevail, they were therefore obliged to place together those that were and those that were not diseased, and in consequence the disease and mortality spread more and more. The captain treated them with more tenderness than he has heard was usual, but the men were not humane. Some of the most diseased were obliged to be kept on deck, with a sail spread for them to lie on: this, in a little time, became nearly covered with blood and mucus,

P. 34. which involuntarily issued from them, and therefore the sailors, who had the disagreeable task of cleaning the sail, grew angry with the slaves, and used to beat them inhumanly with their hands, or with a cat. The slaves in consequence grew fearful of committing this involuntary action, and when they perceived they had done it, would immediately creep to the tubs, and there sit straining with such violence as to produce a prolapsus ani, which could not be cured. The same punishments were inflicted for the same cause on those who were not quite so ill.

Slaves, whose flux was accompanied with scurvy, and such œdematous swellings of the legs as made it pain to move at all, were made to dance, as they call it, and whipped with a cat if they were reluctant.

The slaves both when ill and well, were frequently forced to eat against their inclinations. Were whipped

ped with a cat if they refused. They used other means still worse, and too nauseous to mention.

The parts on which their shackles are fastened are often excoriated by the violent exercise they are forced to take, and of this they made many grievous complaints to him.

That slaves, when first brought on board, are commonly dejected, he shews by an instance of nine purchased on his passage from Bonny to the Isle of Bimbe, who were all very much dejected: one girl in paricular, clung to the neck of her seller, and though only ten or twelve years old, could not be comforted. She continued three or four days in that situation. The whole cargo appeared more or less afflicted on leaving their country.

Some had such an aversion to leaving their native places, that they threw themselves overboard, on an idea, that they should get back to their own country. The captain, in order to obviate this idea, cut off the heads of those who died, intimating to them, that if determined to go, they must return without their heads. The slaves were accordingly brought up to witness the operation, one man excepted, who was at length, against his will, forced up, seeing, when on deck, the carpenter standing with his hatchet up ready to strike off the head, with a violent exertion, he got loose, and flying to the place where the nettings had been unloosed, in order to empty the tubs, he darted himself overboard. The ship brought to, and a man was placed on the main chain to catch him, which he perceiving, dived under water, and rising again at a distance from the ship, made signs, which words cannot describe, expressive of his happiness in escaping. He then went down, and was seen no more. A strict watch over them was now kept, yet still they found means to elude all precaution. One of the tubs being set near where the nettings were lashed to the bulk-head, some of the slaves who had premeditated an escape, under pretence of easing themselves, contrived, while sitting

1791. on the tubs, to unloose the lashing, so that two actually threw themselves overboard, and were lost. A third was caught when three parts over.

Once imagined an insurrection was intended.—(See particulars.)

They sing, but not for their amusement. The capt. ordered them to sing, and they sang songs of sorrow. Their sickness, fear of being beaten, their hunger, and the memory of their country, &c. are the usual subjects; he could even mention their words.—They generally speak the same language, but there was one man who spoke a language unknown to all the rest, which made his condition very lamentable. He never took exercise but when compelled. His situation (he believes) produced a state of insanity, and he died mad.

P. 37. The slaves had not a sufficient quantity of food, owing to the extraordinary length of the passage, which was fifteen weeks. At first they did not like their food, and would not eat, but when used to it, they would have eaten near twice as much as allowed them.

A considerable number of slaves died in the early part of the voyage. After eight weeks at sea, they had only got three days sail from the place they had set out from. On examination, they did not find five weeks provision on board. Two nations being at war, they could not procure food from either. A Dutch ship supplied them with a little bread, and sufficient water. The food, notwithstanding the mortality, was so little, that if ten days more at sea, they should, as the captain and others said, have made the slaves walk the plank, that is, throw themselves overboard, or have eaten those slaves that died.

Fell in with the Hero, Wilson, which had lost, he thinks, 360 slaves by death, he is certain more than half of her cargo: learnt this from the surgeon. They had died mostly of the small-pox. Surgeon also told him, that when removed from one place to another, they left marks of their skin and blood upon

upon the deck, and that it was the moſt horrid ſight 1791.
he had ever ſeen.

They had on board about fifty boys and girls, but P. 38.
without parents or other relations; there was one
inſtance of two ſiſters.

At Rumbie the natives apprehenſive that they were
going to war with them. Did not come off the
coaſt for ſome time. Two canoes at length ventured,
and inquired if they were come to war or trade:
being told to trade, with apparent caution they attempted to come on board, and aſked the captain if
he had not two tongues. Captain aſſured them he
would not hurt them, on which one of them ventured on board, declaring if the captain killed him,
thoſe in the canoes would kill the ſhip's crew. The
reſt followed, and convinced that trade was the ſhip's
object, deſired that two might ſtay to examine the
goods; at the ſame time requiring two hoſtages,
which was complied with. He knew another inſtance
of the ſame kind.

Whilſt lying off the Batteau iſlands he heard of P. 39.
ſome Europeans being cut off a little before by the
natives, and this from a perſon cloſe by at the time,
ſo as to convince him of its truth. The terror of
the natives on ſeeing the veſſel, left they ſhould de-
ſtroy the iſland, afforded a proof of the fact. They
were in arms all night, which obliged the crew alſo
to arm.

The natives have a particular pleaſure in bartering
what they have for European goods of any kind.

The ſlaves were ſold in the Weſt Indies in an in-
fectious ſtate, and ſome that he believes were going
to die, and accordingly out of 14 of this deſcription
only 4 lived. He apprized the ſeller's agent of their
danger, and his anſwer was, it would be beſt to diſ-
poſe of them immediately; but ſuch as afforded
hopes of recovery, he deſired to have purchaſed for
himſelf, which was done.

Witneſs

Witnefs examined—Lieutenant SIMPSON.

1791.
P. 40.

Mr. John Simpfon, lieutenant of marines, went out in his Majefty's fhip the Adventure, and was on the coaft chiefly from Settra Crue to Accra, in 1788 and 1789. From what he faw, he believes the flave trade is the occafion of wars among the natives. From thofe of the windward coaft he underftood that the villages were always at war, and the black traders and others gave as a reafon for it, that the kings wanted flaves. If a trading canoe along-fide the fhip faw a larger canoe coming from a village they were at war with, they inftantly fled, fometimes without receiving the value of their goods. On inquiry, he learned their reafon to be, that if taken they would have been made flaves.

At C. Coaft Caftle, and other parts of the Gold Coaft, he heard repeatedly from the black traders the flave-trade made wars and palavers. Mr. Quakoo, chaplain at C. Coaft Caftle, informed him, that wars were made in the interior parts for that fole purpofe.

There are two crimes which feemed made on purpofe to procure flaves, adultery and the removal of fetiches. As to adultery, he was warned againft connecting himfelf with any woman not pointed out to him, for that the kings kept feveral who were fent out to allure the unwary, and that if found to be connected with thefe, he would be feized, and
P. 41. made to pay the price of a man-flave. As to fetiches, confifting of pieces of wood, old pitchers, kettles, &c. laid in the path-ways, he was warned to avoid difplacing them, for if he fhould, the natives, who were on the watch, would feize him, and as before, exact the price of a man-flave. Thefe baits are laid equally for natives as Europeans, but the former are better acquainted with the law, and confequently more circumfpect.

That

That the Europeans sometimes fraudulently carry off the natives on that part of the Windward Coast where there is no English factory, he believes. The repeated inquiries and disinclination of the natives to come on board the ship, till convinced she was not a slave-ship but a man of war, confirmed his opinion. When they were satisfied, they came on board readily, and in numbers.

The natives sometimes retaliate on the Europeans for such injuries. From Albion slave ship, at Settra Crue, learnt, that two chiefs being at variance, one of them seizing five of the other's party, had sold them to the Albion, for which that party seized three of the Albion's seamen, and would not release them without the slaves were returned.

Believes if the slave-trade were abolished, the indolence of the natives is not such as to prevent a commerce with them in their native produce; for to his repeated inquiries what they would do were it abolished, the black traders answered, they did not care, they should soon find some other trade to live by.

Convinced the treatment of seamen on board Guinea ships is very bad. When at Fort Apollonia, the Adventurer's boat was hailed by some seamen of the Fly Guineaman, begging to be taken in the man of war, for their treatment made their lives miserable. The boat was accordingly sent to the Fly by captain Parry, and one or two men brought on board. The Albion at another time, unable to avoid the Adventure, (which she tried to do) spoke to her, and the captain brought a seaman on board, whom he wished to leave, complaining he was riotous and disorderly. The man, in every instance, proved the reverse, and from him he learned that he had been half starved and cruelly beaten, both by captain and surgeon, who neglected the seamen, saying he was only paid for attending the slaves. Also learned their allowance was increased, and their treatment better, when in sight of a man of war; which was confirmed to him by

1791. by another man from a slave ship, who had been left behind with a shockingly ulcerated leg, and recited various instances of ill treatment he had received. The Adventure's boat having been sent to Anamaboo to the Spy Guineaman, returned with three men concealed under her sail, who fled from the slave ship, where they complained their treatment had made their lives miserable, beaten and half starved. Besides these there were other instances not remembered.

He never heard any complaints from West Indiamen, or other merchant ships: on the contrary, they wished to avoid a man of war; whereas if the Adventure had taken all who complained and offered themselves from the Guineamen, it must have greatly distressed the trade.

Has been in Barbadoes and Jamaica. When first at Bridgetown, his impression as to the treatment of slaves by their general appearance was trivial, they were natives, houshold servants, and their labour very light; but was impressed with the utmost horror on seeing the field slaves, some working in irons, under the lash of an inhuman negro driver, and their backs in general lacerated by his blows. He never saw a gang without one or two of these tormentors, snapping their whips, and threatening to make them feel them.

When at Cape Coast he saw slaves brought from the interior country, who were bought, he believes, by the then Governor, Mr. Norris. He examined them, and they appeared much concerned at coming into the hands of Europeans. Dejection and despair were strongly painted on their countenances. When at Bridgetown, he saw in the poor-house 18 or 20 seamen, from different slave ships. They related various instances of the barbarities of their late commanders, who had left them behind without any means of getting home. They seemed very much emaciated, and some of them ulcerated and in a condition in which they said neither West Indiamen nor

nor men of war would receive them. They had not only been beaten but nearly starved.

1791.

---

Witness examined—Doctor HARRISON, M.D.

He was above 10 years in Jamaica, from 1755 to 1765, and in America from 1765 to 1778: in the medical line in both.

P. 44.

He had every possible opportunity of knowing the situation of the slaves, seeing them in sickness, in health, and often punished. Has been on several sugar works in different parts of Jamaica, at all seasons, for two or three weeks, sometimes only a few days.

P. 45.

The field slaves have land enough for their support, had they time to cultivate it. They had no other food allowed on the estates he was on, except salt provisions at Christmas. New negroes were allowed a year's provisions, that is, till they had cultivated their land. They had only holidays and Sundays to work it, which was not sufficient, for they must work their grounds after dark. Saturday afternoon was not allowed them on any estate he knew. They looked much better than one could expect considering their severe treatment, but, in general very indifferent. Believes on all estates slaves often plunder other's provision grounds for support. In the first instance he knew of this, a slave was cut nearly all to pieces for it; but after he knew the estates better, he heard and knew it to be frequent.

P. 46.

Not the least attention is paid to the religious instruction of the slaves.

They were very badly lodged, and had no clothes but what they get by their own extra labour, except at Christmas, 2 frocks and 2 pair Osnaburgh trowsers for the men, and 2 coats and 2 shifts for the women, and some had 2 handkerchiefs for the head. In general, their masters give them no bedding at all.

Numb. 4. D Some

1791. Some new negroes have a few blankets, but not generally.

They were not married, nor encouraged to bring up families; the univerfal opinion being, that it was better and cheaper to buy than to breed. Humane overfeers allowed complaining pregnant women to retire from work; but he has feen them labouring in the field, when they feemed to have but a few weeks to go. They were generally worked as long as they were able.

P. 47. Does not think proper attention was paid to the children. Thinks the labour he faw pregnant women doing, muft, at fome times, have injured them.

Old flaves, paft labour, if they had no friends to give them neceffaries, muft have wanted every thing. Has feen a number of thofe objects on different eftates.

They ufally work from fun-rife to fun-fet; fometimes 13 or 14 hours, including 2 hours for dinner. In crop they work night and day, without ceffation.

Grafs-picking, when he faw it, was always extra work, and, on fome eftates, was a cruel hardfhip.

He has always feen the driver with a whip in his hand, and fometimes exercifing it feverely.

The plantation punifhments are fevere whippings, chaining them by the neck and leg, putting heavy iron boots on their legs, and iron pothooks on their necks, and putting them in the ftocks. He has often feen thefe punifhments inflicted with what he

P. 48. thought capricious or feverity. On an eftate, at Liguanea, he faw the overfeer whip feveral old, decrepid women very feverely, only for not picking cotton enough. Has often feen negroes in chains, half famifhed, and fcarcely able to walk, compelled to go into the field.

At Kingfton the negroes were flogged in the gaol, round the town, and on the wharfs. He thought the whippings in gaol, and round the town, too fevere to be inflicted on any of the human fpecies. He attended a man, who had been flogged in gaol,

five

five or six weeks before he was well. It was by his 1791.
master's order, for not coming when he was called.
He could lay two or three fingers in the wounds
from the whip. Knows of many similar instances.
The gaol and wharf whippings were by order of
the masters or mistresses, sometimes by the magistrate, but generally the magistrate orders whipping
round the town. The punishments of soldiers (which
he has very often witnessed) were generally mild,
compared to the whipping of slaves in gaol or round
the town.

Never knew slaves had any legal protection. The
only protection they had, was from their masters
against any indifferent person. Formed this opinion
from a multitude of unredressed violences. Among
others, a negro was flogged to death, by order of her
mistress, who stood by to see the punishment. The
negro died a few days after.—A negro man was put
on the picket so long as to cause a mortification of
his foot and hand, on suspicion of robbing his master,
a publick officer, of a sum of money, which it after-
terwards appeared, the master had taken himself.
Yet the master was privy to the punishment, and the
slave had no compensation. He was punished by
order of the master, who did not then chuse to make
it known that he himself had made use of the money.
Neither the mistress nor master were prosecuted for P. 49.
these acts.

A gentleman offended at a negro, named Monday,
for mimicking him, bought him. After buying
him, he ordered him to be flogged; the consequence
was, that Monday cut his own throat.

He thinks the abilities of the negroes equal to our P. 50.
own, and their dispositions much the same. The
free negroes are as industrious as the whites, and he
thinks slavery causes the unwillingness of the others.
In general, slaves are not so good mechanicks as
whites, which he attributes to the same cause. Many
free negroes are very good mechanicks.

He

1791. He has often heard slaves lament their unfortunate situation. A negro man once asked him, whether the old gentlemen of the country had not much to answer for, for not teaching them Christianity, and for treating them so cruelly as they did, not allowing them to obtain their own freedom when they merited it.

A negro boy of his, detested slavery so much, that he refused all support, which brought on a dropsy that killed him. Another negro, who had been a great man in his own country, refused to work for any white man, and being therefore punished by the overseer, desired him to tell his master, that he would be a slave to no man. His master ordered him to be removed to another estate. His hands were tied behind him, and in going over a bridge he jumped into the water, and appeared no more. These are two facts of Dr. Harrison's own knowledge, out of a great many which he cannot now recollect.

P. 51.   A slave of his told him she had been kidnapped, by being put in a bag. A man who was kidnapped told him he was a great many months in travelling to the sea, that there was a traffick for slaves to sell to the whites, even beyond his country, and that kidnapping was common there.

Sales of the slaves of distressed proprietors were frequent over all the island, when families were often separated. He bought a negro woman and child out of compassion, that she might not be taken from her husband. When negroes are seized for debt, the marshal takes them as he can find them, which generally leaves a part of the family on the estate: though when he chances to seize a whole family, he has known them put all up in one lot; but generally part only of a family was so seized.

He has heard several overseers say, the plough would save a great deal of negro-labour, and lament it was not used.

P. 52.   General opinion favoured those overseers who made most sugar, with little or no respect to lenity; but he
knew

knew one overseer, remarkable for humanity, who made more sugar with fewer hands than others did with more. In his opinion, were slaves more encouraged and more humanely treated, they would do much more work.

Slaves were certainly worse treated when their masters were embarrassed; for their distresses obliged them to work their slaves beyond their strength, to make sugars to pay their debts.

The planter's residence was of the greatest advantage to his slaves. They were always the better used for it in every respect. It was the general opinion, that the conduct of attornies was often inconsistent with the interest of non-residents, and in many cases very injurious to them.

It is well known there, that negro women have no security against violation, unless their masters choose to protect them.

He never thought free negroes sufficiently protected against injuries from whites; because their oaths were not allowed, except in cases of debt.

In the outskirts of Kingston, he has always seen several emaciated and diseased sailors, who were left on shore by masters of Guineamen.

The Jamaica slaves were generally treated very ill, and only individuals treated them well. In South Carolina, the slaves were in general treated very well, and only individuals treated them ill. In S. Carolina, they were well fed, well clothed, less worked, and never severely whipped. In Jamaica they were badly fed, indifferently clothed, hard worked, and severely whipped. In S. Carolina, the negroes laboured by task-work, which was often finished by three or four P. M. which enabled them to work their grounds, and to hunt and fish for themselves. He never saw a driver with a whip, for generally there was no occasion for it, as they worked by task.

In Doctor Harrison's opinion, as a medical man, the climate of Jamaica is more favourable to the increase of slaves than that of Carolina, notwithstanding

1791. ing which disadvantage, Carolina increased in slaves, while those in Jamaica decreased. Sufficient attention was not paid to the rearing of negro children even in Carolina, because they were of opinion it was cheaper to buy new negroes than to rear children.

---

Witness Examined,——Doctor Jackson, Physician, Stockton-upon-Tees.

P. 54. Went to Jamaica in 1774, resided there four years, chiefly at Savannah-la-Mar, where he practised medicine; his profession led him daily, eight, ten, or more miles into the country; has occasionally been, for a short time, at most parts of the island.

On his arrival found the condition of negroes hard, and their treatment cruel.

First thing that shocked him was, a creole lady (of some consequence) superintending the punishment of her slaves, male and female; ordering the number of lashes, and with her own hands flogging the negro driver, if he did not punish properly.

Though this the only instance he saw, believes it not uncommon for women of rank thus to superintend punishments of their slaves (p. 55): they were not worse received in society for it; it might be said, " such a one is a termagant," but she was not for that less respected; it was indeed thought necessary for an industrious wife to be rigid in the punishment of her slaves.

The punishment seemed to him very severe, blood flowed at every stroke, and if the allotted quantum could not, without danger to life, be given at once, the negro was put into the stocks for some days, and when a little recruited, received the rest of his flogging.

As to mode of punishing, in some cases the offender was tied and stood upright; in others more severe, was stretched between four stakes, so tight that he could

could not shrink or move; the whip, like what our waggoners use, was thrown at the distance of three or four paces, which of course greatly increased the weight of the lashes: for women too far advanced in pregnancy to be stretched flat on the ground, a hole was dug in the earth to receive their bellies; this last he never saw, but is as certain of it, as one can be, of a fact he has not seen.

Thinks severe whippings sometimes occasion slave's death: recollects a negro dying under the lash, or very soon after; it was generally said the negro was killed by it; no attempt to bring the person to justice: people said it was an unfortunate thing; were surprized the man was not more cautious, as it was not the first thing of the kind that had happened to him; but chiefly dwelt upon the proprietor's loss.

Has seen slaves with a leg cut off, for running away, he was told: law there allows owners to do so. Has heard of negroes castrated for trespass on overseer's black mistress, of which act no account was taken.

Never knew a negro complain to a magistrate of his master: it was understood he could not have legal redress, or if so, negroes were ignorant of it.

In general, no attention paid to the religious instruction of slaves. In the district where he lived, the church was never opened but for a company of soldiers quartered there; nor to introduce marriage among them. Negro men cohabited where they pleased. White men had unrestrained intercourse with plantation females.

Negroes were generally esteemed a species of inferiour beings, whom the right of purchase gave the owner a power of using at his will.

After much knowledge of them, he could not perceive them at all inferiour to unlettered white men in capacity. As to disposition, they possess many amiable qualities. They are charitable to all in distress; parents strongly attached to their children; and many have given strongest proofs of gratitude and

1791. and attachment to their masters. To mention one instance of this; during the American war, in the action at the Cow Pan, a negro who was attached to him, had escaped with the fugitives of the army to a distance of two or three miles; when, hearing from some soldiers that his master had been seen unhorsed, he returned to the field to search for him, and fell into the hands of the enemy.

They often complain they are an oppressed people; that they suffer in this world, but expect happiness in the next, whilst they denounce the vengeance of God on the white men their oppressors: if you speak to them of future punishments they say, " Why " should a poor negro be punished: he does no " wrong; fiery cauldrons, and such things, are re- " served for white people, as punishments for the op- " pression of slaves."

P. 58. Were slaves well used he cannot conceive why they should not keep up their numbers: they are naturally prolifick, and the islands are in general congenial to their constitutions.

The buying system was generally preferred. Supposes, they are frequently lost, from mothers being forced to work while nurses, as at other times, and so becoming indifferent to rearing their children; not that they want parental affection, but hard usage, and the idea of rearing children subject to cruel treatment, leads them to wish their offspring may fail. Has heard them wish them dead, or that they had never been born, rather than be forced to see them daily punished: hence also they are supposed to procure abortion, to which motive may be added, a fear in such as are handsome, to diminish their charms in the eyes of white men.

Slaves whose owners are in embarrassed circumstances are ill clothed, hard worked, and poorly fed.

P. 59. In general, he considers the hardship of negro field labour to be more in the mode, than in the quantity done. A white man in England would, doubtless, though not superiour in strength, do with ease the

work

work of three negroes in the West Indies; because the slave seeing no end to his labour, stands over the work, and only throws the hoe to avoid the lash, he appears to work without actually working.

1791.

P. 59.

A planter's interest well understood, would doubtless prevent his wearing out his slaves by excessive labour; but, there are few in circumstances to attend to this: they look to the immediate returns of the season only; the other is a view too distant for the most of them.

The slaves of resident owners are generally better satisfied than those of absentees.

The criterion of a manager's merit seemed to be the increasing the number of hhds of sugar; keeping up the stock of slaves by breeding, was not the thing principally looked to.

Managers have almost always slaves of their own.

Field slaves have land given them, sufficient if in good culture, for their subsistence, and something over to carry to market. Many are allowed to keep a breeding sow, or some poultry; in general they have no other property.

P. 60.

As a medical man, is of opinion that white artificers may, and actually do, work at their trade in the West Indies; that Europeans are, with proper caution, equal to the ordinary field labour, without any material injury to health; he knows from personal experience, they may safely walk 20, 30, or more miles a day.

The mortality among the troops may be ascribed more to want of discipline, encampments on unhealthy spots, immoderate use of spirituous liquors, and perhaps defects in the medical department, than to climate.

Did not perceive any great defect in the medical treatment of slaves, every estate being provided with a medical person who visits the negro hospital at stated times in the week, and in extraordinary cases gives immediate attendance when called.

P. 61.

Numb. 4.   E   The

1791. The manager vifiting the fick along with the furgeon, from his firft entering as a book-keeper, becomes equal to the treatment of flight complaints: in general there is a flave on each eftate who can let blood, and do other common things.

Superanuated flaves who have no relations, are, he believes, often placed at the corner of a corn field, and have a few plantanes weekly to keep them from dying with hunger; fuch of them as he has feen, were, dirty and emaciated to the laft degree.

What flaves have occafion to carry, they bear on their heads, and can carry great weight in this way.

Runaways are brought back by the Maroons.

P. 62. Has been in America: joined his regiment (71ft) in 1778, at York Ifland, accompanied it to Savannah; traverfed all the fouthern provinces with the army to York-Town, Virginia; on its furrender, paffed through Maryland, Pennfylvania, and Jerfey, to New-York. The negroes of America appeared to great advantage compared with thofe of Jamaica; their ideas were more expanded, and their bodily exertions greater.

Thrice more domefticks are kept in Jamaica than would be in England for the fame work.

---

Witnefs Examined,—Capt. ROBERT ROSS.

P. 63. Captain Robert Rofs was from 1762 to 1786 in Jamaica. For three years and a half he was book-keeper then on Mr. Dawkin's eftate; he was in fucceffion overfeer on Mr. Morant's, Lord Dudley's, Dr. Rofs's, and Mr. M'Lellan's; he then commanded a company of rangers for fix years; settled a property of his own in 1775; refided on it from 1781 to 1786, when he came home.

Firft impreffion on feeing the treatment of flaves was, that they were cruelly treated, and that they might

might do their masters work with less severity, and 1791. without the whip.

Has seen a negro woman flogged with ebony bushes, so that the skin of her back was taken off down to her heels; she was then turned round and flogged from her breast down to her waist, and in consequence he saw her afterwards walking upon all-four, and unable to get up. He also saw a negro man tied up by the wrists, naked, picketted and flogged with two whips; driver stopped for some minutes and then began again. The punishment might last an hour and a half, and was not by order of a magistrate, but privately by the overseer. At Kingston saw a negro flogged by his master with a two inch rope, from his neck to the waistband, so that his back and body rose in lumps as big as a man's finger. He has seen several so severely flogged as to be disabled from working for days, and even weeks after.

Was acquainted with a master who cut off the P. 64. ears of a slave running away, and acknowledged the fact to him. Saw the slave both before and after; and several others he has also seen with one ear cut off. He has known often severity of punishment, with bad care afterwards, occasion the death of negroes.

Law limits number of lashes to be given in private punishment to 39, but has known negroes receive 200 at a time by order of overseers, where the law would only give 39. Never knew an overseer punished for inflicting them.

Is sure they were inflicted by overseers for crimes which the law upon conviction would not have punished with death.

It is understood if a slave applied to a magistrate he could get redress for excessive punishment, or wanton cruelty on the part of his master or other white person. In towns he has frequently known them apply, but not in the country.

1791.   General mode of punishing slaves in the towns is by sending them to wharfs or workhouses, where they P. 65. are punished at the will of their owners. In towns where the magistrate was nigh at hand, understands they gave redress to the slaves who applied as before for it.

For some years he resided near the town, but not in any of them, and in that period he has known many instances of severity. Numbers carried to the wharfs at various times.

Instances of extreme severity already stated were all at that time practised in the country. Generality of the field-negroes in every place were more or less marked with the whip.

Has known many negroes on their first arrival, finding themselves to be slaves, destroy themselves; and some also on seeing their fellow-creatures punished. They often run away too for fear of the whip, and of being flogged for neglect of duty. The overseers are frequently turned out of place for overwhipping, when complaint is made to the master or magistrate, and therefore the overseers are now more lenient in their punishments than formerly.

Overseers also are more attentive now to keeping up the stock of slaves by breeding than formerly. P. 66. Except Lord Dudley's estate, he knows of none which were not obliged to buy slaves.

There has been a considerable increase of slaves on the estate of Messrs. Muir and Atkinson, and on Mr. Malcolm's estate, where the overseers have taken great care of the slaves both old and young, and studied constantly to promote their master's interest. These the only instances of the kind he knows.

A negro can have no redress for punishment from a magistrate. What induced him to say that a slave could obtain legal redress was, that a negro who was flogged at the wharf at Kingston, and afterwards was so beaten about the head, that his eye was knocked out, and lay upon his cheek, said that he would go shew his eye to Mr. French, who kept a negro wench,

and

and had therefore a great attachment to slaves; but as to having redress from Mr. French as a magistrate, he never understood he had any.

Does not know if the person who beat out the slave's eye was his owner or only one hired by him. A dozen white persons were present at the time. Does not know that the man was ever called to an account for it.

There is a law in Jamaica forbidding owners at one time and for one crime, to give more than 39 lashes to a slave, and if sufficient evidence were produced he has no doubt that the transgressor might be called to an account by a magistrate, but the evidence of a negro is not good against a white man.

He has seen overseers give above 200 lashes, and afterwards flog slaves about the head and shoulders with a cow skin; he never heard of one being called to account for it before a magistrate.

He saw Mr. John Shackle a magistrate in Jamaica flog a negro three times in one day; at breakfast time; dinner time; and at six in the evening. The negro was in the stocks between the floggings. No publick notice was taken of it.

As to persons commonly reputed to have murdered negroes——

\* \* \* \* \* \* \*
\* \* \* \* \* \* \*
\* \* \* \* \* \* \*

he had hanged a negro on a post close to his house, and in three years destroyed 40 out of 60 by severity.

\* \* \* \* \* \* \*
\* \* \* \* \* \* \*
\* \* \* \* \* \* \*

He has known slaves severely punished, then put into the stocks, a cattle chain of 60 lb. or 70 lb. weight put on them, and a large collar about their necks, and a weight of 56 lb. fastened to the chain when they were drove afield. They often die in a few days of their severe punishments, for having but little food,

1791. food, and little care, to keep the fores clear after the whipping, their death is often the confequence.

Has known negroes flogged as unwilling to work, who were in fact fick and unable to work, they could not work for many weeks after, and the caufe was often want of food.

P. 69. Where there are many negroes the work muft be lighter, but it depends on the lenity of overfeers.

Bought 59 African negroes, but was never forced to buy any one he did not like, with a view of not feparating relatives.

---

Witnefs Examined,—Mr. HENRY COOR, of Settle, Yorkfhire, Gent.

P. 69. Was in Jamaica 15 years, ending 1774, as a millwright, chiefly in Weftmoreland, but did bufinefs in three other parifhes.

After he had been near 18 months there, he had 16 or 20 flaves under his direction. Had about 20 of his own, whom he made mill-wrights and car-
P. 70. penters, among Mr. Beckford's negroes. After they learnt their bufinefs, he became partner with one David Thomas, who fuperintended his Mr. (Coor's) flaves, with a few of his own.

Had great opportunities of obferving field-negroes' treatment: was on feveral eftates daily, and had people conftantly working there. Generally breakfafted, and often dined with overfeers, and faw all their actions as much as any man poffibly could. Overfeers fetting flaves to work, in the morning, was moftly attended with loud peels of whipping. Obferved when overfeers came early to the field, flaves who came afterwards were fure of whipping over the clothes. Breeches for the men, and petticoats for the women, generally of coarfe linen. In this cafe, a few fteps before they join the gang, they throw down the hoe, clap both hands on their heads,

and

and patiently take 10 to 15, or 20 lashes: but those
who could not stand without shrinking, were sure to
be stretched on the ground, or held by four of their
fellows, till they had received their compliment.
This slight whipping, as it is generally called, is carried on, more or less, all day. In a gang of about 100,
are generally four or five black drivers, with each a
whip; and in most fields, one or two white drivers who
have only sticks to lean on, while they stand along
the line, and direct the black drivers to touch up those
they think remiss. About eight o'clock the overseer goes to breakfast, and if he has any criminals at
home, he orders a black driver to follow him; for
it is then usual to take such out of the stocks, and flog
them before the overseer's house. The method generally is this: the delinquent is stripped and tied on
a ladder, his legs to the sides, and his arms above
his head, and, sometimes a rope is tied round his
middle. The driver whips him on the bare skin, and
if the overseer thinks he does not lay it on hard
enough, he sometimes knocks him down, with his
own hand, or makes him change places with the delinquent, and be severely whipped. Has known
many receive on the ladder, from 100 to 150 lashes,
and some two cool hundreds, as they are generally
called. Has known many returned to confinement,
and, in 1, 2, or three days, brought to the ladder,
and receive the same complement, or thereabouts,
as before. They seldom take them off the ladder,
until all the skin, from the hams to the small of the
back, appears only raw flesh and blood, and then
they wash the parts with salt pickle. This appeared
to him, from the convulsions it occasioned, more
cruel than the whipping; but was done to prevent
mortification. Has known many, after such whipping, sent to the field, under a guard, and worked
all day, with no food but what their friends might
give them, out of their own poor pittance. He has
known them returned to the stocks at night, and
worked next day, successively. This cruel whipping,

1791.

1791. ping, hard working, and ſtarving, has, to his knowledge, made many commit ſuicide. Remembers 14 ſlaves, who, from bad treatment, rebelled on a Sunday, ran into the woods, and all cut their throats together. He could relate ſeveral other inſtances, (p. 74.) He has been often a juryman in ſuch caſes, and remembers no other verdict given that "Felo " de ſe," and except once, never knew it oppoſed, and that was a ſlave on William's Field eſtate, who was whipped by order of the overſeer, and afterwards beaten by him moſt inhumanly with a ſtaff over his head. The negro told him he had broke his arm, which he held up to ward off the blow;

P. 72. yet he kept on beating him, till the man ſprang off, and next morning was found hanging to a tree. An eye-witneſs declared, in evidence, he believed the negro's arm was broke, and that this cruel treatment made him kill himſelf. A doctor agreed the arm was much ſwelled, but could not ſay it was broke. After a long canvas, the verdict was, as uſual, ſelf murder. The Gold Coaſt negroes, when driven to deſpair, by harſh uſage, always cut their throats; and thoſe of the moſt inland country, moſtly hang themſelves.

Once, when dining with an overſeer, an old woman, who had run away a few days, was brought home, with her hands tied behind. After dinner, the overſeer, with a clerk, named Bakewell, took the woman, thus tied, to the hot houſe, a place for the ſick, and where the ſtocks are in one of the rooms. Mr. Coor went to work in the mill about 100 yards off, and hearing a moſt diſtreſsful cry from that houſe, he aſked his men, who, and what it was, they ſaid they thought it was old Quaſheba. About 5 o'clock the noiſe ceaſed, and about the time he was leaving work, Bakewell came to him, apparently in great ſpirits, and ſaid, "Well, Mr. Coor, old Qua-
" ſheba is dead. We took her to the ſtocks room;
" the overſeer threw a rope over the beam; I was
" jack ketch, and hauled her up, till her feet was
" off

" off the ground. The overseer locked the door,
" and took the key with him, until I now returned
" with a slave into the stocks, and found her dead."
Mr. C. said, " You have killed her; I heard her
" cry all the afternoon." He answered, " D—n
" her for an old b—h, she was good for nothing,
" what signifies killing such an old woman as her."
Mr. C. said, " Bakewell, you shock me," and left
him. The next morning, his men told him, they
had helped to bury her; so here it rested, till another affair brought it on the carpet The poultry keeper, a girl about 11 or 12 years of age, brought the overseer a young duck that had died, to clear herself of having killed it; that not satisfying him, he beat her very severely himself, and then forced her to eat up the duck guts, feathers and all, threatening her with 5 times as much beating, if she did not. The girl thinking more would kill her, tore and eat every bit of it. In the evening she complained to her mother, who went, at night, and complained to Mr. Beckford's attorney, of that and other cruelties of the overseer; and for one, the story of old Quasheba, referring for proof of all, to Mr. Coor, who was all the time on the estate. The attorney sent for him, Mr. C. to wait on him next morning, which he did, and told him old Quasheba's story, as related. He was very angry at him, asking him how he could see his master's slaves murdered so, without telling him (the attorney) of it. He said it was not his business to tell him, but such cruelties were so common on the estates, that he had thought no more of it. The overseer suffered no legal punishment. The attorney appeared very angry with him, at the time, but all was settled, and he went on as usual for about half a year, when he was dismissed, Mr. C. cannot exactly say for what.

He thought the treatment by the overseers in general, very severe. He did not think this severity necessary, for many substantial reasons he could give.

1791.
P. 73.

P. 73.

P. 74.

1791. give. He proved it himself from ocular demonstration.

P. 87. One George White, kept up so sharp a discipline over a gang of slaves, which fell under his (Coor's) care afterwards, that he generally flogged them very severely for the smallest faults, so that he reduced them both in their persons and faculties. They were never without sores, from his cruelty. The floggings quite disabled them from using the little leisure they had in working their grounds, which was their chief support. Hence they became poor both in body and property, and subject to theft, which he mostly attributed to want; for their sores from beating made them unwilling to stir, when at leisure. When these slaves came under him (Mr. Coor) he used them kindly, excused small faults, promised rewards for good behaviour; such as allowing them time to work their grounds. His first care was to see them make a good use of this time; but after he found their grounds thriving, he had little more to do, and in a few months, from a poor, scabbed, ill-looking, dispirited gang, they became fat, sleek, lively, and worked as chearfully as ever he saw workmen in England; and he could have done more work with them, in one-third less time, than White could have done with all the force of the whip. Good treatment changed their very morals: he could have trusted them with any thing. Being a lieutenant, he was once ordered out after outlaws, by the colonel, who gave him leave to chuse a serjeant's guard of the white militia; he told the colonel, if he pleased he (Mr. Coor) would arm his slaves for that duty, which he did, and found as much fidelity in them, as he could have expected in Englishmen. They pitched their tents round his, saying, they would all

P. 88. die, sooner than he should be hurt. Those slaves were under his care 13½ years, during which he never flogged one of them. They would have been more ashamed of a small tap, with a supple jack from his hand, than of 100 lashes from their former master. They

They were grateful in the higheſt degree. On Sunday, they often would bring him a fowl, as a preſent, and never killed a hog, but they ſaved ſome choice part for him. He could mention a variety of other inſtances of their gratitude and affection to him.

An eſtate, at which he did buſineſs at times, in his neighbourhood, belonging to a Mr. Dunn, was a ſmall one when he firſt went there, not from want of land, but of negroes. It then made about 50 hhds. of ſugar. He worked his ſlaves moderately, and his wife took great care of the ſick, lying-in women and children, who ſeemed to ſwarm on this eſtate, and he never heard any complaint of the locked jaw there. To Mr. C's knowledge, in a few years, this eſtate doubled its produce, and before he, Mr. C. left Jamaica, he had ſettled another thriving eſtate, under his eldeſt ſon, which then made about 60 hhds. and all, to the beſt of his knowledge, had ariſen out of the ſmall ſtock of ſlaves before-mentioned, except ſix new negroes bought. He could not but have known it, had more been bought. A neighbouring eſtate to this, whoſe ſituation was far ſuperior for health and eaſe in getting proviſions, yet perpetually decreaſed in ſlaves, owing, in his, and other peoples opinions, to inhuman treatment. The owner, who managed it himſelf, very often, to Mr. C's knowledge, bought 20, 30, or 40 new ſlaves at a lot, and, in about 10 or 11 years, the eſtate was very much reduced, both in produce and negroes; ſo that from good circumſtances, his credit was in that time reduced to a very low ebb, which, he verily believes, aroſe from ill-treating his ſlaves. It would be to no purpoſe to tell the particulars. Some inſtances of his capricious cruelties are too bad to relate.

He has always thought the rearing of children well worth the planter's notice; but ſo inattentive did he always find them to it, that he has heard overſeers ſay, they would far rather the children ſhould die than live; nor did he ever ſee any proper preparation for the reception of them. The ſides of the huts

1791.  huts they are born in, are no more defence againſt the cold night damps, than one of our paſture hedges. Bedding they have none, but a board or baſs mat. When the child is born, the midwife aſks the overſeer for ſomething for the woman; a bottle of rum,

P. 90. and 2 or 3 pound of ſalt beef, which does well enough, for they ſeldom fail to recover. But they never put the infant to the mother's breaſt, till 8 days be over, for which time a woman out of the field nurſes it, who probably has a child 2, 3, or 4 months old. Here he ſubmits to medical men, what effect the milk of a woman, hardly wrought and poorly fed, under a vertical ſun, would have on a tender infant. They moſtly die convulſed, generally about the 8th day. This want of care is more lamentable, not only from humanity, but intereſt, for if they ſurvive the 8th day, they moſtly do well, and he very ſeldom remembered any dying, from the 8th day to the 8th year. What convinces him farther it is for want of care, is, becauſe, where they have warm houſes, kind treatment, and the child ſet to the mother's breaſt, he very ſeldom knew any die; and it was neither labour nor expence to raiſe them, after the fatal 8th day was over. It is his firm opinion, that with kind and judicious treatment of the infants, the ſlaves in Jamaica will increaſe, without any importations from Africa.

It was more overſeers object to work ſlaves out, and truſt for African ſupplies, than work them moderately, and keep them up by breeding; for he has heard many ſay, "I have made my employer 20, 30, "or 40 more hhds. per year than my predeceſſors, "and though I have killed 30 or 40 negroes per "year more, yet the produce has been more than "adequate to the loſs."

P. 91. The ſlaves can expect no redreſs, but from the attorney. Many of them have commiſſions on the produce, and, if they give ear to the ſlaves complaints, the overſeer will tell them he will leave the eſtate. If he makes great crops, Mr. C. has often

obſerved

observed the attorney wink at his preſſing the ſlaves to perform more work than human nature could bear.

Moſt of the field ſlaves are marked with the whip, not only Africans, but creoles. Has known many very well diſpoſed creole negroes, that have had wheals from their hams up to the ſmall of their backs; but this is nothing thought of, as it is ſo common.

It is natural to think that ſlaves will ſuffer from their maſter's being in debt; for they are generally hard worked, and ill clothed and fed. He could mention, as inſtances, 2 or 3 neighbouring eſtates.

Domeſticks are very often treated ill, without redreſs, from their maſter's caprice. He has heard many ſay, they would rather be under the field hardſhip, than in the houſe. He boarded about 6 months with a doctor, who uſed his field-ſlaves ill, but he daily ſaw how his domeſticks were treated. He made no more of knocking down his waiting-boy, than if he had been a piece of wood, for what Mr. C. thought no fault at all. Two houſe-wenches were treated the ſame way. One of them having broken a plate, or ſpilt a cup of tea, he nailed her ear to a poſt. Mr. C. remonſtrated in vain. They went to bed and left her there; in the morning ſhe was gone, having torn the head of the nail through her ear. She was ſoon brought back, and when he came to breakfaſt, he found ſhe had been very ſeverely whipped by the doctor, who, in his fury, clipt both her ears off cloſe to her head, with a pair of large ſciſſars, and ſhe was ſet to pick ſeeds out of cotton, among 3 or 4 more, emaciated by his cruelties, until they were fit for nothing elſe. This girl never applied for legal redreſs. The negroes generally thought they could have no redreſs, but from their maſters or attornies. He believes no more notice was taken of the deed, than if he had cut off his dog's ears. Thinks ſome magiſtrates could hardly miſs knowing it; for ſeveral viſited at the doctors. The girl waited at table with her ears off.

P. 91.

He

1791.   He never knew a field slave have more than a breeding sow and a few poultry, and thinks it impossible for such to get any property. Never knew even tradesmen possess any thing, though they have more opportunities of accumulating than a field-slave.

P. 93.   Slaves were forced to carry from their grounds, whatever they could spare from the bread of their family, to buy salt provisions for all the week. One negro would carry about 4 bits worth, more or less, according to the varying market price, which they lay out in eatables or clothes; for, in general, they had only 5 yards of cloth, worth about seven-pence, or seven-pence half-penny per yard.

Slaves were fed many ways, but the most common was, depending on their little grounds. The poorer, who never had spirits or ability to cultivate them, depended on some one of the plantation slaves, for whom they worked all the little time they were allowed. Does not speak of new negroes; for they are generally distributed to the plantation slaves, who have the best grounds, under whom they work all the little time they are excused from their master's business. They have land, which overseers think they should bring into some order, while under the said negroes; but too often, from quarrels with the master slaves, they are turned out of doors before their grounds are in perfection, and obliged to steal

P. 94.   or beg. Thinks this the greatest reason why there are so many bad slaves. Slaves land, wherever he has been, is quite sufficient; but they have not time to work it.

Dead mules, horses, cows, &c. were all burnt, under inspection of a white man. Had they been buried, the negroes would have dug them up in the night, to eat them through hunger. It was generally said to be done, to prevent the negroes from eating them, lest it should breed disorders.

On Shrewsbury estate, the overseer sent for a slave, and in talking with him, he hastily struck him on the

the head with a small hanger, and gave him two stabs about the waist. The slave said, "Overseer, you have killed me." He pushed him out of the piazza. The slave went home and died that night. He was buried, and no more said about it. Mr. C's house was on this estate, near the overseer's house. About 6 months after, the overseer moved thence, to Anchovie-Bottom estate, why, Mr. C. cannot tell; but knows it was not for this. This was about 1770. He was called a very valuable overseer, as he worked the slaves hard, and made great crops of sugar. It was generally believed he had killed 2 more at Anchovie-Bottom; as a proof of this,—it being whispered, among the neighbours, that these two made three slaves he had killed, and it being looked upon then, that the killing of three slaves was capital, he thought proper to go privately away, and Mr. C. never heard more of him. A. Mr. Foot, (an inferior attorney under Mr. Herring) Mr. C. is clear, knew the particulars of the first-mentioned murder, having often talked with him on that, and many similar subjects; but knows not, if Mr. Foot told it to Mr. Herring. He never heard of the least attempt to bring the overseer to justice; but has heard Mr. Foot say, he was a very good overseer, but a d——d wicked dog when drunk. Mr. C. is pretty clear he was drunk when he did that deed.

The slaves allowed food, in Jamaica, was mostly herrings. He has known about 2 barrels among 100, 150, or 160 slaves, at a time; about once a month or six weeks; and he is clear, that every common man's share, was very seldom above 7 or 8 herrings. The field-negroes had no other allowance; and sometimes he has seen herrings so rotten, as to have been measured out, all mashed up like a porridge.

He bought 6 boys and 2 girls from a Guinea ship. He took a slave with him to interpret, and who asked the slaves he bought, if they had had the yaws. They all told him they had, their skin being then

very

1791. very clean and black; but in 6 weeks or two months, they all broke out violently with the yaws. They then spoke a little English, and he asked them, if they had not the yaws in their country. They said yes; but when they came near buccra country, the buccra on board rubbed them with something that made their skin clean. He has known several Guineamen in port 2 or 3 weeks, before declaring sale, or allowing any inhabitant to go on board (which they never allow, until they have declared sale) and it was always reported, that this delay was to get the slaves in proper trim for sale.

P. 96.

Jobbing gangs were increasing much when he left Jamaica. Every overseer or white man, who had money or credit, bought new negroes to job them out. He could have had £14 per cent. for his money, in that way, and have had it insured; but masters that work them themselves in that way, make much more.

Epidemicks are much more fatal to poor and ill fed, than to well fed, hearty slaves. But one fatal epidemick (a flux) prevailed while he was there. It attacked all ranks of whites and blacks; and it was generally poor, ill fed negroes, that died of it. Few well fed negroes died of it, and not one white person.

On some estates, the negroes provision grounds are close at hand; on others tolerably near; but he knows several, where they were 4 or five miles off.

Always observed negroes, who had grounds in tolerable order, work with great pleasure; but those who were turned into them only covered with woods and bushes, had very ill heart to begin upon them, and generally were obliged to spend that time they should have laid out upon their grounds, in working under some other negro, for present support.

P. 97.

Has often known the different offices of overseer, doctor and attorney, on an estate, filled by the same person.

Runaway

Runaway slaves never take refuge among the Maroons; for these are a check on them. They have £3 per head for taking them, and a shilling for every mile they bring them.

On one estate, most of the slaves were christened and instructed by a person sent from Europe, and they were always the best disposed slaves in that neighbourhood; but on no other estates did he ever hear such a thing named. Of a number of slaves taken from Guadaloupe, one family was bought by a neighbour of his, and the doctor told him, the father of that family had prayers in his house night and morning. He does not remember the estate, where the slaves were instructed, buying any new slaves, and they were always very strong handed. He was very well acquainted with the whole gang, as he took care of their mills, &c. for most of the time he was there.

Promiscuous intercourse was very common, both among the slaves, and between the white men and negro women. There was no restriction. It was the greatest disgrace for a white man, not to cohabit with some woman or other. No attempts were made to induce the men slaves to restrict themselves to one woman. It was not considered any way disadvantageous to an estate, for the men to have 1, 2, 3, or 4 wives, according as they could maintain them with the produce of their little spots of ground. The negroes wives were not at all secure from the attempts of the overseer or book-keepers; for though a man might know of his wife having lain with the overseer or book-keeper, he dared not resent it, either to her or to them, for if he did, he would be sure of a very smart flogging for it, though probably on some other pretext.

In Boston, Rhode-Island, New-York, New-Jerseys, and Pennsylvania, the slaves are treated much like farmers servants in England, and he saw them carry on their masters business just in the same way. Where a master had 3, 4, or more slaves, one of them

1791. them was mostly a leading man. He has often conversed with such head man on farming, ploughing, &c. and always found him very intelligent.

Thinks a great deal of his evidence has tended to shew, that the behaviour of the negroes generally correspond with their treatment.

At his first going to the island, a common flogging would put him in a tremble, so that he did not feel right for the rest of the day; but by degres it became so habitual, that he thought no more of seeing a black man's head cut off, than he should now think of a butcher cutting off the head of a calf.

---

Witness examined—JOHN GILES,

Near Hay, Brecknockshire,—Farmer.

P. 74. Was in Montserrat from 1757 to 1762; in Grandterre 1763; in Grenada 1764, and part 1765; in N. America rest of 1765; in St. Croix from 1766 to 1772; in England 1773; in St. Croix 1774 to 1778.

His first impression in the West Indies was, that slaves were cruelly treated, severely punished for trifling offences, and not sufficiently fed.

P. 75. He arrived in crop time; there was then no food allowed, except a furnace of horse-beans or potatoes daily boiled for the weaker part of the gang. Out of crop, the allowance was from four to six pints of horse-beans, rice, or Indian corn, and four to six herrings weekly, to each slave.

A great deal of land allowed them, but no time to cultivate it, except Sunday; when they were also obliged to pick large bundle of grass, morning and night; many too, watched the works in rotation; no other day was allowed in lieu of the time lost to them on these occasions.

Picking of grass is ever a great hardship, particularly in dry seasons: they are forced to do it on week days,

days, in the time allowed for dinner, and after 1791. sun-set.

Has often known slaves steal from hunger.

Knows of no care taken to instruct slaves, or induce them to marry.

Their capacity is good, and their disposition better than might be expected from persons so untutored.

Severe treatment is no ways necessary. On two estates where he lived, the increase of the slaves, under a milder treatment, exceeded decrease by one per cent. There was also more work done, as they did P. 76. not run away as on other estates, where treated ill.

The slaves were very inhumanly treated on the estate he lived on in Montserrat: the field gang was not assorted as to strength, the weak slaves being forced to work as much as the strong.

Recollects several shocking instances of punishment there; in particular, the driver, at day-break, once informed the overseer, that one, of 4 or 5 negroes, chained, in a dungeon, would not rise: he accompanied overseer to the dungeon, who set the others that were in the chain to drag him out, and not rising when out, he ordered a bundle of cane trash to be put round him, and set fire to. As he still did not rise, he had a small soldering iron heated, and thrust between his teeth. As the man did not yet rise, he had the chain taken off, and sent him to the hospital, where he languished some days, and died. Though the owner resided on the estate, never heard that he condemned this conduct, which if he had, he, (Mr. G.) must have knew it. He could, if necessary, relate several other instances. The overseer, so far from being punished, or called to account for this action, was always in great favour with his masters. Slaves often ran away, and when retaken P. 77. were punished by severe whippings, by chains, by very hard work, and often not released from the chain till, being so emaciated, they were in danger of dying. The deaths exceeded the births more than two to one. The estate did not prosper, the gentle-

1791. man was almoſt ruined by it. The mortality was chiefly among the grown field ſlaves, by their being hard worked, cruelly puniſhed, and ſparingly fed.

Thinks the ſlaves were often ſo fatigued by the labour of the week, as ſcarcely to be capable of working their own ground on Sunday.

The marks of the whip were to be ſeen on almoſt all the weaker part of the gang, from forcing them to keep up with the reſt.

Pregnant women puniſhed, but not very ſeverely.

P. 78. When ſlaves were ſo old as to be paſt labour, their owners did not feed them.

Negroes might be managed with comparative eaſe, were their temper and diſpoſition attended to. The buſineſs might then be done in a better manner, and without ſuch frequent flogging.

Never heard that ſlaves had any protection from ill uſuage from owners, or thoſe under them.

Never knew one planter interfere with the treatment of the ſlaves of another.

Never heard any thing of the locked jaw. They had children die ſometimes; but neither overſeer nor doctor interfered; they were left to old women, the midwives.

The treatment in Grenada was exactly ſimilar to that in Montſerrat; he ſaw no difference.

The merit of a manager was eſtimated by the quantity of crops produced on the eſtate.

A manager of Grenada told him of a great cruelty he had committed. Several negroes and mules had died on the eſtate; an old woman was ſuſpected of having poiſoned them. He, (Mr. G.) aſked the manager if they had not given her up to the law, who ſaid no, they had taken a ſhorter method with her. They made a bit of a thatched hut, put her into it, with ſome combuſtibles, and burnt her to P. 79. death. The manager was not diſcharged for this: thinks he told him it was done by the owner's deſire. It was not told him as a ſecret.

Never

Never heard of any care taken at African sales to 1791.
prevent the separation of relations.

Never knew pains taken to improve mode of cul- P. 80.
tivation, or implements of husbandry, except in that
of cutting cane tops by a machine. Plough might
be applied with great effect in these two islands in
easing the labour of slaves.

Slaves in St. Croix were better used than in either
of the two British islands, but not so well as they
ought, were the planters attentive to their interest;
and if properly treated, believes their increase would
be general throughout the islands.

Never heard that the slaves had any protection
there.

Planters there reside on their estates, and do not
live so extravagantly as in the English islands.

Recollects an instance of the effects of treatment of
slaves. Where he was manager, the slaves were
forced to be up at two in the morning, at a time
when canes were cutting, on 80 acres of a rising
ground, which, from a want of mules, they were
also obliged to carry half a mile upon their heads.
This year the slaves decreased. He prevailed on the
owner to buy six mules more against next crop; that
and the following year the slaves increased one per
cent. Was perfectly convinced that the decrease and
increase spoke to, was in consequence of the difference
of labour.

Never heard talk of the Code Noir while in Grande
Terre: if it had been usual for slaves to be any way
relieved by it, they would have sought redress for
the very severe usage of a man who was his partner
in a distillery: the commanders, to whom he was
very obnoxious, would certainly have taken cogni-
zance of his conduct to his slaves, had it been usual
to do so.

Thinks one half of the domestics of the planters
of Montserrat and Grenada unnecessary.

The Chief Judge at Montserrat was the Honourable
John

1791. John Dyer. Grenada, while he was there, was under military law.

The judges were planters—not, he believes, bred to the law—removable at the King's pleasure.

---

Witnefs examined—MATTHEW TERRY,

Of Afkrig, Yorkfhire, Land Surveyor.

P. 82. Was four years in Dominique as book-keeper and overfeer, one at Tobago as a land-furveyor, in the King's fervice, and feven in Grenada, ending in 1781, as a colony furveyor.

His trade gave him full opportunity of obferving the treatment of flaves. They appeared in general to be ufed with great feverity; believes they generally underftood that the law reftricted the number of lafhes to 39; but this was not in the leaft obferved; has feen it broken repeatedly; never knew

P. 83. any redrefs obtained. It was ufual to rub their backs with brine after fevere punifhments.

In his time one Thochard, a French planter, in Grenada, was generally fuppofed to treat his flaves very cruelly, and for trivial offences to cut off their ears and legs, and otherwife mutilate them. Heard of no attempt to punifh him. Saw upon his eftate two men-flaves with wooden legs.

The greateft property he ever knew a field flave poffefs was two pigs, and a little poultry. The flave has not the means of getting much property, (p.85).

Little or no attention was paid to the breeding of flaves; child-bearing, and confequent lofs of labour, was matter of regret to planters; little or no difference in the punifhments of pregnant females and others. The planters appeared to prefer increafing their crop to increafing their flaves, (p. 85) to depend upon African fupplies, and defirous to have as many males as poffible.

Very

Very confiderable loffes were common among the newly imported Africans. One-third die within the firft year. Of a lot of fix, bought by himfelf, two died within the firft year, and at the end of five years two only furvived.

1791.

P. 85.

Suicide is common, particularly among the Ebos. Never heard of an inftance of it among creole flaves. The latter are more induftrious, being inured to it from their infancy.

Seldom run away. Infurrections are confined to Africans.

Never knew a flave buy his freedom.

No allowance of grain or flour given to any but new negroes. Has known a bunch of plantanes (fufficient for a week's allowance) given to each negro once or twice a year.

P. 86.

Many managers poffefs flaves of their own.

Land furveying is exceedingly laborious in the Weft Indies; he purfued it for 7 years without injury to his health: has often feen mill-wrights at work in the fun, whofe health did not fuffer. There are alfo white blackfmiths and coopers there, but the latter only direct negroes working under them.

---

Witnefs examined——Capt. HALL, of the Royal Navy.

Was at Barbadoes and the Leeward iflands from 1769 to 1773, and from 1780 to 1782 at thofe places, and at Jamaica and St. Domingo.

P. 99.

The treatment of negroes on the B. iflands appeared to him tolerable in the towns; on the plantations rather inhuman. Punifhments inflicted were very fhocking to perfons not ufed to fee them: much more fo than on board a man of war. The field flaves he has feen (a great many) were generally marked with the whip.

In cafes of ill treatment by their mafters, it was generally underftood, they could not obtain redrefs;

againft

1791.
P. 100.

against others, their master assisted them. That this severe system was not necessary, nor for the master's interest, he is confident, from the good effects he has seen result from a lenient treatment in the French islands: for instance, the Marquis de Rouvray was particularly attentive to population, and the good treatment of his slaves at St. Domingo: they were never hard pressed in their work: he suffered no improper intercourse between the males and females, every man had his own wife, and no white was suffered to disjoin that union: the parties were punished for separating without cause.

Hospitals were built for the sick and pregnant; the latter, when far advanced, were taken in there, and employed in trifling work to the time of delivery. Here they might remain separated from their husbands, and excused from field labour, till the child could be supported without the mother's help; or when their strength would permit, return with the child to their husbands, and take the chance of work. In consequence, the Marquis had not for some years occasion to buy negroes. Having, however, left his estate to the care of a nephew, upon his return, after an absence of two years, instead of the happiness that reigned when he left it, he found nothing but misery and discontent; the whites had seized upon the pretty women; their husbands through discontent ran away; and the labour falling heavier upon the rest, they became discontented, and their work badly carried on; so that it cost him two years before he could re-establish order. It was a pleasure to walk through this estate, for the slaves used to look up to him as a father.

P. 101.

In the British islands breeding not thought desirable: they rather thought it a misfortune to have pregnant women, or even young slaves. They esteemed the charge of rearing a child to maturity, more troublesome, and greater, than buying a slave fit for work; and it was not uncommon for them to give away a child of two years old, as you would a puppy

puppy from a litter. Has heard an overseer, of some 1791. consequence, express this opinion. It was, in fact, his system to prevent population, as far as in his power; and he understood this to be a general system.

So little care was taken of infants, that mothers deemed it a misfortune to have children. After the month, they were sent to field labour, with their child upon their back, and so little time afforded them to attend to its wants, that he has seen a woman seated to give suck to her child, roused from that situation by a severe blow from the cart whip.

Domestic slaves, from their general good treatment, were understood to increase.

Believes, that slaves suffered from the owner's absence, because it was the business of the overseer, for his own credit, to make as much sugar as possible; to do this, he must work the slaves to the utmost: it being no concern of his whether they died or not.

Knows, from an instance which fell under his eye, that the slave's death may be occasioned by severe punishment, and the master not be called to legal account.

As to the slave-trade being a nursery for seamen, he conceives it to be quite the reverse.

In taking men out of merchant-ships for the King's service, he has from the crew of a Guineaman, 70, been able to select only 30, who could be thought fit to serve in any ship of war, and when those were surveyed, he was reprimanded for bringing such men into the service, who were more likely to breed distempers, than be of use; and this was at a time when they were so much wanted, that almost any thing would have been taken, viz. in 1782, when they had not men to man the prizes taken on the 12th of April. The instance related was not a particular case, he found it generally so; having had many opportunities between 1769 and 1773

1791. 1773 of seeing the great distresses of crews of Guinea ships, when in the West Indies.

Has great reason to believe, that in no trade are seamen so badly treated; from their always flying to men of war for redress, and whenever they come within reach; whereas men from West Indies or other trades seldom apply to a ship of war.

As to peculiar modes of punishment adopted in Guineamen, he once saw a man chained by the neck in the main-top of a slave-ship, when passing under the stern of his Majesty's ship the Crescent, in Kingston-bay, St. Vincents; and was told by part of the crew, taken out of the ship at their own request, that the man had been there 120 days.

Is clearly of opinion, that white men might do the lighter field work, without injury to their health, as seamen go through very heavy work there unhurt.

---

Witness examined—Capt. GILES, of the 19th Regiment of Foot.

P. 103. Was in Barbodoes, Antigua, St. Lucia, and Jamaica, from June 1782 to April 1790, except about 15 months in England.

Thought the treatment of slaves generally severe. Field slaves in general marked with the whip.

P. 104. Punishment by whipping (though fewer lashes given) more severe and cruel than that of the army, because of the size of the whip.

Had once an opportunity of observing the treatment of a jobbing gang, which he thought beyond what human nature could support for any length of time, because their allowance of food, (which he daily saw) was not equal to support them, and this he understood to be generally the case. This gang had the same respite at noon as plantation negroes, but as some of them would eat their week's allowance in 3 or 4 days, they were obliged to carry wood and

and water, between twelve and two o'clock, for the soldiers, for which they were paid in provisions. Has understood it to be calculated, that a jobbing gang, lasting for seven years, would bring a profit to the owner.

1791.

He had no opportunity of seeing that superanuated slaves were not properly taken care of by their owners.

Can speak to the inefficiency of laws to protect slaves against the ill usage of their masters or other white persons. Was told by a planter, that he once heard one of his own negroes was killed by his overseer. He had the body taken up, and there was found upon it some chains or fetters (p. 106.) but the overseer could not be punished for want of a white evidence.

P. 105.

A free woman, and her two children, were claimed by a person in Jamaica, as his property, who confined them, in order to sell them to the Spaniards. He, (Capt. G.) heard of the circumstance, and interfered, knowing the person could have no claim either to the woman or her children. She, with her husband, had joined the royal army in South Carolina: he worked in one of the public departments as a carpenter, and a driver, and she laboured upon the lines at the quarter-house camp.

After two trials at the Surry assizes, Kingston, the woman and her children were liberated; which must have been the case at the first, had black evidence been admitted; of which he could have produced people bred upon the same estate, and neighbourhood, who also had free tickets from the Governor, Sir A. C.

Without his inteference believes this woman and children must have been sold as slaves, because none on the island so well knew the circumstances as himself. Another case, previous to this, was that of a woman claimed by a person in Jamaica, who, supported by Major Nesbit, of the 19th regiment, was also rescued from slavery, after a trial at the Surry assizes.

Once

1791. Once saw, in Jamaica, a negro mason with a wooden leg, at work: upon asking the white people who superintended the work, how he had lost his leg, was answered, that it was for no good, for the fellow used to run away for months at a time.

The slaves situation and treatment will vary according to the disposition and circumstances of the owner; for on one or two estates in the neighbourhood of his station, the slaves were well treated; they appeared much happier than on several others adjoining; (consequently he imagines better fed.) Thinks none of these stole to supply their wants, as was frequently the case with other gangs in the neighbourhood.

Saw the negroes go weekly to market, a distance of 14 or 15 miles.

---

Witness examined—JOHN TERRY, of Askrig, Yorkshire.

P. 107. Was in Grenada from 1776 to 1790. First 7 or 8 years an overseer, then a manager.

Thought the slaves treatment very bad; it hurt him much at first; in time became more inured to it.

Has known slaves punished by managers severely for trifling faults; durst not complain to owner, for fear of worse treatment; has known them punished for so doing by owner, and sent back, though their

P. 108. complaint was just. Field slaves usually bear marks of the whip. Never heard that a slave complained to a magistrate of his owner, manager, overseer, or attorney.

Has known the same person both attorney, manager, and doctor, on one estate.

Never knew a planter or manager interfere with another's treatment of his slaves.

Has

Has known estates, where slaves were worse fed and clothed than on others; in consequence, were great thieves; eat also putrid carcases. Food is the general object of theft among slaves, and at the hazard of their lives. 1791.

Picking of grass a considerable addition to their labour. Done at dinner-time, and after sun-set. P. 109.

An overseer, on the estate where he was, (Mr. Coghlan) threw a slave into the boiling cane juice, who died in four days. He was not punished otherwise than by replacing the slave, and being dismissed the service. Was told of this by the owner's son, the carpenter, and many slaves on the estate. Has heard it often.

Has known entertainments given among negroes; some of which might cost a thirty-six shilling piece, but such were very rare, (p. 110.)

A field slave in favourable circumstances, (he does not mean the commonality) may earn about six bits a week: he has known them so poor as not to be able to buy poultry. Never heard of a field negro buying his freedom, (p. 110.)

Slaves were not allowed to keep sheep on any estate he knew. On some they might keep two or three goats, but very few allowed it. Some keep a few pigs, and poultry, if able to buy any. P. 110.

While a manager, he never received any directions about attention to pregnant women or children. Has heard managers say, it was cheaper to buy African slaves than to breed: that they wished the children to die, for they lost much of the mother's work during their infancy.

The best recommendation of a manager was, that he made the most sugar.

On the estates he knew, the sexes were about equal.

Of imported Africans, women have the best chance for life. P. 111.

On the estates he knew, more men died than women.

Never

1791. Never knew any children die of the locked-jaw.

Free negroes were generally as well-behaved as others in the same rank of society. Those who had learnt a trade, worked as journeymen with white masters: those who had not, went a fishing, by which they earned more than by field work.

The driver's whip is a severe instrument, and will bring blood through the breeches. Twenty stripes severely laid on the bare breech, may unfit a man for work for two or three days.

The opinion in Grenada, upon passing the last slave act there, was, that it never would have the intended effect.

P. 112. Did not observe it make any difference, except in the half-days in the week.

The clergymen of the parish where he resided never performed the duty the act imposed on them.

Never heard of any complaints against them for non-performance of it.

## Witness examined—JOHN BOWMAN,

### Clerk to a Ship-Builder of Whitehaven.

P. 112. Was in the African employ, from 1765 to 1776, mostly on the Windward Coast, as third, second, and chief mate. Sent up the country as a trading mate to buy slaves, ivory, and cam-wood; a distance of 20 to 40 or 50 miles, in the rivers Scassus, S. Leone, Junk, within the rocks of Grand Bassau, and Little Cape Mount River.

Was eight months as a factor at the head of S. Leone; and 17 to 18 months at that of the R. Scassus. Traded in a boat at Junk, Grand Bassau, and Little Cape Mount Rivers.

P. 113. Having settled at the head of Scassus with 10 slaves money, he informed the King, and others, that he was come to reside as a trader, his orders being

being to supply them with powder and ball, and encourage them to go to war. They answered they would go to war in two or three days: by that time they came to the factory, said they were going to war, and wanted powder, ball, rum, and tobacco. They were dressed in some kind of skins, with large caps, and their faces painted white, to make them look dreadful. They asked for a drink of rum, which when given them, they went off to the number of 25 or 30. After six or seven days some of them returned with two women, and a girl, 6 or 7 years old.

1791.

P. 114.

They said they had got these in a small town which they surprised in the night, that others had got off, but they expected the rest of the party would bring them in, in 2 or 3 days. When these arrived, they brought with them two men whom he knew, and had traded with. Upon questioning them, discovered the women he had bought, to be their wives. Both men and women informed him that the war-men had taken them while asleep.

The war-men used to go out once or twice in 8 or 10 days, while he was at Scassus; it was their constant way of getting slaves, he believed, because they always came to the factory before setting out, and demanded powder, ball, gunflints, and small shot; also rum, tobacco, and a few other articles. When supplied, they blew the horn, made the war cry, and set off. If they met with no slaves, they would bring him some ivory, cam-wood, &c. Sometimes he accompanied them a mile or so, and once joined the party, anxious to know by what means they obtained the slaves. Having travelled all day, they came to a small river, when he was told they had but a little way further to go; after crossing which, they delayed till dark. When they had got over, (about the middle of the night) he was afraid to go further, and asked the king's son to leave him a guard of 4 men. In half an hour he heard the war cry, by which he understood they had reached a town;

P. 115.

1791.
P. 116.

town; in about half an hour more they ret
bringing 25 to 30 men, women, and children,
at the breast. At this time he saw the to
flames. When they had re-crossed the river,
just day-light, and they reached Scaffus about
day. The prisoners were carried to different
of the town. They are usually brought in
strings around their necks, and some have their
tied acrofs. Never saw any slaves there wh
been convicted of crimes.

Has been called up in the night to see fire
told by the town's people, that it was war
ing on.

Whatever rivers he has traded in, he has t
passed burnt and deserted villages, and learned
the natives in the boat with him, that war had
there, and the natives taken and carried to the

P. 117.

He has also seen such upon the coast: while
ing at Grand Buffau, he went ashore with four
traders to the town a mile off. In the way,
was a town deserted, only 2 or 3 houses sta
which seemed to have been a large one from tw
plantations of rice. A little further on, they
to another village in much the same state. W
the first town was taken by war, there being
ships then lying at Buffau: the people of the
had moved higher up in the country, for f
the white men. In passing along to the t
town saw several deserted, destroyed, they sa
war, and the people taken out and sold.

Slaves were obtained in the same manner in
rivers where he traded on the Windward Coast

P. 118.

The inhabitants of all these places subsist o
yams, cassada, fowls, deer, fish, and an a
called tomboer. They raise more rice, &c
they consume, and dispose of the surplus to
ships as may be lying in the rivers, sending it
in large canoes. While at Scaffus, he gave fre
orders for goods from S. Leone, which he c
might be sent up by these periocas, having fou

men good and honeſt. Proviſions of every kind were abundant in the town. Has ſeen countrymen carrying baſkets of 40 or 50 lb. weight of rice, beſides fowls, eggs, &c. which he has bought in exchange for tobacco and beads. 1791.

The natives appeared to be induſtrious, and diſpoſed to trade in their native produce. Believes they would have cultivated more ground, if a greater ſupply had been wanted by the ſhipping. When aſked, they have ſaid they would like to trade with good white men in their own produce, and would ſoon make more plantations of rice.

When under Captain Strangeways, the ſhip then lying in the river S. Leone, at White-man's bay, ready to ſail, he was ordered down from the factory, (all the ſhip's company being then dead but five) and the captain, who ſent him on ſhore to invite two traders on board. They came, and were ſhewn into the cabin. Meantime people were employed in ſetting the ſails, it being almoſt night; and the land breeze making down the river. When they had weighed anchor, and got out to ſea; the witneſs was called down by the captain, who, pointing to the ſail caſe, deſired him to look into it, and ſee what a fine prize he had got. To his ſurpriſe, he ſaw lying faſt aſleep the two men who had come on board with him, the captain having made them drunk, and concealed them there. When they awoke, they were ſent upon deck, ironed, and put forward among the other ſlaves. On arrival at Antigua, they were ſold. P. 119.

The natives were afraid to come along-ſide of a veſſel when under ſail. P. 120.

Frauds were practiſed by Europeans in the articles they traded in with the natives; ſuch as in rum, by mixing it; in powder kegs, ſeemingly large, but holding only a little; in falſe ſteelyards and weights.

The natives, where he reſided, were friendly and hoſpitable; juſt and punctual in their dealings.

When he began to ſettle at the river Scaſſus, there were only four or five houſes there, and about 25 people,

1791. people, so that he was doubtful if he could do it to advantage: but informing the king, that a white man was come to trade with them, was told that strangers would come and settle there. In the course of a few days, several people came and built houses, and the town increased fast, (p. 121.) So that there might be 40 to 50 houses, and 120 to 130 inhabitants when he left it.

P. 121. Has been in Jamaica, Antigua, Grenada, St. Vincent's, Dominique, and Barbadoes, in most of which he has seen Guinea seamen lying about in an ulcerated abject state, without means of support.

---

Witness examined,—JOHN DOUGLAS, Boatswain of the Russel Man of War.

P. 121. Sailed to Africa in 1771, in the Warwick-Castle slave ship. Only one voyage in the trade; because he could not bear with the filthiness and disagreeableness of the voyage.

Seamen were well used in his ship; not suffered to lodge between decks when the slaves were on board.

P. 122. Lost 7 out of 53. Had plenty of provisions.

Had reason to believe that the crews of other ships on the coast, were neither so well fed, nor treated; because boats from the Gregson, and others, which he cannot mention, came often aboard, and the seamen begged much for provisions.

As to the ways in which slaves are procured: when ashore at Bonny Point, he saw a young woman come out of the wood to the water-side to bathe; soon after, two men came from the wood, seized, bound and beat her, for making resistance, and bringing her to him, desired him to put her on board, which he did; the captain's orders were, when any body brought down slaves, instantly to put them off to the ship.

When

When a ship arrives at Bonny, the king sends his war canoes up the rivers, where they surprize all they can lay hold of. They had a young man on board, who was thus captured, with his father, mother, and three sisters. The young man afterwards in Jamaica having learnt English, told him the story, and said it was a common practice.

1791.

War canoes always armed.

P. 123.

Slaves sent in the king's canoes, came openly in the day, others in the evening, with one or two bound, lying in the boat's bottom, covered with mats.

Near Cape Coast, the natives make smoke as a signal for trade; they saw the smoke and stood in shore, which brought off many canoes: pipes, tobacco, and brandy, were got on deck, to entice them on board; the gratings were unlaid, the slave-room cleared, and every preparation made to seize them; two only could be prevailed on to come up the ship's side, who stood in the main chains, but on the seamens approaching them, they jumped off, and the canoes all made for shore.

The Gregson's people, while at Bonny, informed them, that in running down the coast, they had kidnapped 32. He saw slaves on board that ship when she came in; and it is not customary for vessels bound to Bonny, to stop and trade by the way.

Does not think slaves are much subject to seasickness.

Has been in the West Indies in the king's and merchants service, from 1766 to 1782.

Has frequently seen Guinea seamen lying or wandering about the streets and wharfs, mostly in Jamaica, in a diseased and miserable condition: they were called wharfingers; it was on the north-side of the island he has seen the most; many of whom were not capable of walking to Kingston for relief.

Recollects to have seen 3 funerals of Guinea slaves in the West Indies, at which they sing and are mer-

1791. ry; and naming the deceased, they say, he is going home to Guinea.

---

Witness examined,—Major General TOTTENHAM.

P. 125. Went out to the West Indies in 1779, with four regiments under his command. Was about 20 months in Barbadoes, and sometime at St. Lucia, St. Kitt's, and St. Eustatius.

Thinks the slaves in Barbadoes were treated with the greatest cruelty. Cannot judge of the other islands, from his short stay there.

All the punishments he saw were remarkably severe. Was at a planter's house, when the jumper came. Heard him ask the master, if he had any commands for him. He said, no. Jumper then asked the mistress, who replied, yes. She directed him to take out two very decent women, who attended at table, and to give each of them a dozen. General T. expostulated with her, but in vain. They were taken out to the publick parade, and he had the curiosity to go with them. The jumper carried a long whip, like our waggoners. He ordered one of the women to turn her back, and to take up her clothes entirely, and he gave her a dozen on the
P. 126. breech. Every stroke brought flesh from her. She behaved with astonishing fortitude. After the punishment, she, according to custom, curtesied and thanked him. The other had the same punishment, and behaved in the same way. About 3 weeks before the hurricane, he saw a youth, about 19, walking in the streets, in a most deplorable situation, intirely naked, and an iron collar about his neck, with five long, projecting spikes. His body, before and behind his breech, belly and thighs, were almost cut to pieces, and with running sores all over them, and you might put your fingers in some of the wheals. He could not sit down, owing to his breech being in
a state

a state of mortification; and it was impossible for him to lie down, from the projection of the prongs. The boy came to the general, and asked relief. He was shocked at his appearance, and asked him what he had done to suffer such punishment, and who inflicted it. He said it was his master, who lived about 2 miles from town; and that, as he could not work, he would give him nothing to eat.

1791.

There were very few slaves that did not bear the marks of the whip. If severely laid on, they retain the marks many years. There is no comparison at all, between plantation and regimental punishments, the former being so much more severe. Military only cut the skin, the others cut out the flesh.

The field negroes were treated more like brutes, than the human species. The house negroes are clothed and better fed.

Slaves in general appeared very ill fed. Was informed, each slave for 24 hours had a pint of grain, which he boiled; and sometimes half a rotten herring, when to be had. When unfit for the whites, they were bought up by the planters for the slaves.

There was no care taken of slaves superanuated and past labour. They are turned adrift, and obliged to live by plunder. He has seen them himself. An old woman, past labour, told him she was set adrift by her master, to shift for herself. He saw her about 3 days after, lying dead in the same place.

P. 127.

No attention at all seemed to be paid to keeping up the stock by breeding. On the contrary, he believes many discouraged it. He saw but a very small proportion of children.

He has seen the women at work with the hoe, and their naked infants lying on the ground, close by them.

In 1780, a Dutch Guineaman was taken, and brought to Barbadoes. He thinks they had about 270 slaves. He attended most of their sales, and observed a number of the sick slaves in an adjoining yard. Those that were not very ill, were put into huts,

1791. huts, and those that were worse, were left in the yard to die, for nobody gave them any thing to eat or drink. Some of them lived 3 days in that state.

The free-negroes seemed very industrious. The greatest misfortune of all negroes is, that they are left in darkness. He observed a vast difference between the negroes at St. Lucia and any others, owing to the attention of the priests, who instructed them in religion and morality.

P. 128. He has seen a great many English seamen in great distress, in Barbadoes; for the captains often set them ashore to shift for themselves. He cannot say from what ships they came; but only from merchantmen. In St. Lucia, while in our hands, he saw several English seamen lying in the same state.

There was no sort of pains taken to prevent promiscuous intercourse, not even with domesticks, waiting on their mistresses.

Is very positive the impression on his mind, of the treatment of slaves, was made at the time, and on the spot; for he repeatedly told the people of Bridgetown, that he hoped to live to see the unfortunate situation of those poor wretches, taken up by some member of parliament; that, should such an event take place, he should look upon it as his duty to offer a voluntary declaration of what he knew of the matter.

He thinks a present abolition of the slave trade, would be attended with very serious consequences; but, if those unfortunate beings were not left to the tyranny of their cruel masters, but were instructed in morality, and their increase encouraged, and they were rewarded for good behaviour, he thinks that, at a future period, the slave trade would die away of itself.

Witness

Witness examined,—ROBERT FORSTER, of Heblethwaite, Yorkshire.

Was in every British island, except Jamaica, in all about 6 years, ending 1778. The first 4 years apprentice in a store in St. John's, Antigua; the rest of the time a midshipman and second master, and pilot of the king's brig, Endeavour.

1791.

P. 129.

He lived among the town slaves, and often went to collect debts, and visit managers in the country. When in the king's ship, he spent much time among them, having known them before.

The general impression on his mind was, that slaves were severely treated, and in a low, depressed state.

In Antigua, the common allowance was, 7 pints of corn, or horse-beans, for able negroes, with about 3 or 4 herrings weekly; occasionally a little salt, sometimes rum, but not very common. Their work is hard. The bell calls them to it at day-break, and they work till sun-set; have 2 hours at noon; but in their hours of rest, grass is expected. They are treated never as fellow-creatures, but merely as property, and are severely punished for slight offences.

They are allowed a few yards square of ground; but only Sundays to cultivate it, except a few, who had Saturday afternoon.

The plough might be advantageously used, and though perhaps not wholly to supercede the hoe, yet might ease the negroes of many difficult parts of their manual labour. The grinding of their corn at night, by hand, was, in crop, a great hardship: they might be much relieved by some trifling mechanism applied in the sugar-mill, and in many other cases. In general, they seem to have no idea of improvements to ease their slaves. Understood it a general opinion, that if negroes were not constantly kept at hard labour, they would become unruly.

P. 130.

The

1791. The instrument of punishment cuts their flesh, and leaves indelible marks.

No attention at all was paid to marriage. It did not appear to him, that they attended as much to the rearing of children, as we do to the rearing of P. 130. calves. He has known exceptions. A widow Sher- P. 131. vington was left in debt, with 5 or 6 negroes, who, by kind treatment, increased, in 15 or 20 years, to 15, or more. He knows several such instances. As to estates, on the whole of Col. Farley's plantations, they had no need of new negroes. He has heard him say, there was a considerable increase on one particularly. A Mr. Tho. Gravener's negroes also increased. He knew captain Thomason, of Sea-cow-bay, Tortola, who has wanted no new negroes for many years.

Little or no attention was paid to instructing slaves in religion. He believes none at all by the established clergy. Where instruction has been attempted, as it has on several Antigua estates, by Moravian missionaries, the advantage was evident in their manners and behaviour.

P. 131. Those were not thought the most flourishing estates, which bought the most new negroes. It was exactly the reverse.

He never knew, or heard, of a field-negro buying his freedom.

Domesticks have much less work than field-negroes; but their situation, in some respects, is perhaps harder; for, being under the hand of capricious, passionate masters and mistresses, they are often punished, not only corporally, but with numberless teazing and mortifications; nor are they so regularly fed. He never knew them allowed above one-half bit a day; and he believes some are often driven to P. 132. theft or prostitution, by want. The women domesticks are expected to dress neatly, and, having no clothes from their owners, they must use indirect means to get them. They are not often whipped publickly; but their private whippings are very severe,

vere, and he has known a creole woman drop hot sealing-wax on a wench's back, after a flogging. He, and many others, saw a young woman of fortune and character, flog a negro man very severely with her own hands. Many similar instances he could relate, if necessary; they are almost innumerable. He has been speaking chiefly of town domesticks.

Slaves have no legal protection at all against their masters, for any injury short of murder. A little before he arrived in Antigua, one Patrick, a huckster, whom he knew, murdered a woman slave, with circumstances of the most attrocious and savage barbarity. He was tried, convicted, and fined. He was universally blamed, but was dealt with as usual. Slaves have no mode of getting redress from daily injuries of whites, nor their owners; and even sometimes their owners cannot get redress for them. A negro woman was drowned by some seamen of the Favourite sloop of war. A negro man was knocked on the head and drowned, for stealing a piece of beef, alongside a merchantman, at St. John's. These facts were well known, but no inquiry made.

He has known negroes, but not many, turned adrift by their owners, when past labour.

Negroes are liable to be taken for their master's debts, and are confined in a close, disagreeable dungeon, till sold. No regard paid, that he remembers, to selling families together. Saw a family of mulattoes and blacks sold at vendue, and sent to different islands. They discovered great sorrow at being separated.

African negroes shewed the most extravagant joy at their friends funerals, from believing the deceased gone back to their country.

He has seen many of those deplorable objects, Guinea seamen, particularly on the beach at Roseau, Dominique. When the Endeavour was at Grenada, there were 7 Guinea seamen, exceedingly emaciated and full of sores, who complained much of their ill

1791. ill ufage in the voyage. In a few months, they recovered fo much, as fcarcely to be known for the
P. 134. fame men. Captains of men of war fometimes take them, to recover their wages, but generally do not keep them, for fear of infection. Such feamen in Antigua, are called wharfingers, and in Dominique, fcow-bankers.

He lived at Lancafter, when flave-fhips were fitted out there. From their ill treatment, and the fmall numbers that returned, the young men were difcouraged from entering on that fervice, and they were obliged to take fome fhips to Liverpool to man them.

The lives of a prodigious number of negroes were carelefsly and impolitically facrificed in clearing the lee fide of Dominique, for fugar eftates. He recollects one planter there who bought 30 new negroes, and loft them all within the year.

P. 135. Negro porters, who pay their owners a weekly fum, having no fixed rates, endure great impofitions and hardfhips. If, on being offered too little for their work, they remonftrate, they are very often beaten, and receive nothing: and fhould they refufe the next call, from the fame perfon, they are liable to be fummoned before a magiftrate, and punifhed on the parade, for refufal, and he has known them fo punifhed. Negroes that bring grafs to town to fell, have often their grafs taken away, without pay, and fometimes with a beating. The indignities the negroes receive in markets, from white failors and others, are frequent, vexatious, and fevere.

---

Witnefs Examined,—Capt. JOHN SAMUEL SMITH, of the Royal Navy.

Was in the Weft Indies in 1772, 1777, and 1778, for above a year altogether.

Had feveral opportunities of obferving the treatment

ment of plantation-slaves, from meeting with an old 1791.
schoolfellow, a manager, who introduced him to
many other managers.

First impression was that slaves were treated more like beasts than the human species. The mode of punishment generally was, a negro stretched on his belly, on the ground, a man at each hand and leg; the punishment inflicted by a negro with a long whip, tapering from the size of one's thumb, to a small lash. At every stroke a piece of flesh was drawn out, and that with much unconcern to the director of the punishment.

Grass picking and theft, the most frequent causes of punishment. Some were punished for not getting so much grass as others, and that at a time when he thought it impossible for them to get half the quantity, having been on the spot. The grass is generally picked after their day's work. His idea is, they seldom leave work till sun-set, let the distance be what it may; and they are obliged to pick grass all the way home.

The plantation-slaves were very generally marked P. 137. with the whip. The only instance to the contrary is what he shall speak to on a Grenada estate.

It by no means appeared to him, or to be generally understood, that slaves could get legal redress for ill usage by their masters, or other whites. A slave who paid his master for leave to work for himself, and kept a shop and slaves under him, was employed on a job, by a gentleman of property; on being displeased with the man, he sent for him and punished him publickly, and the slave had no redress. This he has no doubt often happens. He has heard of many instances of the like.

Has heard of many cases of slaves suffering from their master's bad circumstances, and has heard it often observed, " If you want to know a proprietor's circumstances, look at his slaves."

Thinks a planter's residence a necessary check on managers, and it was generally unsterstood so. Has
seen

1791. seen managers particularly attentive to their own stock and slaves, which he thinks they could not have done had the owner been there. This difference of usage must doubtless cause much jealousy to the field-slaves. Has often seen more food given to managers slaves; and it is commonly observed, that it is easy to know the manager's slaves from the owner's, from their better appearance. Has reason

P. 138. to believe managers often favour their own slaves, in labour, and other particulars, especially in grass picking, as he has often seen; and he has no doubt but the grass is generally appropriated to the manager more than the owner. Managers never employ their own slaves for this purpose. The keeping stock is generally a part of the manager's income, and he has no doubt it is fed at the proprietor's expense.

Planters never appeared careful to keep up their slaves by breeding. Has seen instances which convinced him that managers attended more to the increase of their own slaves. The managers seemed generally prosperous, and that often when the owners seemed to be going behind hand.

It never appeared to him that any attempts were made to check promiscuous intercourse, and to introduce regular domestick habits. He has often known where people from the ships visited managers, and had opportunities given by them of selecting women for their private ends: nor were the wives of negroes secure from the whites on the estates. He has known complaints made of the overseer having infringed in that particular, against the woman's will, without redress.

P. 139. Has seen many slaves neglected, who were aged and past labour. On observing to the inhabitants the state of such objects, he has been told, that building hospitals for them would be endless, as slaves would bring complaints on themselves to leave the estate.

It

It was understood a common practice, and he himself has known instances of women, in respectable stations, standing by to see their slaves punished.

Always considered negroes as keen, sensible, well-disposed people, when their habits were not vitiated by cruel usage.

Never thought it necessary to treat them so severely, having seen an instance where the reverse usage produced a good effect, and which he often mentioned to managers whom he saw acting differently. Was answered it might be practised in particular cases, but it would be impossible to get the work done, were it general. The manager, in that one instance, told him that more work was done than on estates where the treatment was otherwise. He does not remember asking if the pairing of the slaves was attended to on that estate; but he saw religion the first object of the manager, which he thought had a very good effect.

Believes slaves, if used ill, dare not complain to an attorney except in attrocious cases. Firmly believes, the opinion of the slaves is, that the attorney and manager are one and the same, with respect to understanding each other.

Never saw balls or dances among field-slaves; but often among house-slaves.

On the whole, it by no means appeared to him, that the state of slaves could bear any comparison with that of peasants here. He always considered them as treated and spoken of as cattle.

Has often been employed to board Guineamen to impress men; and though he supposes he may have boarded near 20 vessels, at times, he never could get more than two men, who turned out such inhuman fellows, that they were forced to dismiss them, though good seamen. But the chief reason of his not getting men was, the fear of infection, having seen many of them ulcerated very much, and otherwise disordered; and though often solicited by them, and told, that if he did not receive them, they would be sent ashore

1791.

P. 140.

and

1790.
and left behind. To be applied to, by feamen, in any other trade, to be taken out of their own fhips into His Majefty's, is fo uncommon as feldom or never to happen.

---

Witnefs examined—Mr. WILLIAM DUNCAN.

P. 141. Was in Antigua from Jan. 1785 to July 1789, as clerk in a ftore fix or eight months; as overfeer for about two years and a half; the reft of the time, kept ftore for himfelf.

Firft impreffion was, that flaves looked very poorly and ill treated.

The ufual allowance of plantation-flaves is a gallon of Indian corn or horfe beans weekly, with fometimes two herrings; at other times, 24 lb. of yams and a little falt.

The negroes, on the eftate he was on, which were 162, had only fix or feven acres among them, of but indifferent land. They had Sunday to work it, and fometimes Saturday afternoon, out of crop.

Negroes appear in the beft condition rather towards the end of crop. At other times, look ill fed. He fhould fuppofe they are driven by hunger to theft. They ufually fteal provifions, at the rifk of being cut and beat by the watchmen.

P. 142. Thinks about fourteen pence fterling the utmoft fum which an induftrious field-negro can earn for himfelf in a week. He never knew fuch have any confiderable property, nor heard of a field-flave buying his freedom.

Very feldom knew entertainments given by the negroes. Thinks about fix dollars might be the utmoft coft of fuch as he has feen.

Thinks provifions allowed by mafters, and that which flaves raife in their own grounds, are, in general, infufficient to fupport them and their families

*properly*

properly and comfortably. He has often heard them 1791. complain for want of food.

He thought the plantation-slaves cruelly treated, and not sufficiently attended to.

The pregnant women, on the estate where he lived, P. 143. did little work after they were four months gone with child; came out at eight o'clock and went home by four; if wet came not out at all. At times the women work a little, and their children are left with old women, in the field. They are allowed to suckle them. On a neighbouring estate, the usage of pregnant women was the same: cannot say as to others.

He looks on the work generally required of field-slaves as laborious, according to their strength to perform it.

Sometimes slaves have 39 lashes, sometimes they are confined with chains and collars; and sometimes with iron boots on their ancles. Their whippings are severe, sometimes wantonly inflicted, and, at other times, disproportionate to the offences. Many negroes bear about them the marks of the whip. He has seen a negro so cut, that he could not lie on his back or sit down.

He knew of no protection which slaves had against ill usage from their owners, or managers, or overseers. The owner was liable to be punished for murdering his slave. He knew a white man, in in- P. 144. different circumstances, who was fined 100l. currency, and imprisoned 12 months, for murdering his negro boy.

Relates an instance of a slave unjustly beaten by an intoxicated manager. Though laid up in consequence of it some months, he got no redress.

He has known the same man doctor and attorney, and manager and attorney.

The opinion was, that a creole negro, by the time he was fit to work, cost more than one from Africa.

The treatment on the estate he lived on was better than common. The effect was that they increased. Also the slaves on Sir G. Thomas's Belfast estate, and
Carlisle's,

1791. Carlisle's, and several others he cannot name, increased, or kept up their numbers, without addition by purchase.

On a neighbouring estate, the treatment was worse than usual, and the effect was, the slaves decreased.

He thinks the sexes nearly equal, but he believes, most males.

The capacities and dispositions of negroes are much like those of the whites.

They received religious instruction chiefly from Methodist preachers. The island clergy were not so attentive as the Methodists. The negroes so instructed were improved in their morals and behaviour. Such paid more attention to marriage. He has often known negroes desire to have their children baptized. The clergy usually took a dollar from them for baptism.

He has known families sent to different islands, from sales by execution, or otherwise.

He has seen some free negroes very well behaved, and very industrious. They are usually tradesmen and hucksters. He never knew them work in the field. They would think it a disgrace to work with a slave. They can earn more by those employments than by field-work.

He has often heard the slaves say, they were kidnapped; particularly a woman who waited on him, said that when going on an errand, she was carried off in a bag and sold.

He sees no reason why the plough might not be used, especially to loosen stiff land, which would certainly save much labour.

Witness

Witness examined—Captain Thomas Lloyd,

Of the Royal Navy.

Was in the West Indies in 1779. Commanded the Glasgow, and was burnt out of her in Montego bay, Jamaica.  
1791.  
P. 147.

His first impression was, that the slaves were very generally considered as black cattle, and very often treated like post-horses.

Relates instance of a man and woman slave executed at St. Ann's bay, in sight of his ship's company. The former for running away, the latter for secreting him.

At Mrs. Winne's, of Mammee bay, saw a woman slave with one hand only, and asked Mrs. W. how she lost it. She said it had been cut off. She had a female slave to whom she trusted her linen and other valuable effects, from suspecting her indented white servant had abused that confidence. She directed her slave never to issue out linen, without her orders. The white woman wanted a pair of sheets, and attempted forcibly to take them. A scuffle ensued, and six weeks after the supposed offence, the white woman swore the slave had struck her, and she had her right hand cut off, Mrs. W. having in vain endeavoured to suspend the amputation. She spoke of this as an inhuman act, and a great injury to her property.

P. 148.

He was told by a person of veracity, whom he wishes not to name, that it was the practice of a certain planter, whose name he does not now recollect, to frame pretences for the execution of his worn out slaves, in order to get the island allowance: and it was supposed he had dealt largely in that way.

Captain Cornwallis told him, while he was there, that, at a dinner with some of the principal planters, the conversation turning on the profit and loss of

Numb. 4.   L   sugar

1791. sugar estates, one of them said, that in crop he worked his negroes 20 hours out of the 24. Another said, many of them must have died. He granted that, but, on the whole, it answered.

He has seen, about the streets and roads, many old, miserable objects, and was told many of them had their freedom given them, when no longer able to work. The most wretched object he ever saw was at Port Royal.

He had reason to believe, that negroes might be induced to work properly, without severity. A Mr. Greenland had but a few, who looked well and happy. Captain L. asked him the reason. He said, he never punished them, and he did not find but he was as well off as others who pursued a different conduct.

P. 149. He has heard sensible people ascribe the decrease of slaves, on several estates, to the severity of their treatment.

Many instances of the ill treatment of the slaves, have been told him by his brother officers, upon the station; but why they keep back their evidence he cannot tell. He has heard of military combinations to obtain justice, and to resist oppression; but this is the first instance he ever heard of associations for the suppression of truths.

---

Witness examined—Lieutenant BAKER DAVISON,

Of the late 79th Regiment.

P. 150. Was in Jamaica, from the middle of 1771 to the end of 1783, except a few months on the Spanish main. (Practised surgery in Jamaica, many years, before the French war, p. 154.)

Had many opportunities of seeing the treatment both of field and town slaves. Was quartered in many parts of the island; resided some time at a planter's planter's house, given him and his family for a barrack.

1791.

The first general impression on his mind was that the slaves were very cruelly treated, by being most unmercifully flogged by their owner's order. Such punishments never were restricted to 39 lashes. Understands there was such a law, but never knew it abided by, where punishment was really meant.

P. 151.

Sometimes owners in town would have them flogged at home, or send them to gaol, to be punished, or have them tied up to a crane on the wharfs. He has very often seen those punishments inflicted, at all times of the day. In houses and on the wharfs slaves are always punished by order of the owners, and often in gaol.

They appeared much more severe than regimental punishments. He remembers a new negro girl flogged by her mistress's order, and who died of a mortification from the wounds two days after.

In towns the slaves are generally flogged with a cowskin, and on estates with a long whip.

P. 152.

On estates they are fastened to four stakes driven into the ground, and whipped. He has often seen regular punishments in the field, for neglect of work, and other offences committed on the spot.

He has often seen owners send their slaves to be whipped in gaol; and has very often seen them brought home by persons belonging to the gaol. The precise number of stripes to be given in gaol was not ordered. The owners generally told them to flog them well, according to the crime.

He knew many cruelties; but none followed by death, except that mentioned. The clergyman's wife at Port Royal, was remarkably cruel. She used to drop hot sealing-wax on her negroes, after flogging them. He was sent for, as surgeon, to one of them, whose breast was terribly burnt with sealing-wax. A woman next door to him was often flogging her negroes so cruelly, that he has frequently gone in and insisted on her desisting; and, at last, he complained

1791. plained of her to a magistrate, who told him he had nothing to do with it.

P. 153. He is very sure the slave's treatment depends wholly on the owner's disposition; as some were very cruel, and others not so.

He has very often remonstrated to owners and managers on severity, especially to the clergyman's wife, and the clergyman himself, who said they would not do without severity, and even being half starved, which he often knew was the case at his own house. He has often talked to them on their slaves being ill from severity and hunger. He particularly remonstrated to the woman mentioned (whose negro died) when he has seen the negro at work, kneeling, on her bare knees, on the pebbles, a punishment very common in houses there.

He believes the slaves generally understood they had a right to legal redress, for severity, as he has often had complaints, when quartered up the country, from different estates. He never knew such redress obtained, from negroes themselves complaining. When ill used by others, the owners take care to get redress.

P. 154. He saw a slave both of whose nostrils had been slit, by her mistress's order, from jealousy. No attempt was made to punish this woman, as she was of some consequence, being the wife of the engineer of the island.

It was very common for women, in respectable situations, to stand by, at the punishment of their slaves.

He thinks pregnant women were not, in general, properly attended to, having been sent for to several estates, where the mother scarcely had any cloaths to cover her, nor any baby-cloaths, and was in want of every kind of proper nourishment.

He has seen several pregnant women flogged on estates, and a hole made in the ground to receive their belly. He was once sent for to a woman who had

had miscarried from severe flogging, when both child and herself died.

The jaw-fall was fatal to negro infants, in many cases which fell under his notice, owing, he believes, to want of proper necessaries, bad houses, and various other causes. It is impossible to account entirely for it. He is sure it was not equally fatal to white children; as in the different regiments he was in, they had a great many children born, but he never knew one of them die with it.

Thinks, in general, the slaves were very badly fed.

It appeared to him, that when masters were in debt, the slave's food was reduced; as the slaves of several very poor planters near him, used, in the night, to rob him of every kind of provisions. There were several estates where he knew the slaves were better fed, and who never troubled them.

He is sure the slaves were not universally allowed Saturday afternoon, to work their grounds, as he never knew it; and, had it been common, he must have known it.

He has known the slaves, on the estate where he lived, several times obliged to work, even on Sundays, for their master. His house was very near the works.

He has often known them work all night at the boiling-house and mill.

The taylor, who worked for him the whole time he was in Jamaica, bought his own freedom; and when he left the island, had some slaves of his own. He never knew a field-slave buy his freedom.

Has known slaves, (generally Africans) destroy themselves, particularly one at Port Royal, who having been punished over-night, was found hanging in his hut in the morning. He was an African who had not been long bought. He never knew a creole kill himself.

Is sure old negroes, past labour, were not, in general, sufficiently attended to. He knew two old
men,

1791. men, belonging to a woman in Port Royal, who subsisted by begging.

The negroes wives were not secure from the whites; for he has known different book-keepers, just come to the estate, take their wives from them. Believes this was very often a cause of discontent to the slaves. (If there be a law against this, he never knew it inforced. It is common for whites on estates to chuse negro women for themselves or friends. p. 181.)

Both house and field slaves were generally marked with the whip.

A great many instances have fallen within his notice, which proved severity unnecessary. He had always 5 or 6 slaves, whom he never found it necessary to punish, as he used them well. A Mr. Malcolm, who had a large estate, would not allow a negro to be punished, without his knowledge. In an insurrection, Mr. D. expressed his surprise, that he would leave his wife and family on the estate, when
P. 157. he was 8 or 10 miles off. Mr. M. said, he was sure his negroes would behave as well in his absence, as in his presence. Mr. D. has been often at his house, and has known him most days go among his negroes, and hear their complaints. He told him that he had not bought a new negro for 10 or 12 years. That they never ran away, and that his estate and negroes had considerably increased in that time. Has often heard him say, he had as much work done as others, and that his negroes always worked willingly. Is sure he encouraged their pairing, as he gave them every necessary, and kept their houses in good repair. He knew an estate where the negroes were all creoles. Is sure they were treated better than common.

Free negroes were generally tradesmen, and very industrious.

Saw a mother and her daughter separated at a sale
P. 179. by vendue. A negro woman had been sold by her mistress to a Jew, to be sent off the island; but Mr. D. bought

D. bought her from the Jew. She had 2 children, 1791. whom her miftrefs kept from her, and whom fhe often begged him to buy, which he could not conveniently do. He bought a new negro, who found his brother, and brought him to the fort to Mr. D. Mr. Chambers, owner of the brother, begged Mr. D. to part with his, as the brother was a very valuable boiler. This Mr. D. reluctantly complied with, for his was equally valuable.

The Maroon negroes in Jamaica, increafed moft P. 180. certainly. He has often been in all their towns, and always faw great numbers of children. Their numbers were confiderably more when he left, than when he went to, the ifland. He is fure they did not incorporate run-aways among them, as they had a reward and mile-money, for bringing them to the gaols.

Is fure whites, if temperate, could, without material injury, do any kind of out-of-door work. It is well known, that the fhip-wrights and other tradefmen, in the king's-yard, Port-Royal, often work all day long, and he never knew them unhealthier than people in general. White artificers certainly do work at their trades, in the Weft Indies, without materially hurting their health.

He believes thumb-fcrews are very often ufed in the Weft Indies, having feen feveral negro girls at work with the needle, in prefence of their miftreffes, with a thumb-fcrew on their left thumb, and he has feen the blood gufh out from the end of them.

Domefticks certainly are particularly fubject to their owner's caprice. He has often known their miftrefs fend them to be punifhed, without telling them for what. He has been frequently fent for, to the clergyman's flaves before-mentioned, after they have been feverely flogged, and otherwife ill treated, fo that he conceived their lives in great danger: particularly to one woman who had been P. 181. tied up all night, by her hands, and abufed with cayenne pepper, in a way too horrid and indecent to
mention

1791. mention. He lived next door to a washer-woman, at Port Royal, who was almost continually flogging her negroes. He has often gone in and remonstrated against her cruelty, where he has seen the negro women chained to the washing tubs, almost naked, with their thighs and backs in a gore of blood, from flogging. He could mention various other capricious punishments, if necessary.

He is sure means are used, in Guineamen, to suppress the slaves diseases (which afterwards break out still more violently, or bring on other disorders) especially fluxes, as he made it his business to ask the surgeons, who candidly told him their mode of treatment on board. He made this inquiry, on his wife's father having bought a good number of slaves out of a Guineaman, several of whom broke out in violent fluxes.

He has known new negroes put into the field 2 or 3 days after being bought. They sometimes remain on board in the harbour, 2 or 3 weeks before sale.

P. 182. Has seen a great many ulcerated sailors lying about, in most parts of the island, especially at Kingston. They chiefly belonged to Guineamen, for he particularly asked them.

Has often heard planters say, such an overseer had improved the estate, by large crops: but never heard any such thing mentioned, in connection, as his care of the negroes, or keeping them up by breeding.

He has often gone on the estates of absentees, with attornies, and came away with them, and saw very little attention paid, except asking the overseer when the sugars would be ready for market. He never heard any inquiries made into the negroes state and treatment.

Has frequently heard owners of slaves say, that a creole, when fit to work, costs more than a new negro.

The attorney and overseer are not always distinct persons. He has known several that were both attorney

torney and overseer. He knew several in Spanish Town, from 20 to 40 miles off the estates they were attornies for. Attornies are often directly interested in increasing the crops, as he always understood they have a per centage on them.

1791.

P. 183.

Overseers very often have slaves of their own: he has known them have jobbing gangs. Has known the absent master's house-slaves sent into the field, and the overseer's put in their room.

Many more domestics are kept in West India families than in similar English ones. Has known from 12 to 20 in a house, where half as many would do very well.

Domestics certainly increase, from being better fed and treated, and less worked.

Female slaves are very commonly let out, by their owners, for prostitution.

Slaves sell vegetables at market, on their owner's account; as several mountain estates chiefly depend on selling vegetables.

On many estates he is sure proper medical care was not taken of the negroes; as the surgeon often lives far from the estates, and visits them, when he thinks proper.

He brought a Guinea woman to England, who wished much to be sent to her own country. It is common for sick negroes to say, with much pleasure, they are going to die, and are going home from this Buccra country.

P. 184.

Has often known slaves 12 months in gaol, from their master's debts.

Believes owners are very commonly involved with Guinea merchants; for they often stay on the estates, all the week, except Sundays, with their gates always locked. Buyers of new negroes, if planters, are credited, from one crop to another; if not planters, from 6 to 12 months.

He has very often seen refuse-negroes, sold at vendue, in a wretched situation, and very cheap. Several make a trade of it.

Numb. 4. M There

1791.   There was a captain to every Maroon town, and
a fuperintendant over the whole, to keep up order.
P. 185. He thinks runaways could not be harboured, in the
Maroon towns, without coming to the captain's
knowledge, who always lives very near the towns.
He is appointed, by the governor, as guardian of the
treaty with the Maroons.  He is always a white man.

---

Witnefs examined—DREWRY OTLEY, Efq.
His Majefty's Chief Juftice on the Ifland of
St. Vincent.

P. 158.   Refided in the W. Indies fince 1776, chiefly in St.
Vincent.  Has vifited Antigua, Tobago, St. Kitts,
Grenada, and St. Lucia: was in England about ten
months of the time.

Is of the council of St. Vincent's, appointed in
1784, and chief juftice in 1787.

Managed his own eftates there till made chief
juftice; when, often abfent on public bufinefs, he
employed a manager, whofe conduct he conftantly
fuperintended.

As to the laws refpecting flaves; the old flave
acts, which were the general laws throughout the
iflands and which in many ftill continue unrepealed,
have appeared to him in many cafes unjuft and inhuman, as to the perfonal fecurity of flaves; which
appears only to be provided for, in cafes of murders,
difmemberment, and mutilation. And as the evidence
of flaves is never admitted againft whites, the diffi-
P. 159. culty of legally eftablifhing facts is fo great, that
white men are in a manner put beyond the reach of
the law: however, fuppofing the proof full, the murder of a flave in fome iflands is only punifhable by a
larger fine, and difmemberment and mutilation by a
fmaller.  Some of the acts are filent on the murder
of a flave, and it has been fuppofed, in thofe iflands,
that it was punifhable by the common law of England:

land: however, on confidering the latter part of the fecond claufe in the St. Vincent flave act, which is alfo introduced in fome of the flave acts of the other iflands, is of opinion, that by inference from that claufe, the murder of a flave is not punifhable by common law as a capital offence.

There is no law for fecuring the flave's property, againft his mafter, nor againft ftrangers, unlefs the mafter brings an action.

There are laws in moft of the iflands obliging mafters to provide food and clothing for their flaves; but does not think them in general efficient, from the difficulty of bringing proof of the breach of the law.

Some claufes in the St. Vincent's flave act appear to be oppreffive and impolitic; particularly that which obliges the whites, under a penalty, to fearch once a fortnight, the negroe houfes on the eftate, for runaways or ftolen goods; that which prevents flaves from hiring themfelves of their mafters to work on their own account; thofe which lay certain reftriction on free negroes, and deprive them in fome cafes of trial by jury; the claufe which throws obftacles in the way of flaves buying their freedom; and fome others which he does not juft now recollect.

In his anfwers, he confines himfelf to St. Vincent's where named; where no ifland is named, his obfervations extend to all where the old flave acts are yet in force.

The omiffions in the old laws are fo numerous that it is difficult to afcertain them; he will therefore fpeak to fuch alterations and provifions as appear neceffary for the protection of flaves.

He would recommend the paffing a flave act in every ifland, repealing thofe now in force, and eftablifhing regulations upon the principle of the late Grenada act, to obviate the difficulty of bringing evidence againft whites: councils of protection or guardians, fhould be named to fee that the provifions made for the benefit of flaves are enforced: they fhould be empowered to infpect provifion grounds,

1791. sick houses, clothing, negro-houses, and the general condition of slaves; and upon just grounds of suspicion, to have power to examine whites, or other free persons, on oath, and to prosecute offenders, where necessary.

Thinks, if the guardians do their duty, and act with impartiality, that the substitute for the evidence of slaves, (provided by the Grenada act) affords as great a degree of protection and security as persons in a state of slavery can enjoy.

Can devise no means, likely to be adopted, for admitting the evidence of slaves, in their present state of ignorance.

P. 161. The laws lately passed in Jamaica, Grenada, and Dominica, (as contained in the Privy Council report) have supplied most of the omissions now noticed; but the Grenada law seems best calculated to have full effect.

The punishments to be inflicted by the St. Vincent's slave act, must be by order of justices of the peace: recollects no provisions there, which limit the degree, or ascertain the nature, of the punishment which a master or manager may inflict.

The general modes of punishment he has observed on West India estates, were, whipping, the stocks, chains, iron collars; the latter not frequent, nor long worn, because deemed hurtful to the slaves health.

As to whipping in a cruel manner and disproportionate to the offence, overseers striking slaves wantonly, subtracting from his allowance, taking away the provisions he has raised, or other arbitrary and cruel treatment independent of punishment for
P. 162. offences, much depends on the temper and disposition of masters or managers. On all the estates he has known, where the master or manager resided, overseers were forbidden to strike any slave, and were liable to be turned off if they did. Sometimes they do it, but does not think it common.

The

The treatment of slaves, so far as he has observed, is in general humane.

1791.

Instances of cruelty do and will occur, but does not think them common. Certainly thinks them exceptions to general usage.

As to instances of notorious cruelty in the islands going unpunished, never knew but one case where a man was punished by law in St. Vincent's for cruelty to a slave, and that was very lately. Has heard of other cases of cruelty notorious, which have gone unpunished.

In St. Vincent's, industrious field slaves are generally possessed of some property. So far as he can guess, an industrious but ordinary field slave may acquire to the amount of 6l. or 8l. sterling per ann. Of 200 slaves on an estate, not more than one-third can be reckoned field slaves; some of whom will be young and indifferent to property, others lazy. He should suppose 12 to 18 might acquire to the amount mentioned. Has heard of field slaves acquiring to a greater amount, but in general they are careful to conceal their property from their masters. They acquire it by raising hogs, goats, poultry, and by the culture of their grounds, of which they have in general more than they can cultivate, and as good land for the purpose as any on the estate. Out of crop they have half of Saturday, or one day in a fortnight. Thinks the latter better for the slave, as he can go fresh to his work, and has more time to complete any particular job.

P. 163.

In St. Vincent's slaves are never married according to the rites of the Church, but they are very often attached to one woman.

Knows of no law to prevent a white from debauching the wife of a slave: but does not recollect any case of the kind.

P. 164.

As the females, who are not married, do not seem to prize chastity much, he should suppose the men licentious with regard to women.

Slaves,

1791. Slaves, when paſt the time of youth, often live faithfully as man and wife.

The men are in general ſo addicted to the uſe of ſpirituous liquors, that they will get drunk as oft as they can.

Has heard young females ſtudy to procure abortions, but never knew a caſe: they are ſo fond of dancing, that he does not think pregnancy, unleſs far advanced, would prevent their going a great way for it. Dances are common, but ſlaves from diſtant eſtates are forbidden.

The ſlaves are in general very harmleſs and peaceable. Never knew a caſe, even where they have been ſaid to be ill treated, of their attempting to injure their maſter's property from reſentment; tho' were they ſo inclined, they have many opportunities, particularly in crop time. They diſcover a benevolent diſpoſition, and a general good will. On every diſtreſsful emergency, ſuch as fire, which often happens, he has always obſerved negroes from the neighbouring plantations, uncalled, even in the night, ready and active to their utmoſt exertion in relieving the misfortune of the moment. Recollects an inſtance which occurred in 1785: A fire ſuddenly broke out among his canes, at a place the moſt diſtant from where his own ſlaves were working. Thoſe of Sir William Young, who were at work near the ſpot, voluntarily run to the place, and with much trouble and ſome riſque extinguiſhed the flames, which might otherwiſe have deſtroyed 50 or 60 hogſheads of ſugar; nor did they aſk any reward; but of courſe ſome recompence was ſent them.

Thoſe ſeaſoned to the iſlands appear to be of a chearful temper; and are ſo, when well uſed; which may be known by their returning merry and ſinging, from their work.

Thinks, on eſtates well handed with ſeaſoned negroes, and which have a regular ſucceſſion of children to ſupply thoſe who fall off by age, the numbers might be kept up, and probably increaſe without importation,

importation. In many inftances, eftates, humanely managed, and with a fuitable proportion of the fexes, actually have, and do increafe their numbers without importation. (p. 167.)   1791.

Is acquainted with the Caribs of St. Vincent's. They are moftly of the negro race, faid to be defcended from fuch as efcaped from a flave fhip, wrecked upon the coaft.   P. 166.

Believes they do not incorporate runaways, who would be eafily diftinguifhed from the Caribs, who have a peculiar flattening in the forehead, produced in infancy; they have a reward too for bringing in runaways; and there is befides a ftrong antipathy between them and the flaves (p. 169). Their number is faid to be 3000, fo that they muft certainly have increafed, and believes they are ftill on the increafe: they are fond of fpirituous liquors (p. 169).

As flaves can never live fo much at their eafe as the Caribs do, and muft be more expofed while at work, they will be fubject to difeafes, to which the Caribs and free negroes are not; they will therefore probably not increafe fo much, though they may increafe.

W. India eftates are in general deeply mortgaged: in proportion to the weight of debt on them, they will in many inftances be worked with greater exertion of labour, and under difadvantages of credit prejudicial to the fupplies for comfort, or even fubfiftence of the flaves, in many cafes.   P. 167.

He fhould neceffarily conclude, that where flaves are not fupplied equally with the neceffaries and comforts of life, they will of courfe be proportionally defective in increafe.

The proprietors of eftates preffed by their creditors would, he fears, be induced to work their gangs beyond their ftrength, were they cut off from frefh fupplies of flaves, and thus a fudden and total abolition eventually prove oppreffive to many flaves in the Weft Indies.

Believes,

1791. Believes, the question of the slave-trade depending in the British Parliament, may have directed the attention of the colonial legislatures, to the reform of the laws in favour of slaves; and while the question
P. 168. continues pending, believes they will be disposed to adopt any practicable regulations which may be recommended to them; but does not think they would attend to such recommendation with the same good temper and satisfaction were the question decided, and the slave-trade stopt.

Does not think any effectual reform of the slave laws could be made without the co-operation of the colonies, as by the constitution of their governments, their legislative bodies must pass the laws, and the magistrates and others in the islands enforce them.

His letter to Sir William Young, contained in the Privy Council Report, was written in haste, and merely for Sir William's private information.

As the laws now stand in many of the islands, domestick slaves must be peculiarly subject to their masters caprice; and their situation can less be effected by regulations of law, than even that of field slaves, because the conduct of masters to domesticks
P. 169. is not so open to the observation of the world.

As to supposing private punishments to be restricted to a certain number of lashes, and masters and overseers should exceed the limitation, or splitting one crime into many, give the limited number for each; can devise no mode of bringing such master or other to justice, while the evidence of a slave continues inadmissible.

Believes there are 400 or 500 whites in all, exclusive of the military, in St. Vincent's; perhaps 150 more in the small islands now connected with it; and imagines the slaves on those islands, which are not many, are included in the number of St. Vincent's slaves.

Never knew a free negro hire himself to field labour, to hire as mechanicks is common.

The

The stock of slaves on his estate when he first went out have constantly increased; but the new negroes he has bought since 1784, have, in spite of all possible attention to them, decreased at least one in eight. Mr. Robley told him, that on his estate Sandy Point, in Tobago, there has been a constant considerable increase by births, though the situation does not seem healthy. In St. Vincent's, upon Sir William Young's estate, Calliagua, there has been for some years past a constant increase by births; the same on Mr. Haffey's estate, and he believes also upon Mr. Winn's; and likewise upon Mr. Collins's and a Mr. Morgan's estates.

1790.
P. 170.

If proper attention was paid to the religious instruction of slaves, he is convinced it would be of the greatest advantage to the planters. Within these three or four years, some Methodist missionaries, have had access to many estates in St. Vincent's, for that purpose. Has heard that in Antigua the slaves have been greatly improved in their morals by the instructions of the Moravians; insomuch, that the actual value of such slaves, considered as objects of commerce, has been raised. An increase of population from the births, would be an undoubted consequence of the moral improvement of slaves (p. 174.)

Does not think, that even on those estates where he has known the stock kept up and increased by births, such attention has been paid to the subject as he would judge proper (p. 174.)

As to whites escaping punishment in atrocious cases, from negro evidence being invalid, recollects, that in October 1789, a slave in Tobago was said, and universally believed, to have been stabbed by a white (thinks the manager of the estate) in the presence of many other slaves. The man died on the spot, and the white was tried, but, for want of such evidence as West Indian courts of law require, was acquitted. Another case occurred in St. Vincent's; a white, was strongly suspected of having shot his brother-

P. 171.

1791. brother-in-law, the fact was said by two or three slaves to have been done in their presence; and, the coroner's inqueft (he thinks) confirmed this fufpicion, by a verdict of wilful murder, againft this white. At a court where he (Mr. Ottley) prefided, the caufe was tried, and although there fcarcely remained a doubt with the jury of the man's guilt, he was neverthelefs acquitted, for want of fufficient evidence.

Thinks, that flaves in general are better treated, and more fatisfied with their condition, where the owner refides.

Where ground provifions are fcarce, and the owner's embarraffments prevent his getting fupplies of imported provifions, his negroes muft certainly fuffer. In 1779, he has heard, many perfons fuffered in Antigua from this circumftance.

P. 172. Has always heard that in St. Kitt's the chief dependance is on imported provifions, and it muft be often fo in Antigua, from the droughts to which they are fubject.

Where planters, as has often happened, take in more cane land than they can properly cultivate, the labour of the negroes will be increafed, and the land will not be productive.

Never knew a field flave buy his freedom. Never heard of act of fuicide among creoles.

As to infurrections, whether moft to be apprehended from African or Creole flaves, there never was an infurrection in St. Vincent's; but thofe which happened in Tobago, he has heard, originated with the Africans.

The circumftance of being forcibly torn from their families and friends, will frequently have the effect to fhorten the lives of imported flaves; particularly the aged: thofe who deftroy themfelves are always found to be adults.

P. 173. The climate of St. Vincent's, when firft fettled, being covered with wood, was very fatal to Europeans; but now it feems as healthy as any other

of

of the islands; and it has been remarked, that no greater mortality has occurred among the troops, for these five or six years past, than is common in England. The Europeans who are resident, from exposure during the hours of labour, are frequently subject to diseases.

By the court act, slaves may be seized for the owner's debt, but not till his goods, chattels, and produce are found insufficient. Slaves by the laws of St. Vincent's are in general considered as of the nature of real estate, and so descend to the heir, and widows are dowable from them; but where the personal estate is insufficient, executors may inventory slaves, and apply them to the discharge of the testator's debts. But to prevent estates being deprived of slaves, there is a particular law in St. Vincent's, allowing the executors to advance money at 6 per cent. interest, taking security on the slaves.

In case of actual seizure, the marshal is equally responsible for slaves, as for other property.

As to separation of families, by such sales, the law has provided, that a woman and her infant child shall always be sold together. Does not recollect any other provision.

Is of opinion, that the reforms in the treatment of slaves hinted in the preceding part of his evidence, would be for the mutual advantage of owner and slave.

With respect to the interests of the owner and managers being sometimes at variance, it is in general the manager's interest to make large crops, to support his character as a planter; and persons often judging from effects, he may feel himself under a kind of necessity of working the slaves harder than he wishes, to keep up to the produce of former years.

Never lost more than two or three children on his estates by the tetanus, but many by worms between three and six years, which seems the most fatal disorder to children in the West Indies, white as well as negro.

1791.  Want of food and other ill treatment he should suppose to be one great cause of slaves running away:
P. 175. indeed he has heard of a case, where about 20 negroes, who had been long absent, on the death of a master esteemed very severe, voluntarily returned to the estate: however, has known negroes run away without any provocation.

Upon asking his African negroes how they became slaves, some who were imported young, said, they were kidnapped; others, that they had been sold for crimes, or prisoners of war.

---

Witness examined—Reverend Mr. STUART.

P. 175. Has been at Guadaloupe, Dominique, St. Croix, St. Eustatius, St. Kitts, (at the last about a year) and Nevis. Went to the West Indies about the be-
P. 177. ginning of 1778, and left them in 1779 for America,
P. 175. which he left at Christmas 1782. Has had a twenty years acquaintance with the condition of slaves in the different states of N. America.

He is warranted in declaring that the negroes are an oppressed and much injured race, in no better estimation than labouring cattle; and every descrip-
P. 176. tion of their treatment he has met with, falls short of their real state. He read Mr. Ramsay's, in manuscript, at St. Kitts, and comparing it on the spot with the treatment of the slaves, thought it too favourable.

Though there are as humane people in the West Indies as elsewhere, they are from the nature of slavery led into cruel measures. The punishments there often seemed too severe. Has seen many negroes working in chains both in America and West Indies. Has often known runaways put in a dungeon at night, and once saw about fourteen, some of whom were in chains, put into a dungeon, apparently

ly much too small for them. Next morning he saw 1791.
one of them taken out dead.

Slaves in America seem more hearty and robust than those in the West Indies, owing, he supposes, to their being better fed. Their allowance was a quart of Indian corn, pease, or rice, each day, and a little salt. P. 177.

It was generally believed the Carolina slaves increased without importation.

He was told at St. Croix, that the slaves, instructed by the Moravians, were better behaved than the others.

The blacks are not inferior to the whites in abilities or disposition. They have as much generosity, fidelity, gratitude, understanding, and ingenuity; capable of receiving religious instruction, and improvement of every kind. Has found his black servants in nothing inferior to his white ones, and is sure that education and opportunity alone make a difference between the two descriptions.

Nothing had been done to alleviate the situation of the negroes, in general, in the period of Mr. Stuarts's residence in America and the W. Indies.

Witness examined—Captain SCOTT.

Captain Alexander Scott, of the Royal navy, was on the coast of Africa from Senegal to Cape Coast, in the Merlin, 1769, during the rainy season. Out of 90 men they buried there 8, of whom only 4 died of the disorders of the country. The surfs there are not an utter impediment to landing and shipping goods. He has himself landed from his own boat at Dixcove, Commenda, and Cape Coast, and the boats without him, also at Succonda. He has been in the W. Indies longer than on the Coast of Africa, and has of course seen greater surfs there than on the coast. P. 177. P. 178.

From

91. From a tranſaction which happened the ſecond day after his arrival in the Weſt Indies, he thought the negroes very cruelly uſed. He ſaw a white man purſue a negro into the water, bring him out, and take him to the wharf, where he had him hung up to a crane by his hands, which were tied together, and weights tied to his feet. When thus hoiſted up, but ſo as ſtill to touch the ground, another negro was ordered to whip him with a prickly buſh. He walked away from the diſagreeable ſight. The next day he ſaw the ſame negro lying on the beach, and with the aſſiſtance of another taking the prickles out of his breech, ſeemingly ſwelled and bloody. The negro aſſigned as a reaſon for the whipping, that the wharfinger thought he had ſtaid too long on an errand.

179.

---

Witneſs examined—Rev. Mr. DAVIES.

185. Reſided at Barbadoes fourteen years; the three laſt, learning the management of a ſugar eſtate; left it twenty-one years ago.

It was not underſtood that ſlaves had a right to legal redreſs when ill uſed by maſters.

186. As to field-ſlaves being well, or ſparingly fed, it is difficult to judge from appearance only; before crop many ſeemed very emaciated, in crop they looked well. Has ſeen their allowance dealt out; a grown negroe had nine pints of corn and about one pound of ſalt-fiſh per week: ſome principal ſlaves had as far as twelve pints; but the grain of the Weſt Indies is much lighter than wheat.

Never knew field-ſlaves acquire conſiderable property; they had a few houſe-neceſſaries, and were allowed to keep a pig, or a goat, and poultry.

As to its being a ſerious object with planters, to keep up the ſtock of ſlaves by breeding; it was ſo much otherwiſe, as to be generally thought a neceſ-
ſary

sary part of plantation expense to buy a lot of new slaves every six or seven years. Thinks the cause why the number of slaves are not kept up by births is, that females are over worked, in turning dung, carrying it out in baskets of 60 to 70 pound weight on their heads, and that for about eight hours a day, in the season. On their return home, they have to grind their corn by the strength of their arms, rubbing it between two stones: they must rise with the earliest dawn to prepare their food, that they may be in the field in time to escape punishment. Their circumstances (particularly the grinding corn) tended to discourage marriage, the woman's life becoming harder then, from being thus a slave to her husband (p. 187).

1791.

Pregnant women, and such as had children, are allowed to come into the field a little later than the rest.

With very good usage, if the females are to the males as three to four, the stock may be kept up by births; as it was on Kendal plantation belonging to Joshua Steele, esq. though the proportion was as two to three (p. 188).

Though people in general seemed to consider slaves as their most valuable property; yet their attention to them (from a sense of interest) appeared insufficient, because a great number of recruits was necessary.

To produce large quantities of sugar at a small expense, was the chief criterion of a manager's merit; though owners sometimes discharged their managers for too much severity.

Is of opinion they cultivated too much cane land, and too little provisions, as many were obliged to buy American corn: thinks having less cane land would produce better treatment to the slaves, and be ultimately for the master's benefit.

P.

The dependance on imported slaves certainly contributed to embarrass planters.

As to the practicability of keeping up the stock of slaves by births, provided it had been an object of serious attention to the planters; cannot say he attend '

1. to it when on the island, but it does appear to him now (from the facts which then fell under his notice p. 188.) that by general good usage of the slaves, and a milder treatment of females in particular, by the use of cattle and instruments of husbandry, especially the plough, their numbers might be kept up, perhaps increase. Knew a few estates which kept up their numbers without importation.
8. Is of opinion slaves were in general too sparingly fed, whether the master was embarrassed or not.

Understood from common report, that there were few estates that were not more or less embarrassed, from debt to the Eupopean merchant, or from jointures, or fortunes to brothers and sisters.

On asking African negroes how they became slaves, was answered they had been kidnapped.

Thinks their feelings much the same as Europeans. When removed from their habitations and spots of ground, they have been known to pine away.

As to the practice of slaves constantly working under a driver, does not recollect a single exception.

9. The whip is committed to the hands of apprentice boys, as well as to men, who often punish the slaves for very slight faults, arbitrarily.

---

Witness Examined—Mr. MARK COOK.

Mr. Mark Cook arrived in Jamaica in 1774, and left it, 1790; was three years in planting business: rest of the time as clerk and schoolmaster with different gentlemen there.

His first impression of slaves treatment shocking; for he lived close by a cane-piece, where they worked, and constantly heard the whip going. Slaves used cruelly, hardly looked on better than beasts, and often used worse.

Have not sufficient food nor time to cultivate their grounds. Has known both Africans and Creoles

eat

eat putrid carcafes, is convinced through want, would not have done it if they had had other fufficient food: when they have time and opportunity, are very cleanly in their food—are very fond of wafhing themfelves.

1791.

P. 190.

Are but indifferently clothed: one half of them almoft naked in the field; this not from choice but want; are fond of clothes when they can get any; alfo badly lodged; if overfeers can get their work done, they do not attend to fuch matters.

Their ufual punifhments very fevere, more fo than neceffary to procure the work to be done properly: much more of it might be done, were they better fed and lefs whipped.

Common to dung cane pieces by moon-light, and to oblige them to pick grafs after their day's work: this a great hardfhip. Negroe's grounds generally about two miles from the works; common to exact grafs picking for overfeer's cattle; feldom efcape punifhment if they neglect it. (p. 191.)

P. 191.

In crop-time they work in general about 18 hours out of 24: are often hurt through mere fatigue and want of fleep: knew a girl lofe her hand by the mill while feeding it; for overcome by fleep, fhe dropped againft the rollers. Has heard of feveral inftances of the kind.

Has known negroes own grounds taken from them to be put in canes for mafter's ufe, and wood land given them in exchange—a great hardfhip, and certainly the caufe of great diffatisfaction among them.

Thinks they are in general much neglected in ficknefs. There are doctors on eftates, but they feldom attend. Has known negroes, ordered to work by doctor when incapable of doing it, drop in the field, and obliged to be brought back again.

Much the fame work is expected from pregnant women as others; has feen them holing within a few hours of delivery; has known 39 lafhes given them at this time; has heard many of them wifh never to

P. 192.

Numb. 4.          O          have

1791. have children to undergo the hardships they themselves have been subject to.

Superannuated slaves have no allowance, and only what they can get among their relations; has seen them wandering about the beach, left to take care of themselves.

Desert frequently, owing to hunger and fear of flogging when threatened: when brought in are generally severely flogged, and sometimes have an iron boot put on one or both legs, and a chain or collar round their neck. The chain is locked, the collar fastened on by a rivet. When the collar is with 3 projections, it is impossible for them to lie down to sleep; even with 2 they must lie uneasily. Has seen collars with 4 projections. Never knew any injury from the chain and collar, but severely galling their necks; has, however, known a negro lose his leg from wearing the boot.

P. 193. A man and his wife, if industrious, and have their due time allowed them, may earn 3 or 4 bits per week, at the utmost. Never heard of a field negro buying his own freedom.

Domestic negroes are often severely punished, but not so often as field slaves: has known many instances: knew a lady, who had both her men and women domestics laid down and flogged every Monday morning for different slight offences, which happened in the previous week.

Knows of no legal protection slaves have against injuries from their masters.

Has known a field slave receive 200 lashes by order of the overseer, and a domestic 50, by order of his mistress.

P. 194. Once knew a runaway slave brought in, with part of a turkey with him, which he had stolen. His master immediately made two negroes hold him down, and with a hammer and a punch knocked out two of his upper and two of his under teeth. Really thinks negro had stolen from hunger, as he was nothing but skin and bones. Master was not reckoned cruel.

cruel. Witness lived with him three years, and remembers no other cruelty committed by him.

1791.

Never knew any complaint made to a magistrate, or punishment inflicted on owner or overseer in any of the cases mentioned, or in any other case whatsoever, for ill using a negro.

Has known negroes often punished for complaining to the owner or attorney against their overseers.

Chastity of negro women is not at all secure against overseers: if overseer sends for a girl for such a purpose, she must come or be flogged. Has known them threatened and flogged for refusing. Knew a Mulatto girl run away, in consequence of being threatened on that account. She was the wife of one of her own colour. Her husband and children ran away at the same time.

Has known both Mulattoes and Quadroons confined in irons 6 or 7 years, at the sole will of their owner. When they came out, (which was on the death of their mistress) their limbs were so distorted they could not walk. Was informed of it by one who lived two years on the estate, and had seen them often, and with whom he lived afterwards in the same employ.

P. 195.

Greatest recommendation of an overseer is the magnitude of the crop he makes, without regard to working the negroes hard; must work them hard to make large crops.

Some overseers are paid so much upon every hogshead of sugar, and puncheon of rum. Others have a stated annual salary.

Persons sometimes officiate on estates both as attorneys and overseers at same time. Has known attorneys reside 40 or 50 miles from the estates they were to superintend.

A gentleman, on whose estate he lived, bought 25 negroes in one lot, and at two years end had only 8 or 10 left. A great many African negroes die in the first three years after importation.

P. '196.

Has heard African negroes express their praise of

1791. their own country, and grief at leaving it. Never knew one but wished to go back again. Was told by one, when asking him the mode of his capture, that they undermined the house in which he and family lived, and came in upon them in the night, and took them all away.

Knew a negro man who hanged himself, also a woman. On the same property a man had shot himself before witness came to it. Has heard of many other instances of the kind; all Africans. Great rejoicings made by African negroes at the funerals of each other, from a belief that the deceased are gone to their own country again.

Capacity of some negroes is very great: as to disposition, they seem stubborn at first coming, but grow better in time. In both these points they do not differ much from lower white people, when they have been sometime in the country.

P. 197. Knows two estates where, he believes, negroes increased by births, which he ascribes to good usage and their not being worked too hard.

Maroon negroes, believes, are increasing very fast.

Domestic used in general much better than field slaves; thinks they usually increase, but not so fast as field slaves, when well used.

Cultivation of cotton, coffee, and pimento, much more easy than that of sugar; and slaves there look better and increase faster than those on sugar estates.

Jobbing gangs are used in general better than field slaves, if they work under their own masters; but if under the overseer of the estate, much worse.

Slaves of a person embarrassed are worse clothed and fed on that account; thinks in general they are used better, when their owner lives on the estate himself.

Knows of no regulation to prevent separation of families, when slaves are sold by writs of venditioni,
P. 198. or from African ships. Slaves subject to imprisonment when seized for master's debts. Has known
them

them lie long in gaol, and then fold, if the debt not paid. 1791.

Is of opinion white mechanics can do equally as much labour in Jamaica, if under fhelter, as in England out of doors, at proper hours.

Believes there are now more droughts in Jamaica than formerly, on account of fo much land having been cleared. Has heard many elderly natives fay, they never formerly wanted fealonable weather.

Has feen many Guinea failors lying about the towns, and travelling in the country full of ulcers; feemed very miferable people: a very great proportion of thofe in Kingfton hofpital are Guineamen.

Few eftates but what have runaway negroes. When the number is fufficient to make it worth while, book-keepers from the different eftates, armed with a mufket and a couteau, hunt after them in the woods. They fire at them at times, but not with a view of P. 199. killing them. Never knew any killed on fuch occafions.

Witnefs examined—Captain Cook.

Captain Cook, of the 89th regiment, was in Bar- P. 199. badoes, St. Lucia, St. Kitt's, &c. in 1780 and 1781. Thought the negroes in the towns were treated with very great feverity. He faw a woman named Rachel Lawder beat a female flave moft unmercifully; having bruifed her head almoft to a jelly with the heel of her fhoe, fhe threw her with great force on the feat of a child's neceffary, and then tried to ftamp her head through the hole, and would have murdered her if not prevented by two officers. The girl's crime was the not bringing money enough from on board fhip, where fhe was fent by her miftrefs for the purpofe of proftitution.

A domeftick flave, an excellent fervant, and in general well refpected by the officers on whom he attended

1791. tended at mess, having made a mistake on an errand for some cards, his mistress, a person of respectable condition, calling him by name said, 'Go to the jumper (to whom she paid 20s. a year to flog her negroes) give my service to him, and tell him to give you 27 lashes, with which the poor creature was obliged to comply. The company was displeased, and the officers left the house.

Two young ladies of fortune, sisters, one of whom was displeased at the pregnancy of a female slave belonging to the other, by the son of the surgeon attending the estate, proceeded to some very derogatory acts of cruelty. With their own garters they tied the young woman neck and heels, and then beat her almost to death with the heels of their shoes: one of her eyes continued a long while after in danger of being lost. They afterwards continued to use her ill, confining and degrading her. Captain Cook came in during the beating, and was an eye witness of it himself.

Neither in these nor any similar instances (and he could mention others) did the slave obtain any legal redress, nor does he know of any redress from law for the worst injuries, nor even of punishment for the murder of slaves. Two slaves were murdered and thrown into the road during his stay, yet no legal inquiry took place that he ever heard of. This excited his frequent inquiries from persons of all ranks and descriptions, and the universal answer was, that they did not choose to make examples of white men there, fearing it might be attended with dangerous consequences.

He never knew an instance of any endeavour to conceal cruelties of this kind. Being on a visit to General Frear at an estate of his in Barbadoes, and riding one morning with the General and two other officers, they saw near a house upon a dunghill, a naked negro nearly suspended by strings from his elbows backwards, to the bough of a tree, with his feet barely resting upon the ground, and an iron weight

weight round his neck, at least, to appearance, of 14lb. weight: and thus without one creature near him, or apparently near the house, was this wretch left exposed to the noon-day sun. Returning a few hours after they found him in the same state, and would have released him but for the advice of General Frear, who had an estate in the neighbourhood. The gentlemen through disgust shortened their visit, and returned the next morning.

The inferior white people, however, have a general impression, that they are punishable by law if they inflict more than 39 lashes at one time on a negro.

This law may be evaded by splitting a crime into many, and by intervals, dividing the times; and of this where slaves are punished at home, there are daily instances. Returning home one evening late with Major Fitch of the 90th regiment, they heard most dreadful cries, and on approaching the square at Bridge-Town, found they proceeded from the house of a man that sold liquor, and heard the repeated lashes of a whip on a creature whom they conceived to be dying. On their requesting admission, the cruelty seemed to be wantonly increased, which so provoked them that they broke open the door, and found a negro girl of about 19 chained to the floor, almost expiring with agony and loss of blood. The man taking refuge behind his compter from their indignation, and thinking himself free from the law, immediately cried out with exultation, that he had only given her 39 lashes at a time, and that only three times since the beginning of the night. He then threatened them for breaking his door, and interfering between him and his slave, whom he would flog to death for all any one, and have given her the fourth 39 lashes before morning, which must have killed her as she seemed then to be dying.

When masters were embarrassed their slaves always suffered in clothes and food; they often suffered in the same manner from the rapacity of managers in the absence of their masters.

The

1791. The slaves on large estates, the managers being in general more respectable men, seemed happier than those on the smaller.

Female slaves in the towns are very frequently let out for prostitution, or at least on paying a weekly sum to their owners, have leave to go on board the ships of war for that purpose. This is common with the inferiour people, and frequent even among the better sort. He has known a girl severely punished by her owner for returning without the full wages of her prostitution.

On some estates of the better kind, care was taken of those whom age or infirmity had rendered no longer serviceable, and easy offices were assigned

P. 203. them, so that some have grown extremely old, and been useful to the last: but among the inferiour, and sometimes among the most opulent, the reverse is the case; they have been dismissed to poverty and distress: and he does not believe that there is any law to prevent owners from turning such slaves upon the publick, to starve and die in the streets.

He has no doubt, and he speaks from many instances, that white people by habits of temperance, and regularity of hours, might bring themselves to go through nearly as much labour and fatigue in the West Indies as any people whatever.

It does not appear to him that the absence of the owner is in general hurtful to the slave, but that it has sometimes been much so, on one estate in particular, where the manager made a larger fortune than his master.

In general among the white people, and particularly the women, even of the better families, they believe, and endeavour to propagate an opinion, that the negroes are an inferiour species of being.

The clearing of Barbadoes has been thought prejudicial to the fertility of the island, the trees formerly having attracted showers that do not now fall so frequently as before.

He

He has known both mulattoes and African negroes purchase their freedom, but never a field slave.

1791.

When resident at Barbadoes, two instances of negro suicide occurred. A slave who had fled from home for some crime he had committed, was lost for several weeks. Being accidentally met by a man whose business it is to take up runaway negroes, and two assistants with him; the negro too much intimidated to fly, cried out to them, "I will not be taken alive; you and I have lived many years together, and why should we hurt each other." So, brandishing his hanger, he said, "Keep off," and immediately stabbed himself. In the other instance, a slave jumped into a well to avoid punishment for a murder he had committed through jealousy.

P. 204.

When up in the country, he heard it said by the manager of an estate, that an old man, whose office it had long been to flog the negroes, could strike with a whip of 7 feet long or longer, so exactly, as to lodge the point of the lash just within the flesh, where it would remain, till picked out with his finger and thumb. The manager offered to shew the experiment, and tendered wagers that he succeeded once in three times, which were of course declined. Negroes, when flogged in the country, are laid on their belly, with a negro at each hand and foot to raise them from the ground. In towns, they stand bare in the open streets, and expose their posteriors to the jumper. He has been shocked to see in the streets of Bridge-Town, a girl of 16 or 17, a domestic slave, running on her ordinary business, with an iron collar, having two hooks projecting several inches both before and behind.

P. 205.

---

Witness Examined—Mr. WILLIAM FITZMAURICE.

Was in Jamaica from June, 1771, to March, 1786 as overseer the last ten years, the former time bookkeeper,

P. 205.

1791. keeper, except the first six months, when he was clerk to a store in Kingston.

In towns slaves were usually flogged on the wharfs, (where they were sent, because the place was public, and for the conveniency of the crane and weights, p, 206.) They are stript, tied up to the crane, with one or two fifty-sixes to their feet, and a handkerchief round them for decency, and flogged with 39 lashes, probably more. Others were sent to the work-houses and flogged every morning, or every monday morning, according to the master's disposition. The punishment was generally so severe, as to cut them and bring blood, so as to make their frocks, if immediately put on, appear as stiff as buckram. He never knew it inflicted by a magistrate's order.

Pregnant women were very often flogged as described, and frequently miscarried from severe whippings.

P. 206. This mode of punishment continued the same during all his stay in the island.

Negroes provision-grounds were always distant from their houses, sometimes three miles off; and sometimes where it was with great difficulty they got at them.

The slaves of involved masters were always pinched in provisions, at storms or hurricanes.

Slaves provision-grounds, if near the cane-pieces, and the owner wishes to enlarge his estate, are always taken from them, and put into canes. Other grounds are given them, and perhaps a day weekly allowed them to bring it to perfection. This is often attended with the greatest destruction to the negroes, who go about new grounds or to new houses with great reluctance. He has changed negroes to a far healthier situation, and lost many from the effect of the change on their spirits.

Some negro houses are pretty dry, but most of them are open to the weather, being wattled without plaster. They sleep on a board on the ground, near the fire, and after it goes out, they suffer from cold
and

and damp. This causes many disorders, especially
to lying-in-women, who lose more children by this
than any other cause, as they generally die of the
locked jaw.

1791.

Weakly-handed estates, which are far the most
numerous, form their negroes in crop, into two
spells, which generally change at 12 at noon, and 12
at night. The boilers, and others about the works,
cut canes from shell-blow, half past one, till dark;
when they carry cane-top, or grass to the cattle-
penns, and then may rest till 12 at night, when they
relieve the spell in the boiling-house, by which they
themselves were relieved at 12 in the day. On all
estates, the boiling goes on night and day, except
sunday. But well-handed estates have three spells,
and intermissions accordingly.

P. 207.

After crop, they form two gangs, if tolerably well
handed. The shell blows for turning out at 4 or 5
o'clock, or earlier. It depends on the overseer.
They work till 10: have a quarter or perhaps half
an hour for breakfast; work till one, when shell
blows for dinner: if a rainy season, to take advantage of it, they work till the rain falls, which is two
o'clock, perhaps later. He now speaks of the season-
able parts of the island. They have about an hour
and half for dinner, and half an hour to get into the
field, so as that the last shall get there exactly at the
end of two hours; if not they are generally flogged.
They often run to their grounds, which may be distant, to get provisions for supper. Hence loss of
time, and frequent flogging. From dinner they
work till dark, when they trash cattle-penns, or carry
home grass. Then the book-keeper calls the list.
When they get home, it may be about 8 o'clock.
This exaction is grievous, as the willing ones must
wait till the lazy are brought up; and it causes whipping to those who neglect it. Some estates do not
exact this duty, but most do.

P. 217.

Various works are considered as detached jobbs
from the field-work, as hoeing intervals, which they

1791. can do before day; also moulding the cattle-pens, chopping up dung, making mortar, and other preparations for tradesmen. These are called before-day jobbs, which must be done, so as not to hinder the general work.

He never knew but one instance of work being done by task. He hired 60 negroes, all American; from a Mr. Douglas, and they had a task every morning measured out to them by Mr. D. or his overseer, and which they finished by 1 or 2 o'clock, and had the rest of the day to themselves. The driver carried no whip, and only went occasionally to see that the work was properly done. The plantation negroes, on the adjoining land, would not finish till dark (even with the driver) the same quantity of work. From this he thinks, tasks (of work that admit of it) would be to the ease of the negroes.

P. 219. From the negroes working, as they commonly do, in rows, with the driver after them with his whip, it almost necessarily follows that the weak will be hard pushed to make them keep up with the strong. He is sorry to say, that from this cause, many negroes are hurried to the grave; as the able, even if placed with the weakly to bring them up, will leave them behind, and then the weakly are generally severely flogged up by the driver, considered as worthless, and perhaps kept all noon to bring up their rows.

It is the overseer and book-keeper's duty to attend particularly to the negro-grounds. The lazy, or those who give trouble by asking for food, are collected by the driver every Sunday morning, and on the days for working their grounds, (allowed every other week as the overseer chose) and kept to work in a gang, in clearing provision-ground, or putting in order those they have.

Negroes often go 18 or 20 miles to the Sunday market, as he particularly knew the last four years he was in Jamaica. These journies are very hurtful to the Negroes, and it is almost impossible to prevent them.

He

He never heard of a common field-slave buying his freedom. Has known negroes who had saved a little money; generally head-carpenters, &c, endeavour to do it. Some masters have sold them their freedom, when or the border of becoming invalids, and where the estate was not mortgaged. On the last estate on which he lived, a very old, yet valuable man, who was head cattle-man, asked him to speak to the attorney to get him his freedom; but the estate being mortgaged it could not be done. (Africans who have been many years tradesmen or headmen, may probably buy their freedom when old, p. 232).

1791.

P. 220.

Very often, especially in the towns, the poorer whites and Jews let their negroes work out, and pay them a certain weekly sum. Many who have no trades, are pushed very hard to do this, and often skulk into the country, rob on estates, are chopped or maimed by watchmen, or sent to gaol as runaways. Handsome women are obliged to bring home more money than ordinary, it being expected they will be kept by whites or free persons. This is much the practice in Kingston and Spanish town, where he was a good deal. Old negroes past labour, especially those of Jews, are desired to provide for themselves, and he is sorry to say often suffer by hunger, or rough treatment, when caught stealing on the estates.

On some estates, where the proprietor lives, the doctor may attend twice a week, which is generally expected; but where the proprietor is absent, and the attorney 30, 50, or 100 miles off, the negroes often suffer very severely indeed, for want of medical care. The doctors are often young and inexperienced, which is generally attended with very fatal effects and certain ruin to the owner, as he knows from experience. The ordinary care of the sick depends on the hot house (hospital) man or woman, who bleed, dress sores, and give medicine, as directed by the doctor or overseer. Resident planters allow the hot-house per-

P. 221.

son

1791. son a little wine, by the doctor's order; but, on absentees estates, the overseer, even if so humane as to give it out of his own pocket, is perhaps distant from town, and has no wine. Attornies, generally do not give it, alledging it would not be allowed in their accounts: they always told him so, when he wrote for wine for the sick. He knows some, whose estates are in their own possession, who send out wine from hence; but this is not general. After long droughts, negroes are apt to get fluxes, by eating green vegetables, or bad flour, especially the former.

He lived with proprietors who wished to encou-
P. 222. rage propagation; but they are often obliged to push them, for good crops. He lived with others who desired to push them, and with whom the loss of a few negroes or stock was nothing compared to large crops, to satisfy their creditors.

Negroes particularly suffer in the hands of mortgagees. In general people in debt push constantly to get out of it, and to raise their credit to buy negroes, which he has known them buy, when, probably, they could not get credit for any other commodity. There is a custom, in Jamaica, of obtaining negroes on bond and judgment.

Some years ago, it was an old saying, in St. Thomas in the Vale (or Sixteen-Mile-Walk) that if a negroe lived 7 years, he paid for himself. The work was so hard there that it was proverbial, "A " Sixteen-Mile-Walk book-keeper, and a Clarendon mule, are the two hardest animals in the country." Several proprietors told him, they considered a child born and reared on the estate to be a dear negro, and overseers generally dislike breeding, as interfering with the work of the women. He has known other proprietors take pleasure in seeing the women breed. Many infants die of the locked jaw, within the 14th day, which he believes, from his last six years experience, is chiefly owing to cold and uncleanliness. The lying-in women generally have large fires in their rooms, which being often broken, let in the cold,

cold, and when the fire goes out a severe chill follows, by which the infant suffers. A great many die of yaws which require great cleanliness. When overseer, he has been directed to attend to the rearing of children; but speaking generally, from his own knowledge, infants had not the requisite care. Believes the stock of slaves could not be kept up or increased on the present system; it would take some time to bring about. He means the easing the negroes, which he thinks might be done, by using the plough on every estate, and, where it can run, putting in the canes after it.

On Raimesberry estate, in Clarendon, the negroes increased so fast, that a gang of them was drawn off to settle a new estate called Yarmouth, which he had the care of, but the settlement was discontinued, from the change of the attorney. On Orange in St. James's no negroes were bought, for at least 15 years, and they increased; as also on Eden in the same parish. He lived on both these estates. Negroes worked moderately may be increased. He has known estates where the negroes were worked severely hard, they increased and decreased nearly equal.

Nothing is more common, than negroes suffering by change of management; as new overseers, as well as inexperienced overseers, push the negroes to make greater crops than their predecessors.

A gentleman had two estates in Clarendon, one of which Mr. F. managed. He had too few negroes for both, but enough for one. He was also much in debt, and his negroes suffering from being overwrought. He put both gangs on one estate, which were amply sufficient, is now making 400 hogsheads of sugar, and is a clear man. Both estates did not before make 150 hogsheads. Most of the time he was his own overseer. Mr. F. never knew he bought any negroes since then, which is about 13 years ago. But cannot speak of this as a fact.

In St. Thomas in the Vale, on the estate of a gentleman lately deceased, by over-pushing, most of the

1791. negroes were destroyed, while he was in England. On his return, his estates were almost without negroes and those that lived were taken by writs of Venditioni, and judgments against him to a large amount. Mr. F. bought, at a sale, 50 odd, to cover a debt for a house in Kingston. Two of his estates were thrown up when Mr. F. left the island, the other three are in the hands of mortgagees. Another estate, within three miles of Montego bay, was making from
P. 225. 180 to 200 hogsheads, with an adequate strength, when it was put in possession of mortgagees. In twelve years it was reduced to 10 hogsheads. The slaves were destroyed, by making an unnecessary canal in swamps. It was brought to sale in 1788, bought by the mortgagee, and is now brought up to its former crops. The proprietor of the estate was most of the time in England. The overseer of it made 10,000 l. and retired.

When overseer on an estate in St. John's, the estate being short handed, Mr. F. mentioned to the proprietor that he would not take off the crop with the negroes and cattle. He told Mr. F. to drive them without mercy, as the loss of a few negroes and stock was no object compared to sending home his crop in time. Mr. F. left him about the end of crop, because he would not see 100 lashes given to a domestic, not immediately under his direction, and who he did not think deserved this punishment.

He has known the plough used on many estates with advantage, as it eases the negroes, and pulverizes the soil. (But some soils do not require pulverizing, p. 226.) Dove-Hall, in St. Thomas in the Vale, plows 40 or 50 acres every fall. He has known Mr. Edwards only put in canes after the plough without holing, except on an estate Mr. Pinnock is attorney for, and which made great returns. The chief obstacle to the plough is, that managers have not time to adopt it, looking for immediate labour, and often there is not a blacksmith within 15 miles to repair it.

He

He has often attempted plowing and has been obliged, by thefe obftacles, to leave it off.

In fome cafes, the Doctor's vifits are a confiderable check on the overfeers feverity, where the proprietor lives on the eftate. But when the attorney lives perhaps 20, 30, 40, or even 100 miles off, then it is the intereft of the overfeer and doctor, not to find fault with each other.

He is forry to fay, he never knew recourfe had to legal redrefs for wanton cruelty to flaves. Has known people, a Mr. Rufhie in particular, whom he had occafion to fee, almoft daily, commit cruelties which brought negroes to their end. He caught him, one day, in the act of hanging a negroe. On his remonftrating, Rufhie ordered him off his eftate. He rode away and informed his employer, who was a magiftrate and who defired him to go and inquire the next morning, before R. was up, whether the negro was dead. This Mr. F. did; and on privately afking a white man, he defired Mr. F. to go into the curing-houfe, when he faw the negro lying dead on a board. He returned and told what he had feen to his employer, who was very much fhocked; but Mr. F. heard nothing more of it. It was well known this man killed many of his negroes, and that fo faft, as to force him to fell his eftate. Cafes of this kind, he cannot fay, are frequent; but feverity, and hard work certainly caufe a conftant decreafe of the able negroes. No attempt was made to bring Rufhie to punifhment. His character was generally known, and much defpifed by the neighbouring proprietors. He thinks, his employer defired him to make the above inquiry more from curiofity than an intention to inforce the law againft Rufhie, with whom he was on decent terms. He and his employer often vifited him, and always found his negroes laid up with cruelties, and thofe that could work chained to the coppers, or, in gangs linked in the field. Other cruelties he practifed, were too indecent to be mentioned. He often found Rufhie dropping hot lead

1791. on his negroes, but took no notice of it; as he wished nobody to see him acting those cruelties. He did not interfere; because he got his bread from employers, and did not wish to be disliked, or called officious, p. 231). Other acts of cruelty are often practised, according to the disposition or viciousness of the master or overseer. An overseer he knew well, (and who, as before said, brought down an estate, by the countenance of the mortgage-in-possession, from 180 to 10 hogsheads) was charged with gelding a negro on the estate, for riding out his horses at night, and he believes justly; as afterwards Mr. F. knew he gelt a negro of his own: on which the troop of horse he was captain of, and in which Mr. F. served, objected to do duty with him.

P. 228. He cannot say field slaves, in general, appeared to him marked with the whip. Where there are cruel managers, and large crops exacted, the effects are visible on the negroes.

Negroes are often driven by severity to run away. They go to their masters or attornies, if within reach; but when the attorney lives perhaps 70 or 100 miles off, they prefer going into the woods, being generally taken up as runaways before the journey's end. Planters who employ distant attornies, are sure to suffer by it. Runaways, when caught, are whipped and confined, or if the manager is humane, perhaps forgiven; but they are generally punished to deter others.

He never saw mutilation actually inflicted; but on an estate where he was book-keeper, there was a negro, whose master had had his leg cut off, and had made him a blacksmith. The master said he had, by so doing, made him his most valuable negro; as he did all the iron-work of the three estates, and, before that, he was always running away.

It was generally understood that whipping was limited to 39 lashes: but it is often evaded by putting the negro into the stocks, and giving him 39 more, for the same offence, next day. Hasty and
vicious

vicious people would give perhaps 100 lashes, and if the negro died from it, (which however he never knew) where the owner or attorney lived not near enough, they escaped unpunished.

Has known too many suicides, among new negroes especially, both by hanging themselves and by dirt-eating, which they knew to be fatal. He lost, one year, 12 new negroes by it, though he fed them well. On his remonstrating, they constantly told him, they preferred dying to living. A great proportion of the new negroes that go on sugar estates, die in this way.

They are always talking of their being taken away, and kidnapped, from their country, and of the hardship of slavery.

Nothing is more common than persons buying new negroes, before they have sufficient provision-grounds, and other accommodations for them: and the masters finding it very difficult to buy provisions, the negroes feel hunger, before they can establish grounds, and soil and seasons are often against their raising provisions. Hence such negroes are often lost. New negroes in towns, are better off, being generally employed in the house, and fed weekly.

A man may be attorney for from 1 to 20 estates, according to his interest. He knows several who are attornies for a great number, in various parts of the island, perhaps at the distance of 10, 30, 60, or 80 miles, or more, as it happened.

Some overseers have premiums for all they make, above a certain number of hogsheads; but this is not the common mode. Attornies have salaries or commissions. Believes attornies on most mortgaged estates, draw commissions on the net crops, as well as on what they buy on the island for the use of the estates; and they accumulate great riches.

Some overseers have negroes, others have not; but generally they convert their salaries into negroes. If allowed to work them on the estates where they

1791. themselves live, it causes a jealousy between the manager's and the plantation negroes.

Thinks, on an average at least one-third of the new negroes imported into the island, die in the first three years, and three men die to one woman as he has experienced. The men take every thing unpleasant to heart, and often kill themselves. The women have many protections the men have not, as being taken as wives by the plantation negroes, or being made domestics.

P. 231. In the last four years he was in Jamaica, he bought 95 new negroes; at the end of that time, he sold 52, all that were alive, and those not seasoned. Had he kept them till seasoned, he should have lost more, and for this very reason he sold them.

The lower whites too often looked on the negroes as inferior beings, and often beat them, unless checked by the attornies or overseers.

He only knew one attempt made to give the negroes religious instruction, and that was by a proprietor in Liguanea, who encouraged one or two American negroes, who professed to be capable to give his negroes some religious notions. But the neighbours considered this as dangerous, by assem-

P. 232. bling too many negroes, who might be mutinous. The aforesaid gang of 80 American negroes, after work, went to prayers; they were a valuable gang, and worked task-work for him about nine months.

The cane land is generally as fit for cotton, coffee, or other articles.

Though domestics may not be the best slaves, they appear so, as the house soon makes a visible change on them.

He has been at twenty sales by scramble, at least. No particular care was taken to prevent the separation of relations, except sucking children, or those under three or four years.

Sales by venditioni are very frequent, where levies are made. He has known them three months or

longer

longer in prison, before sale. But this depends on occasional circumstances. 1791.

Refuse slaves are sold according to their appearance, some as low as three dollars. They are generally bought by the Jews in towns, at vendue or at private sale.

He has always, as overseer, given in to the vestries, the annual returns of slaves, stock, &c. and, as vestry-man, (in 1756, in St. Thomas, in the Vale, where he possessed land and negroes) has received such returns, in which it was not usual to distinguish the sexes.

Has very frequently seen Guinea sailors wandering about the island, in an abject state.

---

Witness examined,—Mr. THOMAS CLAPPESON.

Was at Jamaica in 1762 and 1763; from 1768 to 1778, and 1786 to 1789. The general opinion he formed, was, that the slaves were severely treated, and in a miserable state. P. 207.

Thinks that, in general, the food which they can obtain, is insufficient.

For the first 2 years, he was in the seafaring line, the rest of the time wharfinger and pilot. P. 208.

Had opportunities of seeing many negroes from the estates; such as he asked, as to their feeding, generally said (particularly in droughts, when provisions were scarce) " Hungry da kill me."

Very commonly suffer both in quality and quantity of food, from the embarrassments of their masters: has known several who had not credit for provisions; others who bought, for cheapness, damaged corn, &c. when better was to be had; which he has himself sold, and which the slaves complained of, when they came to fetch it from the wharf; a neighbour told him his hogs would not eat it.

Knew

1791. Knew a perſon near him, reputed worth £50,000 loſe 10 or 12 ſlaves for want of food, when it was to be had.

P. 209. Slaves generally ſteal proviſions, ſoap, candles, &c. which they ſometimes ſteal to ſell.

They are generally ill clothed; never knew any go naked from choice.

The puniſhments appeared in general ſevere, to the fear of which he chiefly attributes the frequent deſertions.

Knew a pregnant woman whipped, and delivered on the ſpot.

Has heard of very great ſeverities to runaways; has ſeen them wear iron collars on their necks, and pot-hooks, with 3 prongs, both rivetted; the prongs projecting 2 feet; thinks the wearer cannot eaſily lye down.

Never heard of ſlaves obtaining any redreſs for injuries, by maſters or overſeers.

P. 210. An overſeer told him, he had often picketed the ſlaves to extort confeſſion.

Knew a cooper give his ſlave 200 laſhes, for ſtealing a little rice from him. He allowed his ſlaves a herring a day, and a bit a week.

The wharfinger whom he ſucceeded in 1786, allowed his negroes a herring a day only.

Knew, in 1789, a man who had an old decrepid woman ſlave, to whom he would allow nothing. He remonſtrated with him on it, in vain.

Slaves are often impriſoned on writs of venditioni; at the ſale of ſuch, never heard of any attention to avoid ſeparating families.

The general recommendation of an overſeer is,
P. 211. good ſugars and large quantities; has known an overſeer paid a guinea per hogſhead, beſides his ſalary, for all he could make beyond a certain quantity.

Has known ſeveral perſons attorney and overſeer on the ſame eſtate.

Slaves

Slaves are supposed better off where the owner resides; has heard it always supposed, that the better they are treated, the more it is for the owner's interest. 1791.

It is common for persons who have a few slaves, and but little work, to oblige them to earn 3 or 4 bits a day, and punish them very severely if they fail to bring home such sum; has known them steal grass and sell it to do this: knew a man compel his old negro, wanting a leg, to pay him 4 bits a day.

African negroes are capable of being made mechanics.

They destroy themselves sometimes, from various causes; fear of punishment, jealousy, &c. it is a very prevailing opinion with them, that at death they return to their own country. P. 212.

Has often heard of their being kidnapped in Africa: he had a slave who had been a negro-catcher in his own country.

Has seen several slave sales on board, all by scramble. In 1789, saw a sale by scramble in a butcher's slaughter-house on the beach. Never heard of any precautions at scrambles, to prevent the separation of relations or friends Thinks whites, if temperate, are able to labour in Jamaica; he never worked harder than he has done there; no people work harder than our sailors do there.

Has heard, that clearing the lands, has, near the sea coast, caused more drought.

In his returns to the vestry of the number of slaves, he never used to distinguish the sexes.

The free negroes in general behaved well, they were fishermen and tradesmen. P. 213.

Has heard of several people buying more slaves than they could pay for.

Has heard often seamen say, that in Guinea ships, the crews are ill treated, to make them desert; has always understood, that they did not want to carry home as many seamen as they took out; that they
got

1791. got rid of what they could in the West Indies, to save their wages.

P. 214. Was in Jamaica when the assembly passed the consolidated law; he has often heard it was passed because of the stir about the slave trade in England. Never heard that any regard was paid to it, slaves being still treated as before. Never heard of any prosecution for such disregard: recollects an instance of disregard to it, which came under his eye. The owner of an old and decrepid female slave, would allow her neither victuals nor clothing; advised a son of the woman to complain to a magistrate, who would perhaps order her to be taken care of; believes he was deterred from fear of punishment, as that owner treated his slaves very harshly in general.

---

Witness examined—WILLIAM BEVERLEY, Esq.
A Student of Lincoln's Inn.

P. 215. Was born in Virginia, and lived there the first 16 years of his life, returned in 1786, and resided above two years in different parts of America.

The negroes in Virginia always kept up their numbers, and generally increased. His father's more than doubled their numbers. In 1761 he had about 200, and in 1788, he paid taxes on above 540, of whom not above 20 or 30 had been added by purchase.

P. 216. Slaves there had no legal redress, for ill usage by their masters. In other cases they had, on proving the fact by two white witnesses.

In summer, negroes were generally healthier than in winter, when they always complained of the cold, though it did not hurt their health, when well clothed. The diseases most fatal there are agues and fevers, in summer, to which negroes are less subject than whites.

They

They were generally punished with much severity; but that depends greatly on the owner's disposition.    1790.

Each slave had a bushel of Indian corn meal weekly: besides this allowance, they usually had ground to cultivate for their own use; but this depended a good deal on the master. They were all allowed to raise poultry.

He never heard of any attempts to give the slaves religious or moral instruction.

Has heard of some slaves working by task; but, in general, it was not practised.

Never knew a slave destroy himself.

The slaves of distant proprietors were often treated,    P. 232. by the overseers, much more severely, than those under the master's eye. This different treatment was observable in the appearance of the slaves.

Was told in America, that when the abolition of the slave-trade was first agitated in 1774, many doubted the practicability of keeping up the numbers by births; and the persons so doubting have since expressed to him a conviction that their fears were groundless. The slave-trade was abolished in America in 1774.

---

Witness examined—Mr. GEORGE WOODWARD.

Mr. George Woodward is both an owner and    P. 233. mortgagee of W. India property, in Barbadoes; where he resided in 1782 and 1783, and was also    P. 234. in 1777.

Both in town and country he thought the domestics very numerous. There seemed to be more females than males in the island. While resident, he never heard any complaint of the want of negroes to carry on plantation or other business. He does not recollect the sale of a single cargo of slaves while there.

1791. there. The labour of flaves the year round he thinks cannot be reckoned eafy.

It is poffible in a great degree to relieve the labour of flaves by the plough. He has ufed it himfelf: the firft he ever faw, he took over himfelf, and he is fure it tilled the ground better than the hoe did. One plough, two men, and four horfes, will do as much work as thirty negroes, and better. The labour of holding the plough is much eafier than holing. It did not require much negro labour to prepare the ground for the cane after the plough.

P. 235. There is not much difficulty of ploughing to the depth of fix inches, which is the rule, and a fufficient depth for the cane. The plough may be made to plough the ftrongeft clay land that is.

The negroes are capable of learning the management of the plough. He thinks that the largeft part of the cane land and ginger land of Barbadoes may be ploughed to the advantage of the proprietor, and faving of negroes labour. The negroes are not averfe to the plough: he has feen them both hold and drive it. He did not find the cattle injured by the labour. He is acquainted with the ufe of the plough in England, he farms land of his own. Capt. Lee took out fome ploughs about 3 years ago.

He is not apprehenfive that the abolition of the flave trade will injure his W. India property. He thinks it would be of advantage to the ifland of
P. 236. Barbadoes. By ufing them well, and by good management, the ftock of flaves would naturally increafe, without importation.

---

Witnefs examined—Mr. JOSEPH WOODWARD.

Mr. Jofeph Woodward has been in Barbadoes in 1788, 1789 and 1790. He has there feen the plough in ufe by Mr. Henry Trotman, jun. He believes he has ufed it many years.

Mr.

Mr. Trotman informed him that he thought tillage by the plough both better and cheaper than the labour of negroes with the hoe. The foil that he ploughed was not the beft, it was rather rocky. Mr. Trotman told him, that the plough then anfwered his purpofe, and in time would become general, when people became acquainted with its utility. 1791.

He once at Bridgetown faw a negro lying on the wharf, fo very much debilitated that he could not ftand, and heard from him, that his owner would not take him in. He appeared about 60 years old. P. 237.

He has known free negroes hire themfelves to ftow fugars in the fhips hold; he has known them fo employed on board his own fhip. He knows no labour either of blacks or whites more fevere than this is.

---

### Witnefs examined—Mr. JAMES KIERNAN.

Was in Africa in 1775, 1776, 1777, and 1778, to learn the nature of the trade, to carry it on. P. 237.

The trade for flaves in the R. Senegal, where he refided, was chiefly with the Moors, on the northern banks, who got them very often by war, and not feldom by kidnapping; i. e. lying in wait near a village, where there was no open war, and feizing whom they could.

Has often heard of villages, and feen the remains of fuch, broken up by making the people flaves. P. 238.

Has always heard kidnapping fpoken of there as notorious; and has feen proofs of it by perfons fo taken being ranfomed; when, very often, the white trader afks more than the value of the flave, to give him up: never heard of a white trader, before buying a flave, inquire into the right of the feller.

Never

1791.   Never knew any person sold for witchcraft; a belief in it exists strongly on that part of the coast.

P. 239. The first year, by far the greatest number of slaves were offered to sale, from an open war then subsisting between the Moors and negroes: to which the Moors have always a strong inducement, most of the European goods they obtain, being got in exchange for slaves. Hence desolation and waste: in a few years, they extirpated large settlements on the northern banks of the Senegal, and in time they were expected to root out all the black nations between the Senegal and Gambia. The Moors neither follow nor encourage agriculture.

Believes, that to be sold to Europeans, is considered by all negroes from inland, as well as on the coast, as a punishment only short of death.

The inhabitants of the island of St. Louis, are estimated at about 5000, who are supplied with cattle by the Moors, and with corn by the blacks only.

Ships bound to the W. Indies were supplied by the blacks with large quantities of corn, which the slaves preferred to any other food.

The blacks on the south banks of the Senegal raise cotton, indigo, and tobacco, sufficient for their use.

Knows the negroes manufacture cotton, leather, and metals, for they supply Senegal with clothing, articles of leather, and ornaments of gold and silver: they dye some of their cottons very finely, blues and scarlets; believes their consumption of cotton cloths is very considerable.

Never knew the natives backward in supplying any considerable demand for provisions, when properly encouraged.

Never knew the natives encouraged by Europeans to raise for sale other produce than provisions.

Persons of property there, have a great number of persons under the denomination of slaves, whom they

they treat as Europeans would people of their own family.

---

Witness examined—HENRY BOTHAM, Esq.

Went to the W. Indies 1770, and, in about two years, visited all the islands, English and French, and was employed by government in Grenada, to ascertain the difference of property there between the old and new subjects.

He was not long a planter in the W. Indies. He directed Messrs. Bosanquet and Fatio's sugar estate there, in their partner's absence; but he carried on sugar works many years at Bencoolen, in the East Indies.

He has examined the account, in the P. Council's Report, of the mode of cultivating sugar in the East Indies, and it is the same which he delivered in. He drew it up from having long considered the subject, and, since he delivered it to the P. Council, sees no reason to make any alteration in it.

The following is an Abridgment of the said account:

"Mr. Botham on the Mode of cultivating a Sugar Plantation in the East Indies, &c."

Having been 2 years in the English and French W. India islands, and since conducted sugar estates in the E. Indies; it may be desirable to know that sugar, better and cheaper than that in our islands, and also arrack, are produced in the E. Indies, by the labour of free people. China, Bengal, and the coast of Malabar, produce quantities of sugar and spirits; but, as the most considerable sugar estates are near Batavia, I shall explain the improved mode of conducting those estates. The proprietor is generally a rich Dutchman, who has built on it substantial works. He rents the estate (say of 300 or more acres) to a Chinese, who lives on and superin-

1791. tends it, and who re-lets it to free men, in parcels of 50 or 60, on condition that they shall plant it in canes for so much for every pecul, 133¼ lb. of sugar produced. The superintendant collects people from the adjacent villages to take off his crop. One set of task-men, with their carts and buffaloes, cut the canes, carry them to the mill and grind them. A second set boil them. A third clay and basket them for market, at so much per pecul.

Thus the renter knows with certainty what every pecul will cost him. He has no unnecessary expence, for when crop is over, the task-men go home, and, for 7 months in the year, there only remain on the estate the cane planters, preparing the next crop. By dividing the labour, it is cheaper and better done.

P. 243. Only clayed sugars are made at Batavia, which are equal to the best from the W. Indies, and sold at 18s. per pecul. The Shabander exacts a dollar per pecul on all sugar exported. The price of common labour is from 9d to 10d per day. But the taskmen gain considerably more, not only from extra work, but from being considered artists in their several branches. They do not make spirits on the sugar estates; the molasses and skimmings are sent for sale to Batavia, where one distillery may buy the produce of 100 estates. Here is a vast saving in making spirits, not as in the W. Indies, a distillery for each estate: arrack is sold at Batavia at about 8d. per gallon; the proof of the spirit is about 5-tenths.

After spending two years in the West Indies, I returned to the East in 1776, and in the last war conducted sugar works at Bencoolen, in Sumatra, on nearly the same principles as the Dutch; I confined my expences to what they had done, allowing for the unavoidable charges, on a new and sole undertaking.

The cane is cultivated to the utmost perfection at Batavia; the hoe, almost the sole implement of the West, is there scarcely used; the lands are well ploughed by a light plough with a single buffalo; a
drill

drill is then ploughed, and a person with two baskets filled with cane plants, suspended to a stick across his shoulders, drops into the furrow plants alternately from each basket, covering them at the same time with earth with his feet. Young canes are kept often ploughed as a weeding, and the hoe is used to weed round the plant when very young; but of this there is little need if the land has been sufficiently ploughed. When the cane is ready to earth up, the space between the rows, is ploughed deep, the cane-tops tied up, and with an instrument like a shovel, with teeth at the bottom, a spade-handle, and two cords fixed to the body of the shovel, ending by a wooden handle for a purchase, is used by two persons to earth up the cane, the strongest holding the handle of the shovel, pressing it into the ploughed earth, while the other on the opposite side of the plant, by a jirk of the cord, draws up to the plant, all the earth that the plough had loosened. Two persons with this instrument, will earth up more canes in the day than 10 negroes with hoes. The canes in India are much higher earthed than in the West Indies; in moist soils, they, with little labour, earth them as high as the knee, at once making a dry bed for the cane, and a drain for the water.

The improvement in making the cane into sugar, at Batavia, keeps pace with that in its culture: evaporation being in proportion to the surface, their boilers have as much of it as possible. The cane juice is tempered and boiled to a syrup; it is then thrown into vats, which hold one boiling, there sprinkled with water, to subside its foul parts: after standing six hours, is let off by 3 pegs of different heights, into a copper with one fire; it is there tempered again, and reduced to sugar, by a gentle fire; it granulates, and the boiler dipping a wand into the copper, strikes it on the side, then drops the sugar remaining on it, into a cup of water, scrapes it up with his thumb-nail, and can judge to a nicety of the sugar's being properly boiled. The vats I mentioned

1790.  tioned are placed all at the left end of a set of coppers. After running off for boiling all that is clear, the rest is strained on the outside of the boiling-house; what is fine is put into the copper for sugar, the lees kept for distilling.

P. 245.

Claying of sugar is as in the W. Indies. The cane trash is not, as in our islands, carried into sheds, where it loses much of its strength before it is used; but is laid out immediately to dry, then made into faggots, set up in cocks, and used immediately when dry; hence its force of fire is much greater, and the carrying it to and from the trash-house is saved.

The culture of the cane in the West Indies is in its infancy. Many alterations are to be made, expenses, and human labour lessened; the hoe, now used to turn up soils of different texture, is of one construction, cheap and very light; so that the negro, without any help from its weight, digs up the earth, (and, the cane roots, on replanting) by the severest exertion. In the East we plough up the cane roots.

Having experienced the difference of labourers for profit, and labourers from force, I can assert, that the savings by the former are very considerable.

The West India planter, for his own interest, should give more labour to beast, and less to man; a larger portion of his estate ought to be in pasture. When practicable, canes should be carried to the mill, and cane tops and grass to the stock, in waggons; the custom of making a hard-worked negro get a bundle of grass twice a day abolished; and in short a total change take place of the miserable management in our West India islands. By this means following, as near as possible, the East India mode, consolidating the distilleries, I do suppose our sugar islands might be better worked than they now are, by two-thirds, or indeed one-half of the present force Let it be considered, how much labour is lost by the persons overseeing the forced labourer, which is saved when he works for his own profit. I have

P. 246.

have stated, with the strictest veracity, a plain matter of fact—that sugar estates can be worked cheaper by free persons than slaves.

Whether the slave-trade can be abolished, and the blacks freed, is for the consideration of Parliament. In my judgment, these desirable purposes, may be effected without materially injuring the West India planter. He has but to improve his culture, lessen human labour, and the progeny of the present blacks will answer every purpose of working West India estates. [See this account at large in the Privy Council's Report, at the end of Part III.]

The slaves in the French islands appeared to be better cloathed, better fed, and better behaved, than in the British: and their being well fed is chiefly owing to the French planter putting a great proportion of his estate in provisions.

Whether it might or might not be ultimately for the interest of the British planter, and the benefit of his slaves, if he were to allot to provisions, more of the land now destined to sugar, is a question that can only be decided by experiment in the different islands, as the same answer to it would not suit each. In islands that seldom fail in rains, it is no doubt for the planter's interest, to sacrifice a part of the ground allotted for sugar, to provisions; as these feed his negroes better than any dry or other provisions imported: but in islands subject to droughts, he does not think the planter can without materially lessening his crop of sugar, give up any portion of ground to provisions.

In 1764, when the East India Company's possessions in Sumatra were returned to them by the French, they were informed by their servants at Bencoolen, that the public works, and other labours of their settlement, could not be carried on without a large supply of slaves; the Company therefore sent slave-ships to Africa and Madagascar, and transported to Bencoolen nearly 1000 slaves, in much the same proportion of men, women, and children, as are carried,

1791. carried from Africa to the West Indies, that is more men, than women and children. These slaves, on the first years of their arrival, from the unhealthiness of the climate, and other causes, decreased: but when they had been at Bencoolen a few years, where they were well fed, humanely treated, and had very little work, they began annually to increase; notwithstanding, from the little attention that was paid to their way of life, both men and women lived in the most abandoned way. The wonder was, that they did increase, as the young female slaves were common prostitutes to the soldiers and sailors.

---

Witness examined—JOHN SAVAGE, Esq.

P. 247.

Resided in Carolina from 1729 to 1775. Was not a planter, but was repeatedly on many plantations as a visitant for a day or two at a time, and knew the state of negroes there.

P. 248. Understood labour was performed by task in most operations on estates.

Negroes increased greatly where well clothed and fed; is doubtful if they increased where clothed and fed badly. Heard where masters were harsh, they could not raise children, or but a few.

Where masters were prudent, and kept themselves out of debt, negroes were hearty and strong: hence they got more work out of them than those who did not use them so well, and these were they who made fortunes by planting.

A friend of his, Gabriel Manigault, Esq. informed him, that in 1737 he had on his estate 86 negroes, of whom 12 or 14 were superannuated. The latter he replaced by others. With no more addition than this, they had increased to 270 about a year or two before witness left the country. Mr. Manigault's estate (by purchase) consisted of about 18000 or 19000 acres, 6000 of which were settled, and 12000
or

or 13000 not so; for the latter he had taxes and quit 1791.
rents to pay for many years till his son came of age,
to whom he then gave them. Notwithstanding this
charge on the unimproved land, he always made interest of his purchase-money. Mr. M. was a man
of humanity, and gave his slaves sufficient clothes,
food, and accommodations.

In the year 1739 there was a duty laid on the im-
portatation of slaves to Carolina, which amounted to
a prohibition, and which continued to 1744. The
purchase of new negroes having involved the planters greatly in debt, was the reason why the legis-
lature laid it.

### Witness Examined—John Clapham, Esq.

Was upwards of 20 years in Maryland. Negroes P. 249.
kept up their numbers there by propagation, and increased, so that the overplus in some instances were
shipped to the W. Indies. Has known 100 sales,
where proprietors have had too many for their use
in consequence of increase by propagation; yet they
were not thought to be well treated, though better
than to the southward, and the climate was subject to
great and sudden variety of heat and cold.

Attempts were not frequent in Maryland to give
religious instruction to negroes.

### Witness Examined—Robert Crew, Esq.

Is a native of Virginia, and resided there till
1783. Knew the state of the plantation slaves there.

Had sufficient clothing, and as much Indian meal P. 250.
as they could use, and were in general supplied daily
with flesh, fish, or something else added to their meal
or bread.

Overseers on large estates superintended slaves, but

1791. without a whip, as a master on a small estate, or a bailiff would in this country.

Negroes in Virginia increased rapidly without importation, so much so, that it was a general opinion, that it was profitable to hold slaves on this account, exclusive of the profits of their labour.

Treatment was different on different estates. Where the master was involved and did not superintend his own estate, his overseers were directed to make the greatest possible quantities of tobacco, to supply his pressing necessities. Here the slaves were ill used, worked excessively hard, and were not sufficiently fed. Where the proprietor was in good circumstances, and could pursue his own interest, they were not so hard worked, and had better supplies of food and clothing.

P. 251. This severe system in some, though he thinks never so severe in any circumstances (with a few exceptions) as to cause a decrease in their numbers, and indeed small profits of tobacco plantations could not afford fresh supplies, yet had the effect certainly of preventing their increasing so fast as they otherwise would. Such a system was deemed unprofitable.

Spent a few months at Barbadoes and St. Croix. Was struck with the difference of the treatment of slaves there and in Virginia. A driver with a whip stood over them while at work: they were nearly without clothing. These were the obvious differences. No knowledge of particulars. Thinks the use of the whip formed a difference in their treatment considerably to the disadvantage of West Indian slaves.

Thinks the culture of tobacco nearly as laborious as that of sugar; and the climate of Virginia is not so favourable as that of the West Indies, to African constitutions, on account of the severe cold of the winter.

Importation of African slaves into Virginia, has been generally discontinued since 1772.

Witness

Witness examined,—HERCULES ROSS, Esq.

Resided chiefly in Jamaica, from 1761, to 1782, 1791. and occasionally in Hispaniola.

Had occasion to be in every parish of the island, P. 252. and to be acquainted with the state and treatment of slaves, which depends on circumstances: under a man of humanity, and where the numbers were equal to the work, they lived happy; it was difficult under one of a different description.

It was not understood they had legal redress against owners or overseers for ill usage; nor against others, unless the owner or manager stood forward to protect them.

He had the mortification of seeing innumerable P. 253. punishments inflicted, many with severity, and he fears, some unjustly. An uncommon one now occurs, though it was long ago, at Savanna la Mar. Hearing, from an inclosure, the cries of some poor wretch under torture, he looked through, and saw a young female suspended by the wrists to a tree, swinging to and fro; her toes could barely touch the ground, and her body exceedingly agitated. The sight rather confounded him, as there was no whipping, and the master just by, seemingly motionless; but on looking more attentively, saw in his hand a stick of fire, which he held so as occasionally to touch her about her private parts as she swung. He continued this torture with unmoved countenance, until the witness calling on him to desist, throwing stones at him over the fence, stopped it. Thinks it right to say, that on mentioning it on the bay, it was heard with universal detestation: the perpetrator was not a man of character: he was not brought to legal punishment. Does not know that the law then extended to the P. 254. punishing whites for such acts.

Slaves in Kingston, when flogged, were tied up by the wrists; if on the wharfs to the crane-hook, with weights

1791. weights to their feet, and the crane wound up so as to extend them greatly; the whip was a cow-skin at first, and then ebony bushes, to take off the bruised blood. A gaol was also a place of correction: in fact, every man's premises was a place of punishment, if he chose; but the wharfs and gaol were used by such as did not choose to disturb the neighbours with the slaves cries; but it was understood that any owner had a right to order such punishments, without a magistrate.

In his residence in Jamaica, it became more cleared and improved, and of course healthier: the stile of living, and manners of the whites, gradually improved, and extended a favourable influence to the state of the slaves.

P. 255. Negroes are as capable of labour in the West Indies, as other people in climates congenial to them: that they are better adapted than whites to that climate, is certain. Negroes on board ships, fed on animal food as the whites, are capable of great exertions. In the last war, on the expedition to St. Juan's, government ordered a number of negroes to be collected, to ease the military; they were chiefly culprits, many taken from gaols, whom the owners were glad to part with, though exhausted by confinement and low diet when shipped, they returned almost to a man, in health, and much improved in looks (having had rations with the rest) while the whites, on that service, suffered great sickness and deaths. Something similar was the case with a greater body of negroes sent from Jamaica, to the siege of the Havannah.

As to slaves suffering from the bad circumstances of owners, unable to buy provisions, in some instances it may be the case, when from storms or other casulties, ground provisions are injured.

Slaves may be seized and sold for their owners debts: whereby near relations are often separated. In Kingston and Spanish town, they are confined in gaols till sold to the highest bidders; some of whom may

may be foreigners, and carry a part off the island: a hardship which often happens, and to which creoles as well as Africans are subject.

1791.

P. 257.

Has often been at sales of Guinea cargoes. On the day advertised by the agent, buyers attend aboard; at a given hour the sale is declared open, when each exerts himself to get first among the slaves to have a good choice, and the whole of the healthy and likely ones, are often sold that day. There used to be in Kingston many people who bought on speculation those left after the first day's sale, to carry them to the country, and retail them, or to ship them off. Has often seen the very refuse landed and sent to vendue masters in a very wretched state; sometimes in the agonies of death, has known them expire in the piazza of the vendue master. Has seen them sold even as low as a dollar.

Thinks the slave trade has been productive of great destruction to the human race, both blacks and whites; of which he could furnish many instances: one marked with peculiar circumstances of horror, was this.

About 20 years ago, a ship, with about 400 slaves struck on a shoal, half a league from the Morant Keys, (3 small sandy islands, 11 leagues S. S. E. from Jamaica) the officers and crew took to the boats with arms and provisions, and landed. At day light it was found that the slaves had got out of their irons, and were forming rafts, on which they placed the women and children, the men swimming by the side, whilst they drifted towards the little island where the crew had landed; who left the slaves should consume their provisions, came to the resolution to fire upon them, and actually killed from 3 to 400. Of the cargo, 33 or 34 only were saved, which he saw sold at vendue at Kingston. The ship, he thinks, was consigned to a Mr. Hugh Wallace, of St. Elizabeth's parish.

As it is said to be common when ships are wrecked, for the crew to break up the spirit room and get drunk, he is inclined to think the crew of the Guineaman

P. 259.

1791. neaman must have been drunk to have adopted so horrid a resolution, without first dispatching a boat to Jamaica (5 or 6 hours sail) for assistance. But this is only conjecture, from a persuasion that if they had acted with common discretion, there was no necessity for destroying any of the slaves.

Guinea ships, leaving their seamen behind, was so common as to have been a great nuisance and expense to the people at Kingston, and occasioned a law, obliging the masters of all ships to give security against leaving any disabled seamen behind, or provide for the charge of taking care of them. It was not uncommon for Guinea masters to send on shore a few hours before they sailed, their lame, ulcerated, or sick seamen, leaving them to perish. As to the Guinea trade being a nursery for seamen, he has ever

P. 260. considered it the reverse.

As to any compassion between the state of West India slaves and the peasantry of Great Britain, whatever others may think, he considers it as an insult to common sense: the peasantry in this country are obliged to labour it is true; but there is no market for the sale of human beings, where men of all characters may become buyers, and by the laws hold an absolute right in the person purchased. It is impossible to conceive a man so degenerate, as not to prefer the scantiest morsel with freedom and independance, to the luxury enjoyed by the wealthiest slave on earth. A peasant here however poor, cannot be imprisoned for his master's debts; nor purchased without a legal discussion: he beholds his growing family with pleasure, his industry often enables him to give them such an education, as advances them in life, and puts it in their power to comfort his old age: the slave who has reflection, views his offspring with very different feelings; knowing them doomed to eternal slavery, and ignorant of the character of those to whom they may hereafter belong.

His residence in Jamaica for above twenty years of

P. 261. the prime of his life, must have given him as perfect
a know-

a knowledge of the state of slaves there, as it is possible to acquire. As to the information which may have been got by those holding high commands there he cannot speak decidedly; but if it is meant to know, whether such on occasional visits to estates, were likely to obtain a thorough knowledge of the treatment of slaves, he thinks they could not.

He has often accompanied Governors and Admirals on their tours there; when, the estates visited (belonging generally to persons of distinction) might be supposed under the best management; besides that all possible care would be taken to keep every disgusting object from view, and on no account, by the exercise of the whip or other punishments, harrow up the feelings of strangers of such distinction.

As to his opinion of the probable effects of the abolition of the slave trade, he is at some loss to express himself; he thinks however, that as it would tend to prevent making new settlements in the islands, the produce of sugar not keeping pace with the increasing demand for it, the price must rise and of course the present estates became more valuable: the value of the slaves would also be increased and it would become more the owners interest to attend to their health and population.

Finally, as the result of his observations and most serious reflection, he hesitates not to say, that the trade for slaves ought to be abolished not only as contrary to sound policy, but to the laws of God and nature; and were it possible by the present inquiry to convey a just knowledge of the extensive misery it occasions, every kingdom of Europe must unite in calling on their legislatures to abolish the inhuman traffic. This is not a hasty, nor a new sentiment, formed on the present discussion, which has in no respect influenced his judgment. The same opinion he publicly delivered seventeen years ago, in Kingston, in a society formed of the first characters of the place, on debating the following question (proposed he thinks, by the late Mr. Thomas Hibbert, who had been 40

1791. or 50 years the moſt eminent Guinea factor there) "Whether the trade to Africa for ſlaves, was conſiſtent with ſound policy, the laws of nature and morality." The diſcuſſion occupied ſeveral meetings, and at laſt it was determined by a majority, that the trade to Africa for ſlaves was neither conſiſtent with ſound policy, the laws of nature, nor morality.

The chief ground on which the advocates for the ſlave trade reſted their opinion (he thinks) was, that God had formed ſome of the human race, inferior to others, in intellect; and that negroes appeared to have been intended for ſlaves, or, to that purpoſe.

Has been in ſome of the foreign Weſt India iſlands, in N. America, and St. Domingo. The ſtate of ſlaves ſeemed ſimilar to that in Jamaica; in America he had but little opportunity for obſervation: but upon the whole, they appeared decenter in their manners; more domeſticated, and to have ſome notions of religion.

The

The following Evidence is printed at full length, there not being time to abridge it.

Witness examined—THOMAS IRVING, Esq.

Does not your official situation afford you a general view of the commerce of the British empire, and of the relation of its several branches to each other, and particularly to Great Britain?

1791.

The office of Inspector General of Imports and Exports, committed to my management, exhibits a state of the importations into, and exportations from, Great Britain, and the British Colonies and Islands in America and the West Indies, and of all the revenues arising from our commerce. Accounts are transmitted to the office, from the several ports of Great Britain and the colonies, of every article imported into, or exported from, such ports, distinguishing our trade with each respective country, together (in as far as relates to our Colonies) with the number of vessels, their tonnage, and number of men employed in the trade. I am also annually furnished (extra-officially for a special purpose) by the Register General of Shipping, with a similar account of the number of vessels, their tonnage, and number of men, both British and Foreign, which enter and clear in the ports of Great Britain. In a word, the Inspector General's office, as it at present stands, exhibits a complete view of the commerce, navigation, and commercial revenues of the British empire, Ireland excepted. I am the more particular in explaining the nature of the office, in order that it may appear from what sources I draw any information which I may have occasion to offer to the Committee, in the course of the subsequent examination.

Did you ever execute any other office, which afforded you the means of acquiring a knowledge of the

1791. the trade of the British Colonies in America and the West Indies?

In the year 1767 I was appointed Inspector General of the imports and exports of North America, and Register of Shipping, which offices I continued to execute until the year 1774, when I was appointed Receiver General of South Carolina, and a Member of the Council.

This office of Inspector General and Register of Shipping in North America furnished me with the means of acquiring a thorough knowledge of the trade and navigation carried on between the continental Colonies and the British West India Islands, and the books and papers of that office are still in my possession.

Have the British West India islands, in their present state, the means of furnishing the supply of sugar and rum that is requisite for the consumption of Great Britain and her immediate dependencies?

The British West India islands produce annually a greater quantity of sugar and rum than is requisite for the consumption of Great Britain, her immediate dependencies, and the kingdom of Ireland. In testimony of this fact I beg leave to lay before the Committee the paper which I now hold in my hand, containing an account of the quantity of British plantation sugar imported into, and exported from, Great Britain, in the years 1772, 1773, 1774, and 1775, and in the years 1787, 1788, 1789, and 1790. I have selected those years as exhibiting the fairest state of the produce of the sugar colonies; for in the year 1776, our trade began to meet with many interruptions from the war which was then become general on the continent of America: and I am of opinion, that the islands did not recover the shock which they had sustained by capture, and other consequences of war, sooner than about the year 1787.

Do

An ACCOUNT of the Total Quantity of Sugar imported from the British West India Islands into Great Britain, in the undermentioned Years:

ALSO,

An Account, for the same Periods, of the Quantity of Raw and Refined Sugars exported from Great Britain; distinguishing the Quantity exported to Ireland, and other Parts of the Empire, from the Quantity exported to Foreign Parts.

|  | Quantity of British Plantation Sugar imported. | Raw Sugar exported to Ireland, and other Parts of the Empire. | | | Refined Sug. exported to Ireland, and other Parts of the Empire. | | | Raw Sugar exported to Foreign Parts. | | | Refined Sugar exported to Foreign Parts. | | |
|---|---|---|---|---|---|---|---|---|---|---|---|---|---|
| 1772 | 1,786,045 — 1 | 172,269 | 2 | 5 | 27,623 | 3 | 23 | 1,391 | 2 | 26 | 3,677 | — | — |
| 1773 | 1,762,387 3 15 | 184,252 | 2 | 17 | 23,771 | 3 | 17 | 2,397 | 1 | 2 | 5,772 | — | 9 |
| 1774 | 2,015,911 1 15 | 211,304 | 1 | 25 | 28,139 | 3 | 25 | 14,950 | — | 2 | 5,949 | — | 17 |
| 1775 | 2,002,224 3 8 | 255,686 | 2 | 16 | 23,034 | 3 | 26 | 89,325 | 3 | 12 | 46,755 | 3 | 22 |
| 1787 | 1,926,121 — 3 | 196,636 | 3 | 20 | 24,261 | 2 | — | 2,779 | 1 | 16 | 52,473 | 3 | 19 |
| 1788 | 2,065,700 — 12 | 138,681 | 3 | 19 | 17,150 | 3 | 9 | 6,575 | — | 20 | 58,250 | 2 | 6 |
| 1789 | 1,935,223 2 21 | 149,351 | 2 | — | 20,506 | 1 | 17 | 4,461 | 3 | 15 | 118,033 | 1 | 22 |
| 1790 | 1,882,005 — 17 | 127,104 | 1 | 3 | 13,968 | 1 | 17 | 15,011 | 2 | 15 | 105,892 | 2 | 1 |

Do you think that the extention of the West India plantations beyond the degree that is requisite for supplying Great Britain, and her immediate dependencies with the principal articles of West India produce, would materially promote the interest of the British empire?

1791.

This question is of a very extensive nature, and is involved in a variety of objects and considerations, commercial and political, which I am afraid I am incompetent to offer an opinion upon; more especially in the present debilitated state of my health, having only lately recovered from a dangerous illness.

> The Committee informed Mr. Irving, that they did not wish that he should, in answering this, or any other question, make exertions to the prejudice of his health, and that he would therefore confine himself to such facts and opinions as shall readily occur to him.

The Witness then proceeded as follows:

The extension of the culture of the British W. India islands, beyond that degree that is requisite for supplying Great Britain and her immediate dependencies with the principal articles of West India produce, does not appear to me likely to promote the interest of the British empire; and in support of this opinion, I beg leave to offer the following reasons:

The West India islands have been settled upon a system very different from the British Continental Colonies (now a part of the States of America). I allude to the colonies which are cultivated chiefly by slaves; namely, the tobacco, and rice, and indigo colonies. The settlement of these colonies was undertaken upon small capitals, and the increase of their wealth arose almost wholly out of the growing profits of the industry of the proprietors; whereas our islands in the West Indies have, agreeable to the system hitherto pursued, been settled and extended by

1791. by means of large capitals drawn from the mother country. The Ceded Islands were almost entirely settled with the British capitals; and in the island of Jamaica large sums of money have from time to time been borrowed from this country upon mortgage, in order to extend the cultivation of that island. Thus a capital to a great amount, which might have been employed in carrying on and extending the manufactures, the commerce, and agriculture of Great Britain, has been transferred from hence to the most vulnerable part of the empire; and there invested in pursuits which do not appear to me to have been productive of a profit to the proprietor, or of advantages to the public, in any degree adequate to the precarious situation in which such property stands, from the contingencies of climate, the fate of war, &c. For although the planter resident on the spot will most likely abide by his property whatever change of government he may be subjected to, yet the loss of an island by capture is a complete loss of so much capital to the empire. Notwithstanding our general superiority at sea, the precarious tenure on which we hold our colonial possessions was sufficiently evinced in the course of last war. Thirteen great provinces separated themselves for ever from the empire, whereby property to the amount of many millions was lost to the inhabitants of Great Britain, and her adherents. The provinces of East and West Florida, and the island of Tobago, were ceded to Spain and France; and the islands of St. Kitts, Nevis, Montserrat, St. Vincents, Dominica, and Grenada, were all captured, but restored at the peace.

But besides the reasons already offered—the impolicy of extending the cultivation of the West India islands beyond the degree stated in the question, is in my humble opinion strongly marked by some further considerations.

Notwithstanding whatever may be the difference between the British and Foreign sugars at present, or
for

umb. 4.  1.  An

An ACCOUNT of the Quantity of British and Foreign Plantation Sugars, imported into North America, in the following Years; distinguishing each Year, and the British from the Foreign Sugars.

| YEARS. | British Plantation Sugar. | | | Foreign Plantation Sugar. | | |
|---|---|---|---|---|---|---|
| | Cwts. | Qrs. | lbs. | Cwts. | Qrs. | lbs. |
| 1769 | 49,672 | — | — | 45,437 | — | — |
| 1770 | 66,417 | 2 | 3 | 35,035 | 1 | 1 |
| 1771 | 47,870 | — | — | 21,466 | — | — |
| 1772 | 44,611 | — | — | 51,333 | — | — |

for these two or three years past, since the disturbances in France began to convulse her colonies; yet if we take a comparative view of the difference between the price of British and Foreign sugars, even in a period the most favourable to the British islands, namely, before last war, when they received a complete supply of lumber and provisions from the continent of America, it will be found that the French sugars were sold by the planters from 20 to 30 per cent. cheaper than the British sugars could be purchased in our islands. This fact I state from the information which I received time after time from the merchants and others concerned in the trade between America and the West Indies, when I executed the office of Inspector General of the Imports and Exports of North America; and I was the more minute in my inquiries, as the acquiring information of the prices of the several commodities imported into and exported from America formed a part of my duty, in order to enable me to establish a table of the rates of value for the office. But as a further testimony of the Foreign sugars being materially cheaper than the British, I take the liberty of presenting an account of the quantity of British and Foreign sugars, distinguishing each, imported into our colonies in North America, in the years 1769, 1770, 1771, and 1772. The Committee will perceive by this account, that the difference between the quantity of British, and of Foreign sugars imported, was not very considerable, notwithstanding that the Foreign sugars were clandestinely obtained in the French islands by our traders, which enhanced the price in proportion to the risque, and were also subject to a duty of 5s. per cwt. on importation into America: nor were our traders by any means under the necessity of taking these foreign sugars in exchange for merchandize; for they were chiefly purchased with cash which they received for their lumber and provisions sold in our islands. I am the more particular in stating the difference of the prices be-

1791. tween the British and Foreign sugars, because I conceive it is a maxim thoroughly established in national commerce, that it is unwise to push forward by means of monopolies, restrictive regulations, or bounties, any branch of commerce or manufactures, which cannot be carried on, after a fair trial, within 15 per cent. of the prices of other rival countries: and I am of opinion that this observation will strictly apply even to those branches of commerce from which the nation is supposed to derive the greatest political advantages from the smallest capital employed, namely, our fisheries.

The money expended upon West India estates is in general far from yielding a profitable return, and in this opinion I am supported by the testimony of some of the best informed gentlemen connected with the West Indies, particulary the agent for Jamaica, who states, in his examination before the Privy Council, that the planters throughout that island do not make more than four per cent. upon their capital; and the agent of Barbadoes gave it as his opinion, " That after " payment of expenses and plantation losses, even a good crop does not leave the owner more, or so much as six per cent. the interest of the island, on his capital." Besides the return to the proprietor, the publick certainly derives a considerable profit from the freight of the sugars, and the commission paid to the merchants of this kingdom. This latter circumstance I perceive is upon all occasions strongly urged by gentlemen connected with the West Indies; but the same national profit and political advantages appear to me to apply less or more to every other branch of our foreign commerce, and in many instances to our internal manufactures. Indeed, the testimony of the West India gentlemen, which states, that the capital invested in the West India estates is far from yielding a profitable return, is strongly confirmed by the account which I now beg leave to lay before the committee. By this account it appears that the principal article cultivated in the West Indies has,

An ACCOUNT of the Quantity of Sugars, being British Plantation Produce, imported into Great Britain in the following Years; distinguishing each Year, and each Island from whence imported.

| | 1772. | | | 1773. | | | 1774. | | | 1775. | | | 1787. | | | 1788. | | | 1789. | | | 1790. | | |
|---|---|---|---|---|---|---|---|---|---|---|---|---|---|---|---|---|---|---|---|---|---|---|---|---|
| | Cwts. | qrs. | lb | Cwts. | qrs. | lb. | Cwts. | qrs. | lb | Cwts. | qrs. | lb | Cwts. | qrs. | lb | Cwts. | qrs. | lb. | Cwts. | qrs. | lb. | Cwts. | qrs. | lb. |
| Antigua | 115,364 | 1 | 23 | 83,965 | 1 | 20 | 235,815 | 1 | 23 | 255,861 | 1 | 26 | 254,575 | 1 | 12 | 181,813 | 2 | — | 144,204 | — | 11 | 65,022 | 1 | 26 |
| Anguilla | — | | | — | | | — | | | 1,298 | — | — | 2,129 | 2 | 16 | 3,728 | 1 | 2 | 3 | 2 | 12 | 2,150 | 2 | 18 |
| Barbadoes | 141,541 | 1 | 3 | 110,911 | 2 | 4 | 139,564 | 1 | 3 | 70,181 | 1 | 21 | 130,242 | — | 16 | 110,955 | — | 19 | 97,389 | 2 | 27 | 113,038 | 3 | 21 |
| Dominica | 10,170 | 2 | 6 | 26,705 | 1 | 5 | 53,464 | 2 | 12 | 40,583 | 1 | 21 | 5,665 | 1 | 21 | 47,010 | 1 | 24 | 34,709 | 3 | 5 | 50,036 | — | 23 |
| Grenada | 192,362 | 2 | 5 | 202,679 | — | — | 185,542 | — | 10 | 199,824 | 1 | 23 | 172,880 | — | 9 | 193,783 | — | 25 | 164,338 | 3 | 9 | 191,025 | 1 | 6 |
| Jamaica | 874,560 | 1 | 20 | 1,057,956 | — | 23 | 947,073 | 1 | 1 | 995,187 | 2 | 18 | 824,706 | 2 | 15 | 1,124,017 | — | 44 | 1,236,603 | 1 | 27 | 1,185,519 | 2 | 7 |
| St. Kitt's | 220,716 | 2 | 14 | 110,057 | 3 | 3 | 212,467 | — | 15 | 200,040 | 3 | 17 | 231,397 | 2 | 12 | 187,379 | 1 | 25 | 89,755 | 1 | 23 | 113,379 | 1 | 16 |
| Nevis | 63,125 | 1 | 20 | 30,367 | 1 | 20 | 68,408 | — | 9 | 50,488 | — | 10 | 72,475 | 1 | 11 | 30,050 | 1 | 4 | 28,151 | 3 | — | 35,467 | 3 | 1 |
| Montferrat | 58,008 | 2 | — | 33,770 | — | 21 | 47,590 | 3 | 9 | 39,327 | 2 | 9 | 35,149 | 3 | 16 | 25,113 | — | 13 | 25,089 | 2 | 16 | 19,186 | 3 | 24 |
| St. Vincent | 55,909 | 1 | 18 | 61,084 | — | 12 | 65,177 | — | 17 | 54,071 | 2 | 16 | 61,449 | 1 | 27 | 73,735 | 2 | 24 | 81,283 | — | 18 | 76,747 | 2 | 7 |
| Tortola | 31,660 | — | 3 | 30,126 | 3 | 24 | 33,962 | 3 | 4 | 38,065 | 2 | 7 | 78,749 | 1 | 6 | 84,513 | 3 | 22 | 33,704 | — | 23 | 29,830 | 1 | 14 |
| Tobago | 13,625 | 2 | 21 | 14,153 | 3 | 17 | 27,045 | 2 | 24 | 50,315 | 2 | 7 | — | | | — | | | — | | | — | | |
| Total | 1,786,045 | — | 1 | 1,762,387 | 5 | 15 | 2,015,911 | 1 | 15 | 2,002,224 | 3 | 8 | 1,926,121 | — | 3 | 2,065,700 | — | 12 | 1,935,223 | 2 | 21 | 1,882,005 | — | 17 |

Average of the Annual Produce of the first Period.
Cwts. qrs. lb.
1,891,642 1 —

Average of the Annual Produce of the last Period.
Cwts. qrs. lb.
1,952,262 — —

Increase in the last Period.
Cwts. qrs. lb.
60,620 — — equal to about 4,040 Hogsheads.

[To face page 154.]

has, in point of quantity, been in a great meafure ftationary for thefe twenty years, and yet there is no part of the empire in which property ftands in a more favoured footing. Prohibitory laws were early made tending to force the confumption of Weft India produce upon the inhabitants of Great Britain, and the other fubjects of the empire, whereby the proprietors of the iflands obtained (and ftill retain) a complete monopoly of our markets at a very confiderable expenfe to the Britifh confumer, as appears by the difference of the prices between the Britifh and the foreign iflands.

In our colonies in America, in order to encourage our iflands, the ufe of foreign rum is abfolutely prohibited, foreign coffee is fubject to a duty of two pounds nineteen fhillings per cwt. whilft Britifh is chargeable with a duty of feven fhillings; and foreign fugars, as I have already mentioned, pay a duty on importation into the continent of five fhillings per cwt. and into this kingdom one pound feven fhillings and twopence, which is fourteen fhillings and tenpence per cwt. more than the Britifh fugars. The whole duties impofed upon Britifh fugars are drawn back upon exportation, and refined fugars are entitled to a bounty, when exported, of twenty-fix fhillings per cwt. which exceeds the duty collected upon the raw material three or four fhillings. In order to give the planters a more extenfive market for the fale of their preduce, fugars were, by the 12th of Geo. II. taken out of the lift of enumerated commodities, and the exportation of them permitted to all parts fouth of Cape Finifterre, in Europe.

The evidence upon the part of the Weft India planters, before the Committee of Privy Council, ftate many natural advantages which the foreign iflands poffefs, as reafons why our iflands will never be able to enter into a competition in point of price with the foreign plantations.

For thofe, and the reafons which I have had the honour upon this occafion of fubmitting to the Committee,

1791.

1791. mittee, I am of opinion, that however juft and proper it may be to encourage our own iflands to the extent of fupplying ourfelves, and thereby doing that juftice to the proprietors of eftates there which they confider themfelves entitled to; yet the extenfion of the cultivation of thofe iflands beyond that degree that is requifite for fupplying Great Britain and her immediate dependencies, with the principal articles of their produce, is by no means likely to promote the interefts of the empire; becaufe from the great difparity of price between the Britifh and Foreign fugars, the former cannot be made an object of export by any other means than by that deftructive fyftem of policy which has been too much adopted in fome other branches of our commerce, namely, the granting of bounties out of the Exchequer, in order to enable the Britifh exporter to ftand the competition of prices in the foreign market. It is a dangerous principle to force commerce and manufactures like fruit raifed on a hot bed. In fuch cafes, the capital and the induftry of the individual are too often drawn from objects of profit, to purfuits which can only be carried on by the aid of the national purfe.

Do you think, that by a proper attention to the breeding of flaves in the Britifh Weft India iflands, fuch a number of flaves may be obtained and kept up, without the aid of importation from Africa, as will be fufficient to raife the Weft India produce that is requifite for the fupply of Great Britain and her immediate dependencies?

I have long been of opinion, that by proper attention to the breeding of flaves, the ftock might be kept up in the Britifh Weft India iflands, without the aid of importation from Africa. I beg leave, however, to be underftood, that this meafure is not likely, in my judgment, to be effected by putting an immediate ftop to the importations, but by adopting

such

such a system of policy as will gradually do away the necessity for importation.

1791.

Prior to the late war, the provisions for feeding the slaves were chiefly imported from North America, the attention of the planters being almost wholly directed to what is called the crop, namely, sugars, &c. and as these provisions were bought at a considerable expense, the planters did not consider it their interest to encourage the breeding of slaves at the expense of feeding them ten or twelve years before they were capable, by the produce of their labour in the cane walks, to support themselves. Hence grown slaves, whose labour can be brought into immediate effect, were, and still continue to be, imported from the coast of Africa; and of these a greater proportion of males than females.

If a different system of policy were adopted with respect to the cultivation of the plantations in the West Indies, and which system I have many reasons for thinking would be attended with advantage to the planters themselves: I am persuaded a sufficient number of slaves might be bred at least to keep up the present stock; I allude to the cultivating of a proportion of land sufficient to supply the negroes with provisions, in which the little slaves, from seven years old and upwards, might be useful. In that part of America where I was resident, and which was cultivated as much by negroes as the West Indies, the breeding of slaves was considered so advantageous, that the planter generally valued a child on the day of its birth at five pounds. The prevailing opinion, to the best of my recollection, in South Carolina, at that time was, that the increased population of slaves by birth was from two to ten per cent. and yet the climate of Carolina, particularly of the rice plantations, is, I believe, more hostile to the human constitution than any part of the West Indies.

In order gradually to check the importation of negroes from the coast of Africa, I would submit that a slight duty, in the first instance, should be laid upon

all

1791. all slaves imported; the duty imposed on males to be considerably higher than upon females; or perhaps that the latter should for a time be imported free; and that the rate of this duty should be progressively increased as the means should be provided of supplying the deficiency which this check would give to the importation. And in order to encourage the raising of plantation born slaves, and cultivating provisions for their support, which latter circumstance I consider to be materially connected with the breeding of the negroes, I would propose that the produce of the duties collected upon slaves imported from the coast of Africa should be applied as bounties for promoting the above purposes. The raising of provisions in some of the islands, would, no doubt, be less advantageous than others; but I am of opinion, that the cultivation of a sufficient quantity for the use of the slaves would be profitable and politick. Anterior to the late war, the negroes in the West Indies depended in a great degree for their supply of food on the continent of America. When the disturbances broke out, this source of supply was at once cut off, and the importations from Europe, through captures at sea and other causes, were rendered very precarious. The planters, thus impelled by necessity, were obliged to deviate from their former system, and to turn their attention more towards raising provision upon their own estates. The good effects of this plan has been so forcibly felt, that the importation of Indian corn, which may emphatically be stiled the bread of life, with respect to the food of the slaves, is reduced from about 600,000 bushels, the quantity annually imported before the war, to somewhat under 300,000 bushels, the medium importation of the last three years; and peafe, &c. in a similar proportion. In a political sense, I conceive that no country capable of producing corn to feed itself, ought to be dependent upon any other for any article which it cannot do without, even for a day.

Numb. 4.                X                       An

An ACCOUNT of the Quantity of Rum and Melasses exported from the British West Indies, to all Parts, in the Years 1787, 1788, and 1789, distinguishing each Year, and the Countries to which exported.

|  | 1787. | | 1788. | | 1789. | |
|---|---|---|---|---|---|---|
|  | Rum. Gallons. | Melasses. Gallons. | Rum. | Melasses. | Rum. | Melasses. |
| Great Britain | 2,251,346 | — | 3,646,667 | — | 3,396,653 | — |
| Ireland | 344,150 | — | 688,050 | — | 754,700 | — |
| British Colonies | 885,186 | 26,380 | 652,200 | 24,889 | 658,470 | 20,192 |
| States of America | 1,660,155 | 4,200 | 1,541,093 | 3,923 | 1,485,461 | 1,000 |
| Foreign West Indies | 345,750 | — | 222,512 | — | 143,443 | — |
| Southern Parts of Europe | 9,560 | — | 19,810 | — | 43,450 | — |
| Africa | — | — | — | — | — | † |
|  | 5,496,147 | 30,580 | 6,770,332 | 28,812 | 6,492,177 | 21,192 |

If the British West India islands should in future raise a quantity of provisions sufficient to feed the slaves, in what manner do you think the planters would be enabled to dispose of that part of their rum and molasses, which is at present supposed to be applied to the purchasing of provisions?

Before I reply to this question, I beg leave to lay before the Committee an account of the quantity of rum and molasses exported from the British West India islands, to all parts, for the three years preceding the 5th of January, 1790, which is the latest period to which the account can be made up.

The quantity of provisions suitable for feeding of the slaves raised in the British Colonies in North America is very inconsiderable, and the barrelled mackrel and other fish exported from those Colonies to the West Indies, would almost in any event be in demand, more especially as it is now sufficiently proved, that the produce of the British Herring Fishery is far from being equal to the demand of our islands. The Continental Colonies would, therefore, be very little affected by any change of system in raising provisions for the negroes in the West Indies; and so far from its being probable that the demand for rum in these Colonies is likely to be lessened in future, I am of opinion that the consumption will increase in proportion to the growing population of the country.

By the account which I have just now laid before the Committee, it appears that upon a medium of three years, about 1,500,000 gallons of rum have been taken off by the subjects of the United States; which rum, including the freight, as it can be only imported in British bottoms, may be valued at about 3s. 3d. sterling per gallon in America; the total value at that rate would be £.243,750. This sum is by no means more than equal to the purchasing of lumber, flour, and other articles which have little or no connection with the food of the slaves. In a long examination which I underwent before the Lords of the

1791. Committee of Privy Council, in the year 1784, relating to the opening an intercourſe between the States of America and the Britiſh Weſt Indies, I had occaſion to look very minutely into the nature and value of the articles which the Weſt Indies receive from the States, and into thoſe which the States take in return from the iſlands, and it then appeared to me, (and nothing has ſince occurred to alter my opinion) that the Weſt India planters will always find a ſufficient demand for their rum.

The quantity of melaſſes exported from our iſlands is too inconſiderable to merit notice.

If a ſufficiency of ſlaves for the culture of the Britiſh Weſt India ſettlements ſhould be raiſed within thoſe ſettlements, do you think that the diminution of Britiſh exports to Africa, which may be the conſequence of ſuch a change, would be materially prejudicial to the manufacturing intereſts of Great Britain?

I feel more diffidence in anſwering this queſtion than any of the preceding, as nothing is more difficult to foreſee than the conſequences that may ariſe from any alteration of ſyſtem in a trade long eſtabliſhed. Caſting, however, a retroſpective eye to the effect which the changes in other branches of our commerce have undergone in the courſe of public events, and comparing the probable conſequences which may take place in the caſe in queſtion, by thoſe which experience has afforded an opportunity of determining upon, I ſhall ſubmit ſuch ideas as occur to my weak judgment, as to the tendency that a probable diminution of the Britiſh exports to the Coaſt of Africa, in conſequence of the change propoſed, is likely to have on the manufacturing intereſts of this kingdom.

The medium value of the Britiſh manufactures exported to Africa, chiefly for the purpoſe of purchaſing ſlaves, amounts to about £.400,000 a year, agreeable to the rates of value in the Inſpector General's neral's books; but I mention with regret, that from 1791. the loose manner in which the entries of free goods are made in the Custom-house, the Inspector General's value of such goods is not absolutely to be relied upon, and therefore the value of the exports to Africa may have been less or more; however, the Committee will please to observe, that in the £.400,000, I include the value of the goods exchanged for gold dust, ivory, cam and redwood, gum, drugs, &c. imported from Africa, either directly into Great Britain, or through the circuitous passage of the West Indies.

An immediate stop being put to our exports to Africa, would doubtless be felt in a very considerable degree by those artificers, who are at present employed in manufacturing goods for that branch of our export trade; because they would find the channels through which their industry passed to a market shut up before they had time to turn their attention, labour, and capital to other pursuits. It was not less with a view to this object, than to the consequences which the planters in the West Indies might experience by their being at once deprived of their usual supply of slaves, that I took the liberty of suggesting the crude ideas offered in my answer to the preceding question.

In cases of war breaking out, and being of long continuance with countries with which we had been in habits of carrying on commercial intercourse, temporary inconveniences are doubtless experienced, but not to the extent which theoretical reasoning would induce us to imagine. The enterprise of our merchants soon discovers fresh means of vending the produce of the labour of our manufacturers. The superior capital, ingenuity, industry, and integrity of the British artificer, will ever command a market for the produce of his industry. The late revolution in America, affords striking proofs of the justice of this observation. With the independence of these states, it was very generally apprehended, that Great Britain
would

1791. would also lose the benefit of their commerce; but experience has proved the fallacy of that opinion. The exports of our native manufactures to that part of the world, instead of being lessened since the separation of the two countries, are increased; and as a proof of the delusion of the idea, that the employment of the capital of this country has for some time past been at its ne plus ultra, I beg leave to inform the Committee, that the value of British manufactures exported from this country of late, exceeds that of the most flourishing period before the late war, when the laws of trade confined those colonies, which now constitute the American States, in their supply of merchandize to Great Britain, the sum of upwards of £2,500,000 annually; and that our shipping has also increased between two and three hundred thousand tons, over that which the empire possessed when the American States formed a part of its dominions. Nor has this great increase of trade and navigation arisen from any special or temporary cause, for it will appear by the books of my office, that the value of our exports has been gradually increasing every year since the late war.

For the facts and reasons which I have thus set forth, I am under no apprehensions that a gradual check to the importation of slaves would materially affect the manufacturing interests of this country.

Do you not know the price of sugars has doubled in Great Britain within the last eighteen years?

I believe the price of sugars in Great Britain is very considerably increased within the last eighteen years; but to what amount I am not prepared to give an answer. A considerable addition has been made within that period, to the rate of duties upon sugars, which will consequently increase the price; and I am inclined to think, that the prices at present, and for two or three years past, have been materially affected, as I have already observed, by the disturbances in the French islands.

Do

Do you not think, if a more ample ſupply of ſugar were ſent from the Weſt Indies to Great Britain, that the price in the home market would decreaſe? 1791.

I have already informed the Committee, that the Britiſh Weſt India iſlands, in their preſent ſituation, raiſe a quantity of ſugar more than adequate to the conſumption of the whole Britiſh empire. If the quantity of ſugars in the Britiſh Weſt India iſlands were conſiderably increaſed, ſuch increaſe might probably have ſome effect in lowering the prices to the Britiſh conſumer; but the natural conſequence muſt be a diminution in the price to the Weſt India planter, which would tend greatly to diſcourage him in the extenſion of his plantation.

Do you not believe, that the conſumption of ſugar, and conſequently the revenue ariſing from that article, would increaſe very conſiderably if the prices were lower?

I conceive I have already anſwered this queſtion.

---

☞ *Should any errors have crept into the foregoing Work, it is hoped they will be candidly attributed to their true cauſe—the want of time to correct the preſs.*

F I N I S.

www.ingramcontent.com/pod-product-compliance
Lightning Source LLC
Chambersburg PA
CBHW022017240426
43667CB00042B/561